Hoover Institution Publications

RURAL PEOPLE'S COMMUNES IN LIEN-CHIANG

RURAL PEOPLE'S COMMUNES IN LIEN-CHIANG

Documents Concerning Communes in Lien-chiang County, Fukien Province, 1962–1963

Edited, with an Introductory Analysis, by
C. S. CHEN
Translated by
CHARLES PRICE RIDLEY

HOOVER INSTITUTION PRESS
Stanford University • Stanford, California

The Hoover Institution on War, Revolution and Peace, founded at Stanford University in 1919 by the late President Herbert Hoover, is a center for advanced study and research on public and international affairs in the twentieth century. The views expressed in its publications are entirely those of the authors and do not necessarily reflect the views of the Hoover Institution.

CONTENTS

PART TWO: DOCUMENTS

(NOTE: The titles of the documents are translations of the titles in the original texts, except that in cases where the original had no title a descriptive title has been supplied in brackets. Dates added to titles are similarly indicated.)

Group I: Policy Statements and Production Plans

PREFACE

It was Dr. Yuan-li Wu of the Hoover Institution, Stanford University, who instigated the translation of these documents. The translating was done by Charles Price Ridley, a native of Maine, who graduated from Bates College at Lewiston and received his master's degree in Chinese from Stanford University. During the academic year 1963/64 Mr. Ridley studied at the Inter-University Program for Chinese Language Studies in Taipei, Taiwan. After returning to the United States he worked in the Library of Congress. He is now a Research Associate of the Hoover Institution.

The documents, although many were written by cadre members at the commune or brigade level, are often surprisingly clear in thought and expression. Yet their literary qualities are by no means even. Some passages are difficult to understand and would be unintelligible if rendered into English word for word. At these points the translation is not strictly literal.

A selection of the documents has been printed by a government agency in Taiwan. One or two items of minor importance which appeared in the Taiwan volume are not translated here. On the other hand, the present volume contains several items (Document I, Appendix, and Documents III, XV, and XVI) which either are not included in the Taiwan volume or are included in an incomplete form. These additional documents are mostly statistical tables. It should be noted that these statistical tables are not always internally consistent or consistent with one another. Parts, for example, do not always add up to the exact totals.

The Chinese Communists are very skillful in coining catchy slogans and expressions, such as the Three Red Banners, the Two Road struggle, the Small Freedoms, and "rat work." As far as possible such terms have been preserved in the translation. A glossary compiled by the editor is printed at the end of the book.

The manuscript was reviewed by Dr. Dennis Doolin of Stanford University, by Dr. John Lossing Buck, author of *Land Utilization in China* and *The Chinese Farm Economy*, to which latter work our introductory analysis makes frequent reference, and by Lord and Lady Michael Linsay. The comments of these reviewers have led to a number of improvements. Of course, the reviewers are not responsible for the shortcomings that may still remain.

Many other persons both inside and outside the Hoover Institution have assisted in our work. Our thanks go to all of them.

C. S. C.

INTRODUCTION

Advocates of the Great Proletarian Cultural Revolution which Mao Tse-tung unleashed in the winter of 1965–66 have accused many Communist Party cadres and high-ranking officials in mainland China of serious "cultural lags." They indulge in capitalistic ideas and practices; they have not completely forsaken traditional mores and values; they have, in short, failed to live up to the spirit of Communist ideals as Mao Tse-tung sees these ideals, and they have not immersed themselves in a continuing revolution without which they cannot hope even remotely to approach the desired image of the Maoist Communist. Yet various economic, political and social manifestations of "economism" and "corrupt practices" can be found in great abundance in the documents contained in this volume. These instances occurred during the 1961–63 period and were targets of the Socialist Education campaigns which antedated the Cultural Revolution by several years. It is safe to assume that there had been many similar instances before this period and that there will be many more in the future.

The 1961–63 period is of special interest because it was a period of serious adjustment of economic and social institutions throughout Communist China. The excesses of the rual commune and the Great Leap Forward had to be corrected. Short of an extensive field survey, there is no better way to learn what it was like in the rural society of China of this time than by a careful study of the documents which follow. These documents, and the introductory analysis which serves as a very useful guide to them, provide an in-depth microcosmic view of rural China. While they deal with only a minute part of a vast country, there is no reason to believe that the phenomena they record were in any sense unique. Taken together as a source book, they should provide some invaluable insight to any serious student of contemporary China, be he interested in economics or sociology or local administration, or in the perplexing and ubiquitous "contradictions" of communism and the Communist society.

Yuan-li Wu

Stanford, California
August 1968

PART ONE
INTRODUCTORY ANALYSIS

I

BACKGROUND TO DOCUMENTS

Location of Lien-chiang. The hsien or county of Lien-chiang, in Fukien Province of southeastern Communist China, is situated at longitude 119° 30′ E. and latitude 26° 12′ N. It is about thirty kilometers northeast of Foochow, the capital of Fukien Province, and forty kilometers west of Matsu, one of the two offshore islands still under the control of the Nationalist Chinese, the other being Quemoy, which has been the object of artillery shelling by the Communist Chinese. Until recently Lien-chiang formed part of the Foochow municipality. [1]

Origin of the documents. On the night of March 4, 1964, Chinese Nationalist commandos staged a raid on Lien-chiang and captured certain documents relating to the communes in the country, among which were the twenty-five documents translated here.

Some of the captured documents have been omitted, either because they are repetitious of those selected for printing, or because our microfilms of them are illegible, or for other reasons such as their fragmentary character. As far as possible the contents of these omitted documents are utilized in this introductory analysis.

The documents included here are divided into three groups, dealing respectively with policy statements and production plans, the general aspects of the Socialist Education movement, and the expanded cadre meetings held during the Socialist Education movement. Within each group they are arranged as far as possible in chronological order.

Scope of the documents. Agricultural and fishery production in Lien-chiang was organized in communes. It has been reported that there were fourteen rural communes in the county, namely, the communes of Ao-chiang, P'u-k'ou, Kuan-t'ou, P'an-tu, Tan-yang, Shih-k'ou, San-yang, Ma-pi, Lai-chiang, Fei-lung, Huang-ch'i, Hsiao-ch'eng, Ao-feng, and Tung-ch'ing. [2] The number evidently was or is greater than fourteen; communes named in the documents included Hsiao-yü, K'ang-yuan, Liao-yen, and Ch'ang-lung.

Communes were divided into production brigades, and brigades into production teams. In 1962 there were 240 brigades in Lien-chiang and a total of 2,898 teams.

---

[1] The term "Municipal Committee" appears frequently in the documents. It refers to the Party Committee of the Foochow municipality.

[2] Ta-lu Fei-ch'ing Chi-pao (Mainland Conditions Quarterly), Taipei, July 1964, p. 2.

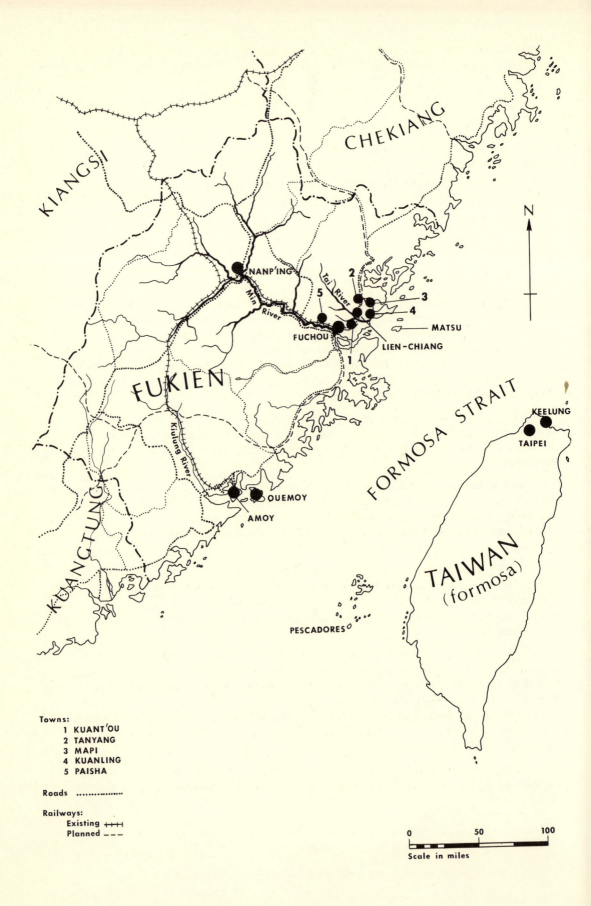

CHEKIANG

KIANGSI

NANP'ING

Min River

Tai River

2

5

3

4

MATSU

FUCHOU

LIEN-CHIANG

1

FUKIEN

N

FORMOSA STRAIT

Kiulung River

KEELUNG

TAIPEI

KWANGTUNG

QUEMOY

AMOY

TAIWAN
(formosa)

PESCADORES

Towns:
1 KUANT'OU
2 TANYANG
3 MAPI
4 KUANLING
5 PAISHA

Roads ·················

Railways:
Existing ┼┼┼
Planned ───

0   50   100

Scale in miles

Of the 240 brigades, only twelve are mentioned by name in the documents.[3] Thus the brigades (and teams) covered here represent a very small proportion of the total.

Period of the documents. The earliest of the documents printed here is dated February 1962; the latest belongs to March 1963. These dates are important for two reasons. First, the depression which, following the Great Leap Forward, gripped the economy of Lien-chiang along with that of the whole Chinese mainland reached its trough in 1961, after which the economy began to turn up.[4] The conditions and problems described in the documents are those belonging to the initial stage of an economic recovery. The optimism expressed in some of the documents was, therefore, not entirely propaganda but had a basis in the improving economic situation.

Secondly, 1962-63 were years during which the center of the commune system was in the process of being shifted from the brigade to the team. The implications of this shift will be analyzed at the appropriate place in subsequent pages.

Comparison with the early 1930's. Information about Lien-chiang during the early 1930's can be found in Chinese Farm Economy by John Lossing Buck.[5] Buck's data were collected during the twelve months which ended July 1923 from the three Lien-chiang villages of Shan-tsang-shan, Tung-hu, and Shan-hsia, the present names of which cannot be identified. It would be a pleasant surprise if the earlier data are, strictly speaking, comparable with those contained in this volume. Comparisons between the two will nevertheless be made in the following pages in the hope of gaining some light, however dim, on the changes that occurred over the period.

It should also be noted that many of the figures quoted in this analysis are only planned figures, not actual ones. It is not always possible to tell a planned figure from an actual one, but in general the two can be distinguished even where no explicit distinction is made between them in the text.

Communes in China. As of 1963, there were in Communist China a total of 74,000 communes, divided into 700,000 brigades and 5 million teams.[6] On the average, there were 7 teams in a brigade and 9.5 brigades in a commune. The

---

[3] They are: the Shan-k'ang, Hung-t'ang, Hu-p'ing, Hu-li, and Ch'ang-sha brigades of the P'u-k'ou commune; the Hua-wu, Lien-teng, and Shang-shan brigades of the Ao-chiang commune; the Ch'ih-shih, P'o-hsi and Tung-an brigades of the P'an-tu commune; and the Chu-ch'i brigade of the Kuan-t'ou commune. A few other names mentioned in the documents may be those of brigades, but they cannot be identified as such.

[4] The food-grain output in Lien-chiang County, 160 million catties in 1959, dropped to 109 million catties in 1961 and rose to 130 million catties in 1962. On the basis of these statistics the course of the economic depression in Lien-chiang can be roughly delineated: (a) the peak of the cycle was reached in 1959 and the trough in 1961; (b) during the two years of the depression the food-grain output declined 31.9 per cent, which may be taken as a measure of the magnitude of the depression; (c) during the first year of the recovery, from 1961 to 1962, food-grain production rose 19.3 per cent. The pace of the recovery naturally differed from sector to sector of the economy. Data in Documents V and VII show that during the same period of recovery fish production rose 2.4 per cent; the money income of the fishing industry, 13.9 per cent; number of pigs, 44.6 per cent; number of poultry, 33.3 per cent; total income of 71 brigades, 3.7 per cent; supply of manufactured goods, 23.0 per cent; supply of the means of production used in fishing, 63.3 per cent; and basic food ration, 26.1 per cent. On the other hand, the supply of the means of production used in agriculture declined 13 per cent.

[5] Published by the University of Chicago Press in 1930; hereafter cited as Buck.

[6] New China Yearbook, 1964 (in Japanese) (Tokyo, 1965), p. 319, and Ti-ching Yen-chiu (Studies in Enemy Conditions) (Taipei), No. 234, which are also the sources for the data presented in table 1.

size of a commune and its subdivisions can be gauged by reference to table 1.

Table 1

CROP LAND AND HOUSEHOLDS OF RURAL
COMMUNES IN COMMUNIST CHINA, 1963

Unit	Average area of crop land (in mou)	Average number of households
Commune	20,760	1,622
Brigade	2,180	171
Team	310	24

The average rural commune in Communist China was 4.7 times larger than a Russian collective farm in the number of households, but its area of crop land was only about half (53 per cent) the size of the Russian one.[7]

In extent of crop land, the brigades and teams in Lien-chiang were below the national average, the former by almost two-thirds (61 per cent) and the latter by three-quarters (77 per cent).[8]

Three stages of the commune. Since its establishment in 1958, the rural commune system in Communist China has passed through three stages, each characterized by a different accounting unit.

During the first stage, from August 1958, when the "Resolution on the Establishment of Rural People's Communes" was passed by the Central Committee of the Chinese Communist Party, to March 1959, the accounting unit was the commune. Another document, the "Resolution on Some Questions Concerning Rural People's Communes," adopted by the Central Committee on December 10, 1958, was of importance during this stage, but introduced no basic change in the commune system.

The second stage of the commune system began in March 1959, when the Central Political Bureau decided to shift the accounting unit from the commune to the brigade. The shift was formalized in the "Draft Regulations Governing Rural People's Communes" (hereafter referred to as "Draft Regulations") promulgated May 12, 1961. This stage ended a few months later, in November 1961, when the Central Committee issued a directive establishing the production team as the accounting unit.[9]

With the team as its accounting unit, the third stage began in November 1961 and is still continuing at this writing (1966). Its basic directives were set forth in the "Revised Draft Regulations Governing Rural People's Communes" (hereafter referred to as "Revised Draft Regulations"), promulgated in September 1962.

---

[7] New China Yearbook, 1964, p. 319, according to which a Soviet collective farm in 1959 averaged 343 households and 2,608 hectares, or 39,000 mou, of crop land.

[8] The average holding of crop land in Lien-chiang was 850 mou per brigade and 70 mou per team, in contrast with the national averages of 2,180 and 310 mou. See section III.

[9] Ta-lu Fei-ch'ing Chi-pao (Taipei), July 1964, pp. 8-9.

The accounting unit. An accounting unit, roughly defined, "carries on independent accounting, is responsible for its own profits and losses, organizes
production, and distributes income."[10]

The unit can be conveniently identified by reference to two of its characteristics,
namely, ownership of the means of production and the manner in which the output is
being distributed among its members. We shall illustrate these characteristics by
reference to the "Draft Regulations" of May 12, 1961, the basic document for the
second or brigade stage of the commune system. However, what is said below will
apply, mutatis mutandis, to situations in which the accounting unit was not the
brigade, but the team or the commune.

(1) Ownership of land, plow cattle, and agricultural implements. As the accounting unit, the brigade was given the ownership of the principal means of production ("Draft Regulations," Art. 17), including land, plow cattle, and agricultural
implements. The teams were given the use of these means, but they did not own
them. Only when the team became the accounting unit was the ownership in these
means of production--with perhaps the exception of ownership in land--transferred
("sent down") from the brigades to them.

(2) Distribution of the output. The second characteristic of the accounting unit
can be described as equality of distribution among members of the same unit. Distribution could not be equal in all matters. Basically, equal distribution applied to
the basic food ration, except for possible differentiation according to age and the
value of the work-points. In the first stage, when the commune was the accounting
unit, the basic ration was to be the same for all members of the same commune.
In the second stage, when the brigade was the accounting unit, the basic ration was
to be the same for all members of the same brigade, though it might differ from
brigade to brigade in the same commune to allow for differences in productivity.
Lastly, in the third stage, when the production team became the accounting unit,
the basic ration was to be the same for all members of the same team, though it
might differ from team to team in the same brigade.

The same principle of equal distribution applied to the value of the work-points.
When the commune was the accounting unit, the work-points received by members
of the same commune would have the same value, and when the brigade or the team
was the accounting unit, work-points received by their members were likewise to
have the same value.

Accounting units of the communes in Lien-chiang. Ownership of the means of
production and equality of distribution of output appear, then, to be two criteria
which can be used to identify an accounting unit. Chronologically, all documents
included here belong to the third stage, when the accounting unit had shifted from
the brigade to the production team, but in actual fact the transition had not yet been
completed in all cases.

In the few cases referred to in the documents, ownership of agricultural implements and plow cattle had been transferred by the brigades to the teams.[11] In the
Hu-li brigade of the P'u-k'ou commune, agricultural implements and cattle to a
total value of 21,202.55 yüan were transferred ("sent down") by the brigade to the
teams under it. No mention was, however, made of the transfer of ownership in
land.[12]

---

[10]Document VII.

[11]See Documents I and II.

[12]Document III, table 8.

In respect to the distribution of the output, there were instances in which the basic ration varied from team to team under the same brigade. This was an earmark of the third stage in the evolution of the commune. In the Hu-li, Hung-t'ang, and Hua-wu brigades the basic ration was, however, still equal for all members of the same brigade, indicating that the transition to the third stage had not been completed.

II

POPULATION AND LABOR

According to Document V, there were 10,480 babies born in Lien-chiang in 1962, and these represented 3.45 per cent of the population. By this ratio the population of the county in 1962 was about 304,000,[13] which can be compared with the figure of 220,000 reported around 1940.[14]

As the area of Lien-chiang totaled two million mou, the population density was 0.15 persons per mou or 583 persons per square mile.

The density of population in the farm area can only be roughly estimated. According to a pre-1937 report, 55.4 per cent of the households in Lien-chiang were farm households.[15] Applying this ratio to the 1962 population, there would be 168,000 farming persons, while the crop area was 204,000 mou or 525 square miles,[16] giving a population of 3,250 per square mile of crop area, compared with a corresponding figure of 1,277 for the 1920's.[17] The density of population in the individual brigades was even higher. It was 3,857 per square mile of crop land in Hu-li and 5,230 in Shan-k'ang.[18]

Number and size of households. It was stated in Document V that "In the entire county this year [1962] there were 4,576 households (6.5 per cent of the total number) either building new homes or making repairs." From this it can be inferred that the number of households in the county was 70,400. With the population at 304,000, the average number of persons per household in Lien-chiang would be 4.32.

The number was 4.00 persons per household in the Shan-k'ang brigade and 4.29 in the Hu-li brigade, the average being 4.15 persons, which may be taken as the

---

[13] Among the population there were 5,407 (1.6 per cent of the total population) Communist Party members and 13,169 (4.3 per cent) cadres. See Document XVIII.

[14] The Chung-lua New Geographical Gazetteer (Shanghai: Chung-lua Book Co., 1940), p. 108.

[15] Statistical Monthly (Nanking), January-February 1932. The reference was furnished by Dr. John Lossing Buck.

[16] See section III.

[17] Buck, p. 351.

[18] In the Hu-li brigade the crop area was 1,770 mou, or 0.456 square miles, and the population was 1,759. See Document III, table 1. In the Shan-k'ang brigade the crop area was 410 mou, or 0.106 square miles, and the population 552. See Document I.

average in the rural districts.[19] As the size of a household in the county as a whole was larger, at 4.32, the size of the average household in the urban regions thus should be slightly larger than that in the rural districts.

During the early 1920's the average farm household in Lien-chiang comprised 5.02 persons.[20] Allowing for the fact that the two sets of figures are not strictly comparable, it is probable that the size of families had declined over the years. In the earlier period, most (62.1 per cent) of the households in Lien-chiang were of the "large family" type, including relatives of the male head as members.[21] The partial disintegration of the large family was undoubtedly an important factor affecting the size of families in recent years.

Rate of population growth. According to the information already noted, the natural birth rate was 34.5 per thousand of the population. But the number of babies referred only to those born in the first ten months of 1962. For the full year, the natural birth rate works out as 41.4 per thousand, higher than the national average estimated at 34 per thousand for 1957. The death rate in Lien-chiang is not known. That for the mainland as a whole was estimated at 11.0 per thousand for 1957. If the same rate held true for Lien-chiang in 1962, then the natural increase of the Lien-chiang population would have been 3.14 per cent (41.4 minus 11.0), appreciably higher than the national average for 1957 estimated at 2.3 per cent.[22]

Sex composition. In 1962 the Hu-li brigade of the P'u-k'ou commune had a population of 1,759. Of this total, 902 were males and 857 females,[23] giving a sex ratio (number of males per 100 females) of 1.05 and a percentage of 51.3 male in the total population. This proportion conforms closely with that of the country as a whole in 1953, when males were estimated to exceed females in the ratio of 51.8 to 48.2,[24] but is drastically lower than Buck's findings, which put the sex ratio in Lien-chiang during the early 1920's at the unnaturally high figure of 137.[25] Buck's figures for the sex distribution during the 1920's by age group are summarized in table 2.

Apart from errors in counting, the explanations advanced by Buck to account for the high variations in the sex ratios among the age groups are these: under four years, infanticide affecting girls and better care given boys; 5-19 years, sale of girls to cities as slaves, concubines, prostitutes, and sing-song girls; 20-49 years, emigration of able-bodied males; and 50 years and above, longer life

---

[19] Derived from the population and household statistics given in Document I for the Shan-k'ang brigade and in Document III, table 1, for the Hu-li brigade.

[20] Buck, pp. 317, 327.

[21] Ibid., pp. 318 ff.

[22] The 1957 estimates are from S. Chandrasekhar, China's Population: Census and Vital Statistics (2d ed., Hong Kong, 1960), p. 53, quoted in Y. L. Wu et al., The Economic Potential of Communist China (Stanford, Calif.: Stanford Research Institute, 1963), I, 20. It may be interesting to note that for India the birth rate was officially given as 40 per 1,000 and the death rate as 16 per 1,000, giving a growth rate of 2.4 to 2.5 per cent, which Chandrasekhar considered too low. U.S. News and World Report, Apr. 3, 1967, p. 90.

[23] Document III, table 1.

[24] Data given by Chinese experts and quoted by John S. Aird in U.S. Congress, Joint Economic Committee, An Economic Profile of Mainland China, p. 364. Hereafter cited as Aird.

[25] Buck, p. 338.

of females.[26] A restoration in 1962 of the sex ratio to a more normal level of 105 may indicate that some, at least, of the factors mentioned by Buck have disappeared.

Table 2

SEX DISTRIBUTION IN LIEN-CHIANG (THREE VILLAGES)
DURING THE EARLY 1920's

Age group	Males	Females	Sex ratio
Under 4	38	20	190
5–19	205	83	243
20–49	199	195	102
50 and above	25	43	58

Source: Buck, pp. 337f.

Age composition. The Shan-k'ang brigade apportioned the basic ration according to age. Of the 552 persons in the brigade, 178 (32 per cent) were below the age of 14, and 374 (68 per cent) were 14 years of age or older.[27] For the country as a whole in 1953, persons aged 14 years or less constituted 35.9 per cent of the total population. On a pro rata basis, persons aged 13 years or less should be equal to 33.6 per cent of the total.[28] The proportion of persons 13 years or younger in the Shan-k'ang brigade was thus 1.6 percentage points below the national average. The difference might be due to causes peculiar to the Shan-k'ang brigade, but it may also indicate either that the depression of 1959-61 had adversely affected the marriage and birth rates, or that it had taken a relatively heavier toll of the younger generation.

Labor participation rate. The Hu-li brigade of the P'u-k'ou commune had a labor force of 675 out of a total population of 1,759. The proportion of the population which participated in agricultural work was therefore 38.4 per cent.[29]

In the Shan-k'ang brigade, also of the P'u-k'ou commune, the total agricultural labor force of 215 persons amounted to 38.9 per cent of a total population of 552.

The labor participation rates in the two brigades were, therefore, very similar to each other. Their average (38.6 per cent) will be taken as the labor participation rate for the whole commune system in Lien-chiang.

Full- and part-time agricultural workers. The labor force was made up of full-time and part-time agricultural workers. A full-time worker presumably referred to a male between the ages of 16 and 60 years or a female between the ages of 16 and

---

[26] Ibid., pp. 345-346.

[27] Document I, Appendix, table 2. The corresponding ratios for the early 1920's were 28 and 72 per cent respectively. See Buck, pp. 337-338.

[28] There appears to be a gap in the statistics for persons between 13 and 14. The gap is, however, more apparent than real. According to Chinese custom, a person, regardless of the month and day of his birth, would be counted as 13 years of age from New Year's Day to New Year's Eve and would become 14 when New Year's Day came round again. See semiofficial Chinese data quoted by Aird, p. 364. The national figure in 1953 for the age group below 14 years was 35.9 per cent. This has been reduced to 33.6 on a prorata basis to arrive at the percentage for the age group below 13 years.

[29] Document III, table 1.

50,[30] who worked full time in agricultural production. A part-time agricultural worker might mean one or both of two classes of persons: (a) those of working age who for one reason or another (such as having children to care for, being employed in nonagricultural work, and so on) were not working full time in agricultural production, and (b) those not of working age (youngsters and older people) who worked part time in agricultural production.

Of the 675 workers in the Hu-li brigade, 341 or slightly more than half (50.5 per cent) were full-time workers and 334 or slightly under half (49.5 per cent) part-time workers. In table 12 of Document III, the labor force of Hu-li in terms of full-time workers is given as 528, implying that one part-time worker was equivalent to 0.56 full-time workers on the average.

The Shan-k'ang brigade's labor force of 215 persons was made up of 93 (43.3 per cent) full-time and 122 (56.7 per cent) part-time workers.[31] The lower proportion of full-time workers in Shan-k'ang cannot be explained. Shan-k'ang had a high proportion of persons aged 14 years and older; it ought therefore to have had more full-time workers unless the proportions of old men and females in the population were abnormally high.

Male and female workers. In the Hu-li brigade, there were 373 male workers out of a male population of 902 and 302 female workers out of a female population of 857, indicating a labor participation rate of 41.4 per cent for the male population and 35.2 per cent for the female population. Corresponding figures for the U.S.A. were 50.9 and 27.1 per cent.[32] Although the two sets of ratios are not comparable except in the most general way, it appears that in the Hu-li brigade the rate of female participation in the labor force was comparatively high while the rate of male participation was comparatively low. Although the Hu-li ratio took no account of males engaged in nonagricultural work and was, to that extent, understated, probably the number of nonagricultural workers in Hu-li was not large and the understatement not great enough to affect this conclusion.

As is to be expected, most male workers were full-time workers and most female workers part-time workers. In the Hu-li brigade, for example, 272 (72.9 per cent) of a total of 373 male workers worked full-time and 233 (77.2 per cent) of a total of 302 female workers worked part-time.

Labor force in Lien-chiang compared with the 1920's. A rough comparison may be made between the labor force in the Hu-li and the Shan-k'ang brigades in 1962, and that in Lien-chiang in the early 1920's as reported by Buck, whose figures are in man-equivalents. This unit was defined by him as "the equivalent of one man working for a period of twelve months."[33] In converting the 1962 labor force into man-equivalents, a male worker, regardless of whether he worked full- or part-time is counted

---

[30] Document II.

[31] Document I.

[32] The U.S. ratios are estimated on the basis of a population (1965) of 194.6 million and a sex ratio of 98 (1950), whereby males would number 96.3 million and females 98.3 million, hence:

	1965 civilian labor force	Rate of participation
Males	49.0 million	50.9 per cent
Females	26.6 "	27.1 " "

Economic Report of the President (Washington, 1966) and Encyclopedia Britannica, 1966 ed., Vol. 22, p. 818.

[33] Buck, p. 20.

as one unit and a female worker as 80 per cent of a unit.[34] On this basis, the 373 male workers and 302 female workers of the Hu-li brigade becomes 615 in man-equivalents, or 9 per cent less than the combined total of 675 male and female workers. By the same ratio the Shan-k'ang brigade's labor force of 215 becomes 196 in man-equivalents. The labor forces of these two brigades are compared with conditions in the 1920's in table 3.

Table 3

MANPOWER IN LIEN-CHIANG

	Hu-li brigade (1962)	Shan-k'ang brigade (1962)	Average of the two brigades ((A)	Lien-chiang in early 1920's (B)	A/B (per cent)
(a) Number of households . . .	411	138	275	—	—
(b) Man-equivalent per household . .	1.50	1.42	1.46	1.68[a]	87
(c) Number of persons per household . . .	4.29	4.00	4.15	5.02	—
(d) c/b	2.85	2.82	2.84	2.95	96

[a]Per farm. Buck, p. 49.

Source: Data for Hu-li based upon Document III, table 1, and those for Shan-k'ang upon Document I.

The table indicates that the households in the two brigades concerned had only 87.0 per cent of the labor force of the 1920's. This may be partly due to the smaller size of households in Lien-chiang today. When this latter factor is allowed for, there appears to be no significant difference between the labor force now and then as indicated in the last line of the table.

The work day. The workers were required to work a certain number of days each month on the collective fields. Labor quotas of the Hung-t'ang brigade are shown in table 4.

In this brigade the distinction between a full-time and a part-time worker seemed to rest on the number of days a person worked in a month. In an unnamed team referred to in an omitted document, full-time workers were distinguished from part-time ones by the length of time worked per day. The labor quota for eight workers in this team was 56 man-days for an eight-day period, but they worked a total of only 27 man-days, indicating an absentee rate of 48 per cent. However, they performed the equivalent of 32 man-days in night work. Including the night work, the labor quotas were slightly overfulfilled. What probably happened was that they took time off during the day for private pursuits and made up their required labor quotas on the collective farm by working at night. Because of absenteeism, the people were able to attend to their private business; but despite absenteeism, thanks to night work, their labor quotas were fulfilled. Since night work cannot match day labor in quality or intensity, collective production probably suffered.

---

[34]Ibid., p. 17, table 8.

Table 4

LABOR QUOTAS IN THE HUNG-T'ANG BRIGADE

Workers	Number of required working days per month
Males:	
Age 16-50 years	26
Age 51-55 years	20
Age 56-60 years	13
Females:	
Age 16-40 years	22
Age 41-45 years	18
Age 46-60 years	15

Source: Document II.

Work-points. For labor on the collective land the workers were paid work-points which, so to speak, were their money wages.

Data concerning work-points for the Hu-li brigade are summarized in table 5.

Table 5

WORK-POINT BUDGET OF HU-LI BRIGADE

Class of worker	Number of workers	Number of work-points	
		Daily	Monthly
Male workers:			
First class (8 points each)	222	1776	—
Second class (7 points each)	87	609	—
Third class (6 points each)	62	372	—
Female workers:			
First class (6 points each)	90	540	—
Second class (5 points each)	102	510	—
Third class (4 points each)	109	436	—
Total	672	4243	102,294

Source: Document III, table 2.

The work-point system in the Hu-li brigade seemed to operate as follows:

(a) Work-points were paid on a time basis, not at a piece rate.

(b) Male and female workers were each divided into three classes. In the case of male workers, the remuneration was 8 work-points per day for a first-class worker, 7 for a second-class worker, and 6 for a third-class worker. For the same class, female workers received two work-points (one-fourth to one-third) less than the male workers. There was thus a differentiation in wages according to sex.

(c) The monthly wages were, it appears, reckoned on a twenty-four-day basis.[35]

According to data relating to the unnamed team mentioned above, part-time workers received half pay. There were ten workers in that team, of whom six were full-time workers, two part-time workers, and two with no labor quota. They were paid a flat rate of 100 work-points for full-time work and 50 points for part-time work, which rates were unusually high. In addition to the regular pay, they received extra work-points as follows:

(a) All except the two with no labor quotas were given an extra day's pay (100 points for the full-time workers and 50 points for the half-time workers) plus an extra bonus of 20 points at the end of an eight-day period from May 24 to May 31, 1963.

(b) Throughout the eight-day period there was night work, for which the workers were paid the part-time rate of 50 work-points per shift.[36]

_____

[35] (a) Monthly wages . . . . 102,294 work-points
(b) Daily wages. . . . . 4,243 work-points
(c) a/b . . . . 24.1 days
Data from Document III, table 2.

[36] The pay was not entirely uniform. For the first night the pay was only 30 work-points and for another night it was 40 work-points. There seemed to be two shifts of night work. For those who worked two shifts, the pay was more than twice that for the single shift.

III

THE MEANS OF PRODUCTION

What is called the "means of production" in communist literature is referred to as input (excluding labor) in Western terminology. It includes land, machines, equipment, and materials used for the production of other goods and services. The term is, therefore, broader in scope than what we would classify as capital goods, in that it includes also land and intermediate materials.

LAND

Crop area. The total area of Lien-chiang was two million Chinese mou, or 1,333 square kilometers. In Document V it is stated that 4,178 mou was equal to 2.05 per cent of the crop area. On the basis of these figures, the crop land of the county would be 204,000 mou, or about 10 per cent of the total area.

As there were 240 brigades and 2,898 teams in Lien-chiang, there would be an average of 850 mou of crop land for each brigade and 70 mou for each team. The last is a significant figure. In the commune system the team was the operating unit, comparable to the farm of the early 1920's, whose area averaged 15 mou.[37] The land used by a team was thus 4.7 times the size of a former farm.

During the early 1920's "large farms" (33 mou) in Lien-chiang were more profitable and produced greater yields per unit area than "medium" farms (10 mou), and medium farms more profitable and productive than "small" ones (5 mou).[38] There thus appeared to be increasing returns to scale. Since the operating unit in 1962, the production team, was twice the size of the earlier large farms, it is quite possible that the optimum size of an operating unit had been exceeded. True, a farming unit of 70 mou (11.5 acres) would be extremely small by United States standards; yet in China it would be unusually large. Whether Chinese peasants possessed the knowledge and experience required for managing such a "large" farm is questionable. To the increase in the scale of agricultural operations can perhaps be traced many of the problems which confronted the commune system in its earlier years.

Planted area. Most of the crop area in Lien-chiang was paddy land which could be planted twice a year. The planted area could thus be larger than the crop area.[39]

---

[37] Buck, pp. 35, 44.

[38] Ibid., pp. 115, 133.

[39] One mou of crop land when used for two crops in the course of the same year is counted as two planted mou, and so on.

The Hu-li brigade's total crop area of 1,770 mou included 1,252 mou of paddy fields, of which 1,030 mou could be used for two crops a year. The planting of two crops thus could increase the planted paddy area by 82.3 per cent and the total planted area by 58.2 per cent.

The Shan-k'ang brigade's total crop area of 497 mou included 337 mou in paddy fields, of which 326 mou could be used for two crops a year. The planting of two crops a year thus could increase the planted paddy area by 96.7 per cent and the total planted area by 65.6 per cent.

The double-cropping index for the Hu-li brigade was thus 1.58 and that for the Shan-k'ang, 1.66, giving an average of 1.62.[40] If the last figure can be taken to be the double-cropping index for the county as a whole, then the planted area of Lien-chiang, with a total crop area of 204,000 mou, should come to 330,000 mou.

The autumn crop was more productive than the spring crop. In the Hsiao-yü commune, the areas scheduled for early and late planting in 1960 were about equal, but 64 per cent of the total output was expected to come from the late crop, and only a little more than one-third (36 per cent) from the early crop.[41]

Ratio of land to man. The land-to-man ratios in the Shan-k'ang and Hu-li brigades in Lien-chiang are shown in table 6.

Table 6

LAND-TO-MAN RATIOS IN LIEN-CHIANG
(in mou)

Basis	Shan-k'ang Brigade	Hu-li Brigade	Average
Crop area per household	3.6	4.3	4.0
Crop area per person	0.9	1.0	1.0
Crop area per worker	2.3	2.6	2.5
Crop area per man-equivalent of the labor force.	2.5	2.9	2.7

Source: Shan-k'ang data based upon Appendix to Document I, Hu-li data upon Document III, table 1.

For many purposes, the crop area per person is the most significant figure. It averaged 1 mou, or one-sixth of an acre, in the two brigades, slightly larger than the size of an average residential lot in the suburbs of New York, which is one-eighth of an acre. It is common knowledge that the small ratio of land to man underlies most of China's economic ills, but it is not generally realized that the average per capita holding could be so small.

In this respect Lien-chiang was probably not a representative county. The East Flower commune in Kwangtung Province, which was also a double-cropping rice district, had in 1962 a population of some 50,000 and crop lands of 84,000

---

[40] During the 1920's the average crop area per farm in Lien-chiang was 1.01 hectares, while the average planted area was 1.14 hectares, giving a double-cropping index of 1.14. Buck, p. 46.

[41] Unpublished document.

mou.[42] There were, therefore, 1.7 mou of crop land per person, which was 1.7 times the per capita holding in the Lien-chiang brigades.

As has been noted, the average crop area per farm in Lien-chiang in the early 1920's was 15 mou. There was an average of 5.02 persons in a farm household and hence a crop area per person of 3 mou. Over the forty-year period, the crop area per person thus declined by two-thirds. Even though these figures are subject to error, they point unmistakably to the serious effect of population growth on the land-to-man ratio.

Private plots. The crop area can be classified according to the part collectively held under the commune system and the part held privately by the peasants.

By law, the area of private plots could not exceed 5 to 7 per cent of a team's crop area.[43] Nevertheless, in the Hu-li brigade the private plots amounted to 9.5 per cent of its crop land. The situation varied from team to team in the brigade. At one extreme, the private plots in one team amounted to 11 per cent of its crop land and at the other, 7.6 per cent.[44] In the Shan-k'ang brigade, the private plots in the individual teams ranged from 12.1 per cent to 15 per cent of the crop area, the average being 13.1 per cent.[45] For the two brigades, the private plots averaged 11.3 per cent of their crop land, which was substantially higher than the limits set by law.

In area the private plots in the Hu-li brigade averaged 0.45 mou per household and 0.11 mou per person. Corresponding figures for the Shan-k'ang brigade were 0.46 and 0.12 mou. For the two brigades the average private plot was 0.46 mou per household and 0.12 mou per person. These averages will be taken as representative of the county as a whole.

Besides the private plots, team members might also hold reclaimed land and land for growing animal feed. In addition, some land collectively owned by the teams was farmed out to the members for cultivation.

The reclaimed land in the county amounted to 40,000 mou,[46] or 19.6 per cent of the crop area.

Farmed-out land was 4,178 mou,[47] or 2.05 per cent of the county's crop area.

Private plots (11.3 per cent), reclaimed land (19.6 per cent), and farmed-out land (2.05 per cent) together constituted the "Small Freedom" land, which amounted to more than 30 per cent of the crop area. In some teams the proportion was more than 50 per cent.[48]

Private plots and the economic recovery of 1961. The documents contain information which may help show the role played by private plots in the economic recovery of the early 1960's.

---

[42] Anna Louise Strong, The Rise of the Chinese People's Communes--And Six Years After (Peking: New World Press, 1964), pp. 177, 181.

[43] "Revised Draft Regulations," Art. 40.

[44] Document III, table 3.

[45] Document I, Appendix, table 1.

[46] Document V.

[47] Document V. According to Document XVIII, the total was 4,326 mou.

[48] Document V. The total area of private plots, reclaimed land, and land for growing animal feed was restricted to a maximum of 15 per cent of a team's land, "Revised Draft Regulations," Art. 40.

What turned the economic tide in Lien-chiang, as in the country as a whole, was the increase in food-grain production. The food-grain output in Lien-chiang in 1962 was given as 130 million catties, of which 111 million catties were grown on collective land.[49] By implication, the remaining 19 million catties came from privately held land.

Of the land held privately, 40,000 mou represented reclaimed land and 23,000 mou (11.3 per cent of crop land) were in private plots. On a prorata basis, the food-grain output of the private plots should be 7 million catties (19 x 23/53) or 5.4 per cent of total output, which seemed to be too small a tail to wag the dog of the economy. What was more, the 7 million catties did not represent a net gain in output. Since the private plots were carved out of the collective land,[50] their contribution to the economic recovery should not be equated to their total production but to their total production minus what they would have produced had they remained under the collective system. The difference, which is attributable to the greater efficiency of the private plots, should have been less than the 7 million catties just mentioned.

Thus, in the light of the experience of Lien-chiang, the role of the private plots in the economic recovery of the early 1960's was probably not too important. Yet to say this is not to imply that private plots, along with other forms of private enterprise, made no contribution to the economic recovery. Their contribution can be summed up under three headings as follows:

(a) Reclaimed land. The most important contribution of private initiative lay in the opening up of waste land, which was entirely due to private efforts. As the food-grain output of privately held land was 19 million catties, of which 7 million catties were attributable to the private plots, the food-grain output of reclaimed land can be put at 12 million catties or 9 per cent of the total output.

(b) Better land use. Probably less than half the privately held land, both private plots and reclaimed land, was used for food-grain production and more than half for higher-valued products.[51] To the extent that the private plots would have been used for growing grains had they remained under the collective system, their being used for higher-valued products represented better land use. Better land use not only increased the national product but also made available a larger variety of foodstuffs, such as poultry, pork, and vegetables, for the local diet and for export.

(c) Higher productivity. It should be true that the privately held land was more productive because it was worked with more care and labor. But against this gain in the productivity of the privately held land must be set the accompanying loss to the productivity of the collective land. A case has

---

[49] Document V. It is not clear whether the amounts quoted here represented the actual or the planned output.

[50] Document V.

[51] The 63,000 mou of privately held land produced 19 million catties of food grains. The average output per mou was 301 catties, or less than half the average output for all cultivated land, estimated at 693 catties per mou. Assuming that the privately held land was at least as productive as other land, this would indicate that less than half of it was devoted to the growth of food grains.

been cited in which the peasants were suspected of taking time off to attend to private business during the day while making up their work for the collective at night.

Land use. The crop area in Lien-chiang was partly paddy fields and partly dry land. Paddy fields were fields in which rice was produced with irrigation or by retaining rainfall and runoff. Apart from rice, fruits and vegetables were also grown in paddy fields. The dry fields were used for growing sweet potatoes, peanuts, and fruit trees. The vacant land between fruit trees was also utilized, presumably for sweet potatoes although the sweet potato is a deep-rooted crop for which such land might not be suitable.

Most (92 per cent) of the crop area in Lien-chiang was used to grow rice and sweet potatoes, as table 7 shows. [52]

Table 7

LAND USE IN LIEN-CHIANG

Crop	Area (Mou)	Per cent of crop land
Rice	141,033	69.2
Sweet potatoes	46,060	22.6
Economic crops (jute, peanuts, etc.)	10,802	5.3
Other	5,910	2.9
Total	203,805	100.0

Source: Derived from data given in Document V.

From the table it is seen that 91.8 per cent of the crop land in the county was used to grow rice and sweet potatoes. The corresponding proportion was lower in some of the brigades for which information is available, being 83 per cent for the Hu-li brigade and 82 per cent for the Shan-k'ang brigade. [53]

Output per unit area. As mentioned above, Lien-chiang's output of food grains (including sweet potatoes converted to grain-equivalents at the ratio of 4 catties of sweet potatoes to one catty of grain) in 1962 was given as 130 million catties. With

---

[52] During the early 1920's the planted area in Lien-chiang (three villages) was distributed as follows (Buck, pp. 184-185):

	Per cent
Rice	43.8
Sweet potatoes	33.9
Subtotal	77.7
Wheat	7.3
Economic crops	4.5
Other	10.5
Total	100.0

Over the years there thus appears to have been a decline in the relative importance of sweet potatoes and wheat and an increase in that of rice.

[53] Data for Hu-li are based upon Document III, table 4, and for Shan-k'ang upon Document I, Appendix, table 1.

the crop area at 204,000 mou and 92 per cent[54] of that area planted in rice and sweet potatoes, the output of food grains would be 693 catties per mou, or 5,198 kilograms per hectare.[55]

CAPITAL

The scarcity of land was undoubtedly the key factor retarding economic progress in Lien-chiang, as it was elsewhere in China. Three possible remedies for the situation would be emigration, development of industries, and increased use in agriculture of capital and new technology.

The communes not only refused to condone emigration, which would deplete them of the labor force needed for agricultural production, but actually acted to stop it.

As to nonagricultural industries, Lien-chiang was reported to have a fair-sized cotton textile factory with 10,000 spindles. There were also shipyards at K'uan-t'ou and T'a-t'ou.[56]

The commune system also operated industrial enterprises of its own. Thus, the Hung-t'ang brigade had a shell-ash workshop. Other commune units operated the industrial enterprises listed in table 8.

Because of their small size and the limited varieties of goods they produced, the nonagricultural enterprises do not lend support to the view that communes were self-sufficient economic units, or that they played any important part in helping raise the economic level in the countryside.

Aggravating the situation was the paucity of capital equipment and the lack of new investments.

Construction. In 1962, dwellings amounting to a total of 8,747 rooms were newly built or repaired by 4,576 households.[57] Houses, however, were not capital goods used directly in production.

With respect to productive construction, irrigation and water conservation were emphasized.

Water-conservation work planned for 1963 required 380,000 man-days of labor, averaging 1.25 days per person per year for the total population, or 2.25 days per person among the rural population on the basis of the pre-1937 ratio that 55.4 per cent of the population in Lien-chiang was rural.[58] In addition, the work would entail a cash outlay of 700,000 yüan and would benefit 85,000 mou of land, with the cash expenditure averaging 7.4 yüan (US$3) per mou.[59]

Agricultural implements. The establishment of the commune system was conceived as paving the way for the mechanization and electrification of agriculture.

---

[54] See p. 16 and 20, above.

[55] This agrees with the official figure of 695 catties per mou for double-cropping rice fields (Document V). According to Buck (p. 204), the output in Lien-chiang was 1,090 catties per mou in the early 1920's. Buck's figure related to the output of rice only.

[56] Ta-lu Fei-ch'ing Chi-pao, July 1964, p. 3.

[57] Document V.

[58] See p. 9, above.

[59] Document VII.

Table 8

NONAGRICULTURAL ENTERPRISES,
HSIAO-YÜ COMMUNE AND HU-LI BRIGADE

Workshops	Hsiao-yü commune Budgeted revenue in 1959 (yüan)	Hu-li brigade Budgeted revenue in 1962 (yüan)
Agricultural implements	18,100	
Shipyard	13,000	
Construction	31,900	
Mattress	10,000	
Sewing	6,000	
Others	2,000	
Total	81,000	
Rice mill		3,000
Bricks and tiles		4,000
Total		7,000

Sources: Data on the Hsiao-yü commune are from an unpublished document. Data on the Hu-li brigade are from Document III, table 11.

In Document V there was reference to 11 new tractors, which were presumably under the management of the communes or brigades for the common use of the units under them. As shown by table 8 in Document III, the agricultural implements whose ownership was transferred or "sent down" from the Hu-li brigade to the teams under it were all the conventional type, including deep plows, old-style plows, large wheelbarrows, small wheelbarrows, hoes, scuffle hoes, wooden racks, sprays, scales, and old-style rakes. The deep plows and old-style plows "sent down" numbered 48 and the scuffle hoes, 1,007. As there were 1,770 mou of crop land in the Hu-li brigade, there were thus one plow to every 37 mou of land and one scuffle hoe to every 1.8 mou of land. As compared with conditions in 11 localities in East Central China during the 1930's, where there was one plow for every 30.8 mou of crop land and one scuffle hoe for each 12.4 mou, [60] the Hu-li brigade was equipped with 6.8 times as many scuffle hoes but only 83 per cent as many plows. The scuffle hoe was a simple tool, while in the Chinese countryside the plow could be considered a relatively heavy implement. There was thus a tremendous increase in light tools and a relative decline in the heavier implements.

---

[60] T. Ogden King, Farm Implements in East Central China (University of Nanking, Bulletin 53, New Series, February 1938), pp. 108, 112. The editor is indebted to Dr. Buck for furnishing this reference and for suggesting the comparison.

Table 9

LABOR-ANIMAL UNITS IN THE HU-LI AND
SHAN-K'ANG BRIGADES, COMPARED WITH THE EARLY 1920's

	Lien-chiang, 1962			Lien-chiang, Early 1920's
	Hu-li	Shan-k'ang	Average	
Labor-animal units . . .	98[a]	24[a]		
Planted area (mou) . . .	2,797[b]	825[b]		
Planted mou per animal unit	29	34		12.9[c]
Labor animal unit per planted mou . . .	0.035	0.029	0.032	0.078

Sources: [a]Footnote 25, above. [b]See above. [c]Buck, p. 312.

Animal power. In table 9 the supply of draft animals (plow cattle) in two of the brigades in Lien-chiang is compared with the supply in the early 1920's as reported by Buck. The recent data have been converted to labor-animal units as used by Buck, so as to facilitate comparison.[61] As is evident from the table, the average number of labor-animal units for each planted mou in the two brigades was 0.032. This is about 40 per cent of the animal power available in the early 1920's, when the labor-animal unit per planted mou was 0.078.

OTHER MEANS OF PRODUCTION

Fertilizer. The main sources of plant nutrients were organic fertilizers (including marine fertilizers) and mud dug up from ponds and river beds. In the / Shang-shan brigade the scheduled application was 2,500 catties per mou,[62] as compared with an early 1920's figure of 1,200 catties per mou.[63]

Chemical fertilizer of unspecified nature was applied only on a limited scale-- 16.5 catties per mou.[64] The optimum application of chemical fertilizers can be put at about 500 kilograms per hectare,[65] equivalent to 67 catties per mou. Measured against this standard, the actual application of chemical fertilizers in Lien-chiang was only a fourth of the optimum quantity. Assuming that each additional catty of chemical fertilizer used could increase grain output by 2.5 to 3 catties (that is, a yield-response coefficient of 2.5 to 3), the optimum use of chemical fertilizers could raise the output of each mou by 125 to 150 catties, or by 18 to 21 per cent of the 1962 output.

[61]See Buck, p. 25. In computing the labor-animal unit, an adult yellow ox is counted as one unit and a water buffalo as one and a third units. Nonadult animals are not counted. According to data furnished by Dr. Buck, adult and nonadult animals in the double-cropping rice regions before 1937 were in the proportion of 76 to 24. Yellow oxen and water buffaloes in Lien-chiang during the early 1920's were in the proportion of 88 to 12 (Buck, p. 219). These ratios have been applied to the data for the Hu-li and Shan-k'ang brigades, which had 126 and 30 draft animals respectively. (Document I; Document III, table 8.)

[62]Document XI.

[63]Buck, p. 224.

[64]Document V.

[65]The amount would vary with the kind of fertilizer used. The optimum combination of plant nutrients is 60 kg. of N, 30 kg. of P_2O_5, and 15 kg. of K_2O for each hectare of land.

Conclusion. Some of the conclusions concerning the economy of Lien-chiang as reached in the preceding pages are summed up in table 10.

Table 10

SUMMARY OF FACTORS AFFECTING
PRODUCTION IN LIEN-CHIANG

Factor	Lien-chiang, 1962	Three villages, early 1920's
Labor force:		
Man-equivalent per household	1.46 (2 brigades)	1.68
Persons in household per man-equivalent	2.84 (2 brigades)	2.95
Crop land per person (in mou)	1.00 (2 brigades)	3.00
Fertilizer (catties per mou)		
Traditional	2,500 (1 brigade)	1,500
Chemical	16.5 (whole country)	. . .
Agricultural implements:		
Light (scuffle hoes, number of mou per unit)	1.8 (1 brigade)	12.4
Heavy (plows, number of mou per unit)	37 (1 brigade)	30.8
Labor-animal unit per planted mou	0.032 (2 brigades)	0.078
Output per mou (catties)	693 (whole country) 815 (2 brigades)	1,090

If we examine table 10, we shall see that in two respects (fertilizers and light agricultural implements) the year 1962 was in better shape than the 1920's; but in other respects, especially in the land-to-man ratio, in animal power, and in unit-area output, conditions had deteriorated over the years. The decline in the ratio of land to man was the inevitable result of population growth, while the decline in animal power and in unit-area output were attributable, in part, to the great depression of the preceding years.

IV

PRODUCTION AND DISTRIBUTION

PRODUCTION

All stages of a commune's work, from production to distribution, were planned. The production plan of the Hu-li brigade is summarized in table 11.

Table 11

PRODUCTION PLAN OF THE HU-LI BRIGADE
(In thousands of catties)

Crop	Planned output	Quota output
Food-grain equivalents:		
Rice		
Collective land	904.1	837.5
Private plots	79.6	-
Sweet potatoes[a]		
Collective land	264.1	241.2
Private plots.	54.2	-
Economic crops:		
Jute	-	11.8
Vegetables	-	126.0
Peanuts	-	3.6
Fruits	-	128.6

[a]Converted into grain equivalents at the ratio of 4 catties of sweet potato to 1 catty of grain.

Source: Planned output—Document III, table 3; quota output of food-grain equivalents from table 5 and economic crops from table 7 of the same document.

In respect to food grains, the plan contains not one but two series of production targets, here called the planned production and the quota production. The quota production differed from the planned production in three respects. First, the quota production did not include the output of the private plots, whereas the planned production did. Second, the quota production included only part of the output of the collective land, whereas the planned production included the whole of it. In this example the planned production of the collective land totaled 1,168,000 catties, of which only 1,079,000 catties (or 92.4 per cent) were counted as the quota production. What factors determined the spread between the two is not clear. Third, it was the quota production, not the planned production, which governed the distribution of the food-grain output. This point is discussed in the next section.

DISTRIBUTION OF FOOD GRAINS

General view. As distribution was based upon the quota production of the collective land, the output of private plots was not included in the total to be distributed. The quota production of the Hu-li, Hung-t'ang, and Shan-k'ang brigades was scheduled to be distributed as shown in table 12.

From the table it will be seen that the quota production of the three brigades was allocated between two main uses, namely, state levies and purchases, and the three retained foods.

State levies and purchases. State levies were the agriculture tax, while state purchases were the compulsory purchases made by the state, in quantities and at prices fixed by it. Products subject to state purchases included food grains, cotton, and other crops specified by the authorities.

It has been reported that state levies ranged from 21 to 25 per cent of the quota production.[66] During the years under consideration state levies were a much lower percentage than 21 to 25 and the major part of the combined total of levies and purchases represented purchases made by the state. In the Shan-k'ang brigade, the combined levies and purchases in 1962 were scheduled at 148,000 catties, or 48.7 per cent of the quota production. Of the quantity, only 15,735 catties, which equaled 5.2 per cent of the quota production and 10.6 per cent of the combined levy-purchase total, represented levies and the rest purchases.[67]

In the Hu-li brigade, rice was valued at 8.6 yüan per tan of 100 catties[68]--which might also be the price paid by the state for its purchases. At the official rate of exchange of 2.46 yüan to one U.S. dollar, the state's purchase price amounted to US $70 per ton of unshelled rice.

The Three Retained Foods. The Three Retained Foods referred to the quantities set aside for seed, feed, and human rations.

An average of 3.0 per cent of the quota production was retained as seed. The quantity thus retained was calculated on the basis of all collective land, not only on that part of it used for the quota production.

---

[66] Ta-lu Fei-ch'ing Chi-pao, Taipei, January 1965, p. 4.

[67] Document I, Appendix, table 2. According to Strong, op. cit., p. 179, taxes were less than 5 per cent of the gross income and about 7 per cent of the net income. Similar figures were given in the South China Morning Post, Hong Kong, February 17, 1966. In Strong's study, gross income referred to the total income to be discussed below.

[68] During the early 1920's the price of rice was 3.50 the then Chinese yüan per 100 catties (Buck, p. 214). In rice, the Communist yüan is thus equal to 40 per cent (3.50/8.60) of the 1920 yüan.

Table 12

DISTRIBUTION OF FOOD-GRAIN PRODUCTION IN LIEN-CHIANG

	Hu-li brigade		Hung-t'ang brigade		Shan-k'ang brigade		Average of three brigades
	Quantity (catties)	Per cent of total	Quantity (catties)	Per cent of total	Quantity (catties)	Per cent of total	Per cent of total
Seed	24,794	2.3	29,500	3.5	9,000	3.0	3.0
State levy and purchase . .	530,900	49.2	372,000	44.3	148,000	48.7	47.4
Feed	24,340[a]	2.3	18,300	2.2	6,000	2.0	2.2
Ration	487,897	45.2	421,500	50.0	-	45.7	46.9
Work . . .	(71,143)[b]	(6.6)	(50,500)	(6.0)	(14,881)	(4.9)	(5.8)
Basic . . .	(416,754)[b]	(38.6)	(371,000)	(44.0)[c]	(123,936)	(40.8)	(41.1)
To the brigade . .	2,058[d]	0.2	-	-	-	-	-
Others	8,774[e]	0.8	-	-	1,919	0.6	0.5
Total	1,078,763	100.0	841,300	100.0	303,736	100.0	100.0

Sources: Document III, table 6; Document II; and Document I, Appendix.

[a]Including feed for fowls owned by the brigade. [b]Includes ration for brigade enterprise personnel. [c]The percentage given in Document II is 42.9, which seems to be incorrect. [d]Exclusive of feed for fowls owned by the brigade and ration for brigade enterprise personnel. [e]A computed residual amount.

A slightly lower percentage (2.2 per cent) of the quota production was set aside as feed. The eighteen teams in the Hu-li brigade reared a total of 21 pigs, 1,770 ducks, and 40 geese. The pigs belonged to the individual teams; the fowls were brigade property. Presumably these were in addition to animals and birds privately kept by the households. The retained feed per head per year was 40 catties for pigs, 3 for ducks raised for meat, 60 for ducks raised for eggs, and 70 for geese.

For human rations an average of 46.9 per cent of the quota production was allotted.

Human rations were divided into the basic ration and the work ration. The basic ration was the same for all members in the same brigade. It was 234 catties per person per year for the Hu-li brigade, 198 catties for the Hung-t'ang brigade, and 225 catties for Shan-k'ang brigade.[69] The work ration, distributed presumably in proportion to the number of work-points earned by the peasants,[70] averaged 5.8 per cent of the quota production, or 12.4 per cent of the total ration in the three brigades.

It appears that in the Hu-li brigade the provision for seed took precedence over state levies and purchases, and that in the Hung-t'ang brigade state levies took precedence over the Three Retained Foods, while the Three Retained Foods took precedence over state purchases.[71]

DISTRIBUTION OF ECONOMIC CROPS AND FRUITS

Economic crops and fruits were also subject to production quotas and state purchases. Economic crops included jute, peanuts, and vegetables such as taro, ginger, and eggplant.[72] What proportion of them was subject to compulsory purchases by the state is not known. As for fruits, the Hu-li brigade's quota production in 1962 was set at 128,631 catties. Of this, 52,560 catties (or 41 per cent) were to be retained by the peasants at 30 catties per person, while 76,071 catties (or 59 per cent) were to be sold to the state.[73]

INCOME AND ITS DISTRIBUTION

Total income. The value, in monetary terms, of the food grains, economic crops, and fruits, together with the revenues from nonagricultural enterprises, constituted the "total income" of a team or brigade, out of which appropriations were to be made for the three funds, namely, the reserve fund, the welfare fund, and the administrative fund. When computing the total income, no allowance was made for the part of output which was taxed away by the government or for costs of production.

The income of the teams under the Hu-li brigade totaled 148,294 yüan[74] and

---

[69] See footnote 83.

[70] See, for example, Document I.

[71] Documents II and III.

[72] See Document III, table 12.

[73] Document III, table 7.

[74] Document III, table 11. The total income for 71 brigades mentioned in Document V was 8,780,000 yüan, averaging 123,661 yüan per brigade and 10,305 yüan per team. These compared with 148,294 yüan for the Hu-li brigade, which averaged 8,239 yüan per team and 84 yüan per head of population.

was derived to the extent of five-eighths from food production and to the extent of one-eighth each from the production of economic crops, fruits, and nonagricultural enterprises, as shown in table 13.

Table 13

TOTAL INCOME, HU-LI BRIGADE

Source of income	Quota production (tan)	Unit price (yüan)	Amount (yüan)	Per cent of total amount
Food grain	1,078.6	8.6	92.761	62.6
Economic crops . . .	-	-	18,078	12.2
Fruits	1,286.3	15.0	19,295	13.0
Brigade enterprise . .	-	-	18.160[a]	12.2
Total			148,294	100.0

[a]This is a residual sum derived by deducting all other items from the total. The actual figure, given in Document III, table 10, is 18,200 yüan.

Source: Document III, table 10.

Each team was to set aside 3 per cent of its total income for the reserve fund and 2 per cent each for the welfare and administrative funds.[75] The funds thus set aside were to be shared by them with the brigade. Table 14 shows the detailed allocations.

Reserve fund. The reserve fund was to be used for purposes of further production. Capital construction and the purchases of cattle, tools, implements, and fertilizer were to be paid for out of this fund. It was moderate in amount, ranging from 75 to 135 yüan per team per year.[76] This paucity of funds was undoubtedly a major cause of the backwardness of the county's agriculture. Its effect was mitigated by various means. The county's construction plan for 1963, for example, envisaged the repair and completion of 182 projects, which required 380,000 man-days of labor, 230,000 cubic meters of earth and stonework, and 700,000 yüan of cash. The larger of those works were to be carried out by the municipal (Foochow) and county (Lien-chiang) governments, while the units of the communes were responsible for only the smaller jobs, which could be done mostly by labor without large outlays in cash. Moreover, loans were given by the state. For these reasons, the commune system was able to get by with relatively small amounts of reserve funds, but its investments had naturally to be confined in the main to the labor-intensive types.

---

[75]In the Shan-k'ang brigade the corresponding distributions were: reserve fund, 5 per cent of total income; welfare fund, 5 per cent; and administrative fund, 2 per cent (Document I). In the Hung-t'ang brigade, the corresponding percentages were: reserve, 4.0; welfare, 2.0; and administrative, 1.5 to 2.0 (Document II).

[76]Document III, table 11.

Table 14

ALLOCATIONS FOR RESERVE, WELFARE, AND
ADMINISTRATIVE FUNDS, HU-LI BRIGADE

Fund	Per cent	Yüan
Reserve	3.0	4,458
To brigade	(1.5)	(2,229)
For teams	(1.5)	(2,229)
Welfare	2.0	2,986
To brigade	(1.0)	(1,493)
For teams	(1.0)	(1,493)
Administrative	2.0	2,986
To brigade	(0.8)	(1,194)
For teams	(1.2)	(1,792)
Total		10,430

Source: Document III, table 11.

Welfare fund. The welfare fund was to be used for social activities, entertainment, and the relief of persons in need.

Some households in the communes were deficient in food. For example, 115
persons in 27 households in the Ch'ang-sha brigade were each deficient in food for
one month out of the year, and 62 persons in 16 households for half a month.[77]
Since other households might have more food than they consumed, food deficiency
in part of the households does not necessarily mean that the whole brigade had a
food deficit. Assuming that it did, the food shortage would amount to 1.84 per
cent of requirements.[78] The families in hardship were provided with food from
the welfare fund at the rate of 30 catties for each person with a one-month deficiency and 15 catties for each person with a half-month deficiency. The relief
cost a total of 4,520 catties of food at a total value of 389 yüan. The details are
given in table 15.

_____

[77]Unpublished document.

[78](a) Number of households (Document XV, table 8).   153
(b) Number of persons (a x 4.32, the average number of persons
        per household for the county as a whole).   661
(c) Food requirements in man-months (b x 12). 7,932
(d) Food deficiency in man-months:
        115 persons with one month deficiency . . . .   (115)
        62 persons with half-month deficiency . . . . (31)
    Total food deficiency in man-months   146
(e) Per cent of food deficiency (d/c) 1.84

Table 15

FOOD-DEFICIENT HOUSEHOLDS, CH'ANG-SHA BRIGADE

Type of household	One-month deficiency	Half-month deficiency	Total
"Five Guaranteed" households:			
Number of households	2	2	4
Number of persons	2	3	5
Deficiency in food (catties)	60	50	110
Military, cadre, worker, and "sent down" households encountering hardship:			
Number of households	4	2	6
Number of persons	17	12	29
Deficiency in food (catties)	510	200	710
Households encountering hardship because of illness or too many children:			
Number of households	16	4	20
Number of persons	80	13	93
Deficiency in food (catties)	2,400	200	2,600
Other households:			
Number of households	5	8	13
Number of persons	16	34	50
Deficiency in food (catties)	500	600	1,100
Total:			
Number of households	27	16	43
Number of persons	115	62	177
Deficiency in food (catties)	3,470	1,050	4,520

Source: Unpublished document.

As can be seen from the table, more than half of the aid went to households encountering hardship because of illness or too many children. The next largest groups receiving aid were the group of unclassified households and the group of military, cadre, worker, and "sent-down" households which were encountering hardship, while relatively little aid was allotted to the aged, the weak, the orphaned, the widowed, and the infirm and disabled--the so-called Five Guaranteed households.

Administrative fund. Of the total administrative fund of 2,986 yüan (table 14), 896 yüan was used to pay the wages of the brigade cadres, 1,345 yüan to pay the wages of the team cadres, and the remaining 745 yüan for all other administrative expenses.[79]

The fund available for the remuneration of team cadre members thus amounted to an average of 74.8 yüan per team per year (since there were 18 teams in the brigade), or 6.2 yüan per team per month. Elsewhere in the documents, the monthly wages of a cadre were mentioned as 33 yüan[80] and 28 yüan.[81] The earmarked fund of a team was obviously not large enough to pay such wages. In actual fact, however, the remunerations of cadres were not paid out of the administrative funds. Some cadres were paid by the government, while others were paid in kind (basic rations) and in work-points in the same way as an ordinary peasant. The administrative fund earmarked as wages for cadres was probably used for their benefit in other ways than as wages.

---

[79] Document III, table 11.

[80] Document XI.

[81] Document XXIV.

V

ECONOMIC LIFE UNDER THE COMMUNES

A peasant's economic life under the communes can best be depicted by an analysis of his income and of the sources from which he got it. His income and its sources will indicate, on the one hand, the kinds of activities in which he was engaged and, on the other, the level of living standard he could afford.

In the following analysis, an estimate of the average per capita income in the Hu-li, Hung-t'ang, and Shan-k'ang brigades is attempted.[82] The selection of these brigades was dictated by the availability of data.

Peasant income came from both the collective system and from private sources.

INCOMES FROM THE COLLECTIVE SYSTEM

The following elements of peasant incomes came from the collective system.

(1) <u>Basic ration</u>. The basic rations in the Shan-k'ang, Hung-t'ang, and Hu-li brigades were respectively 225,[83] 198, and 234 catties per person per year, the average being 219 catties. At a price of 8.6 yüan for each 100 catties, which was the price of rice in the Hu-li brigade,[84] the per capita basic ration was worth 18.83 yüan.

(2) <u>Work ration.</u> The average work ration per head of population (including the nonworkers who were not entitled to the work ration) was 32 catties, being 40 catties in the Hu-li brigade, 28 catties in the Hung-t'ang brigade and 27 catties in the Shan-k'ang brigade. The value in money of the average work ration was 2.75 yüan. As the work ration had presumably to be paid for in work-points, to avoid double counting it will not be counted when we add up the total income of the peasant.

(3) <u>Excess-output ration</u>. The basic ration and the work ration were calculated on the basis of the quota production. The actual production might exceed the quota production, and this excess, or the greater part of it would be retained

---

[82] Per capita income means the average income of the whole population, including nonworkers. Data for the Hu-li brigade from Document III; for the Hung-t'ang brigade from Document II; and for the Shan-k'ang brigade from Document I.

[83] Document I, Appendix, table 2. The figures represent the average rations for persons under 13 and over 14, weighted by the number of persons in each group. It is given as 218.4 in Document I.

[84] Document III, table 10.

by the brigades or teams as an incentive reward and distributed to their members as excess-output rations.

In a Liu Yu-sai team the excess-output ration per worker amounted to 12 catties, with a value of 1.03 yüan. On a per capita basis,[85] the excess-output ration would be 5 catties worth 0.43 yüan.

Many commune units, including the Hu-li and Hung-t'ang brigades, distributed no excess-output ration. In some cases their individual households could nevertheless enjoy excess-output rations in a disguised form under the Household Contract Production system, under which the households contracted to farm a fixed piece of land for the commune system and to produce the quota production in return for a fixed amount of costs in material and money and a fixed number of work-points. Any production in excess of the quota would belong to the households concerned.

(4) <u>Harvest ration</u>. Special rations might be distributed during harvest time. In the Liu Yu-sai and the Yang Li-en teams, the harvest ration amounted on the average to 17 catties per worker, or 7 catties per person, with a value of 0.60 yüan.[86]

The basic ration (219 catties), the excess-output ration (4.5 catties), and the harvest ration (7 catties) add up to a total of 231 catties per person per year,[87] with a monetary value of 19.87 yüan.

(5) <u>Retained fruits</u>. In the Hu-li brigade, each person was allowed to retain 30 catties of the fruits grown in the brigade. At a price of 15 yüan for each 100 catties,[88] the value of the retained fruit would be 4.5 yüan.

The manner in which the economic crops are distributed is not known. Their value will be taken into account when we consider the value of the work-points.

---

[85] Document XI. The labor participation rate is taken to be 38.6 per cent. The per capita excess-output ration is obtained by multiplying the ration per worker by the labor participation rate.

[86] Document XI.

[87] This compares with an official figure of 29 catties per month or 348 catties per year, which appears to be excessive. See Document V.

[88] Document III, table 10.

(6) <u>Work-points</u>. When a member performed work on the collective fields, he earned work-points. The value of a work-point in the Hu-li brigade worked out at 0.060 yüan,[89] or 0.60 yüan for each ten work-points. This compared with 1.07 yüan for each ten work-points in the Liu Yu-sai team, 0.96 yüan in the Yang Li-en team, and 1.477 yüan in an unnamed team.[90] The value of a work-point would vary with the number of work-points issued by the units concerned and their "total income."

In the Hu-li brigade, the average number of work-points per person (including nonworkers) per year amounted to 698, which would have a value of 41.88 yüan.[91]

INCOMES FROM THE PRIVATE SECTOR

Besides earnings derived from the collective system, a commune member could also get income from private sources.

(7) <u>The private plot</u>. The average size of the private plots was estimated at 0.12 mou per person,[92] which could produce 83 catties of food grain (the average output per mou being 693 catties) with a value of 7.14 yüan.

(8) <u>Reclaimed land.</u> As mentioned before, there were 40,000 mou of reclaimed land in Lien-chiang. Divided among an estimated 168,000 rural population,[93] the average per capita holding of reclaimed land would be 0.24 mou. Assuming that the holdings were used for growing food grains, it could have grown

---

[89]The value is estimated as follows: In the estimation, allowance is made for only some but not all of the costs of production. All amounts are in terms of yüan.

Income	Cost of production (seed, feed, chemical fertilizer only), estimated at 7 per cent of income	State levies	Basic ration and fruit distribution	Income available for the redemption of work-points
Food grain				
92,761	6,563	4,824 (5.2%)	41,959	39,415
Economic crops				
18,078	1,265	----	----	16,813
Fruits				
19,296	1,351	----	7,911	10,034
Brigade enterprise				
18,160	1,271	----	----	16,889
Total				
148,295	10,450	4,824	49,870	83,151
Retained for Three Funds				10,430
Income available for redemption of work-points				72,721

According to Document III, table 2, a total of 1,227,538 work-points was scheduled. As the (planned) income available for the redemption of the work-points totaled 72,721 yüan as shown in this table, the value of each work-point amounted to 0.06 yüan.

Sources: tables 12 and 13, above, with the cost of production assumed to be as follows: 3 per cent of income for seed, 2 per cent for feed, and an assumed 2 per cent for chemical fertilizers. The allowance here made for seed and feed is somewhat higher than that officially allotted. See table 12.

[90]Document XI. In the unnamed team a family earned a total of 2,200 work-points which were converted into 325 yüan indicating that each 10 work-points were worth 1,477 yüan.

[91]Since the number of work-points scheduled was 1,227,538 and the total population was 1,759 (Document III, tables 2 and 1).

[92]See p. 18, above.

[93]See p. 9, where the estimate was made on the basis of pre-1937 ratios.

166 (0.24 x 693)[94] catties of food grains, worth 14.28 yüan, though the reclaimed land and the private plots were more often used for higher-priced products such as vegetables, pigs and fowls.

(9) Subsidiary domestic enterprise. Households were permitted to engage in such subsidiary domestic enterprises as embroidery, sewing, knitting, and bee-keeping. The products, except for the kinds and quantities subject to state purchase, could be disposed of in the free market.[95]

(10) Miscellaneous private income. A surprisingly large variety of private activities, which would be thought impossible under a socialist system, was pursued by members of the commune system. Many commune members engaged in peddling (er pan shang). Selling what was produced by oneself was permitted, but reselling what one purchased from others (er pan shang) was generally viewed with disapproval. Some members did odd jobs ("rat work") outside their own commune units. Half the 106-member labor force of the Lien-teng brigade in the Ao-chiang commune worked outside: 31 in stonemasonry and earth-work, three in carpentry, 44 in peddling, and 27 in miscellaneous jobs. The profits from peddling totaled 8,200 yüan, averaging 186 yüan per peddler (four of the peddlers made profits of more than 1,000 yüan each).[96] Members who worked outside the team would have to surrender their earnings to the team. Failing to do so, they would be given no ration and would have to buy food at high prices and be subjected to certain fines.[97] Lending money at high interest was fairly prevalent. It was reported that in the three communes of Ao-chiang, Kuan-t'ou, and Huang-ch'i, 384 households engaged in lending at high interest, involving a total of 72,440 yüan in principal. The rate of interest ranged from 1 to 1.5 per cent per month.[98]

ESTIMATED INCOME PER CAPITA

We can now sum up an individual's income from the sources just enumerated (table 16).

The sources listed in the table yielded an average income per person of 88 yüan in round numbers, which was equal to US$36. This estimate is overstated in one respect--in computing the value of the work-points only part of the costs of production has been allowed for. On the other hand, the income is underestimated in several respects. The price of rice was based upon the official price of 8.6 yüan per tan, which might be too low. The private plots and the reclaimed land were assumed to be planted in food grains whereas they were more likely used for raising higher-priced products. Lastly, the estimate does not take into account the income from subsidiary domestic enterprises and from miscellaneous private sources. As indicated above, miscellaneous income was, in individual cases, substantial in amount.[99]

---

[94] See p. 21, above, 693 being the average output per mou in catties.

[95] Revised Regulations, Art. 41.

[96] Document X.

[97] Ibid. See also Document II.

[98] Document V.

[99] See p. 36, above.

Table 16

ESTIMATED INCOME PER CAPITA

Source of income	Quantity (catties)	Value (yüan)
Collective:		
Rations	231	19.87
Retained fruits	30	4.50
Work-points	-	41.88
Income from collective system		66.25
Private:		
Private plots	83	7.14
Reclaimed land	166	14.28
Subsidiary domestic enterprise		(unknown)
Miscellaneous private income		(unknown)
Income from private sources		21.42
Total income per person		87.67

In cases cited earlier, [100] the salaries of cadre members were mentioned as 28 and 33 yüan per month or 336 and 396 yüan per year.   The salary of 396 yüan per year was looked down upon by a mother who forbade her daughter to marry a cadre member because he earned no more than that amount.   But in all probability a cadre's income is an above-average income in rural communities.   A salary of 336 yüan would become 130 yüan on a per capita (including nonworkers) basis, while a salary of 396 yüan would become 153 yüan. [101]   The average for the two estimates is 142 yüan.   Assuming that our estimate of a per capita income of 88 yüan (US$36) was on the low side and that a cadre's average salary of 142 yüan (US$58) was an above-average income in a rural community,   then we should not be too far wide of the mark if we say that the average per capita income in rural Lien-chiang probably lay between those two limits.

---

[100] See p. 32, above.

[101] A household in the agricultural districts averaged 4.15 persons, of whom 38.6 per cent or 1.6 persons were working.   If 1.6 persons earned 336 yüan per person per year, the total household income would be 537.6 yüan (336 x 1.6).   Dividing by 4.15 gives a per capita income of 130 yüan.   The average of 153 yüan is derived similarly.

VI

CLASS STRATIFICATION IN LIEN-CHIANG

<u>Classification of households</u>. The correct analysis of social classes was one
of the secrets which helped the Chinese Communist Party to win the mainland. Thus
said Mao Tse-tung in the opening paragraph of the first essay in his <u>Selected Works</u>:
"To distinguish real friends from real enemies, we must make a general analysis of
the economic status of the various classes in Chinese society and of their respective
attitudes toward the revolution." Only then could the revolutionaries "unite their
real friends to attack their real enemies."

During the period under consideration, six main categories of rural households
were recognized. In the definitions of these social classes given below, the word
"exploitation" as used by Marxists means the making of money not by one's own
labor. Hence, interest, rent, and profit are regarded by them as forms of exploitation of man by man.

(a) Landlords were those so classified during the land reform of 1951-1952 and
before the rural cooperative movement of 1954-1956. A landlord was originally
defined as a person who owned land, performed little or no labor himself, and lived
chiefly on the rent of his land. [102]

(b) Rich peasants were those so classified before the rural cooperative movement. A rich peasant owned all or part or none of his land, but possessed a relative abundance of the means of production and working capital. He participated in
the performance of labor, but a part, perhaps a large part, of his income was
derived by exploiting the labor of others. [103]

(c) Upper-middle peasants were those who possessed a relatively large quantity
of the means of production, practiced exploitation to a moderate degree, and enjoyed a higher standard of living than the peasant classes below them. [104]

Upper-middle peasants were further classified as "old upper-middle peasants"
and "new upper-middle peasants," according to whether their status was acquired
before or after the rural cooperative movement of the mid-1950's.

---

[102] "How to Analyze Rural Classes," in <u>Selected Works of Mao Tse-tung</u> (Chinese version), I, 123.

[103] <u>Ibid.</u>

[104] Definitions <u>c</u>, <u>d</u>, and <u>e</u> are based upon the Central Committee of the Chinese Communist Party's
"Decision on Certain Concrete Policies Regarding Socialist Education Movements in Rural Districts,"
which was adopted in September 1963, a few months after the period covered by this volume; hereafter
cited as "Decisions on . . . Rural Districts."

(d) Affluent middle peasants were those who derived no income from exploiting others, did not have to submit themselves to being exploited by selling their own labor or by borrowing money, and were economically self-sufficient.

(e) Lower-middle peasants were those who possessed relatively little means or production, had to submit themselves to being exploited to some extent by selling their own labor or borrowing money, and had a relatively low standard of living.

Lower-middle peasants were also classified as "old" and "new," according to whether their status was acquired before or after the rural cooperative movement.

(f) Poor peasants differed from lower-middle peasants in that while the latter's standard of living was low, the former actually encountered hardships in their economic life.

A theme repeatedly harped upon during the Socialist Education movements of 1962 and 1963 was the continued existence of classes and class struggle. A document printed in this volume characterized the class struggle as "protracted, complex, repeated, alternately resurgent and recessive, and sometimes acute."

Official policy toward the social classes. The official policy was to rely upon the poor and lower-middle peasants and to "unite" the affluent middle and upper-middle peasants. Although the latter peasants were considered to be imbued with the spirit of capitalism, Chinese Communist leaders believed that the majority of them would follow their socialist line. Their support, accordingly, was to be gained, though their capitalistic ideas and habits had to be changed through various means, including education, criticism, and struggle.

Landlords and rich peasants were classified along with the "counterrevolutionaries" and the bad elements (thieves, vandals, murderers) as the "Four Class" elements.[105] Not only the landlords and the rich peasants themselves but also their spouses were forbidden to become party members or cadres. Their children were permitted to become cadres, but were in general ineligible for working in the communes as accountants, work-point recorders, inventory controllers, or in other key positions.

Statistics of poor and lower-middle peasants. According to official estimates, the poor and lower-middle peasants comprised from 60 to 70 per cent of the peasants in the country as a whole.[106]

The fragments of information that the documents provide on the stratification of social classes in Lien-chiang are collected in table 17. The poor peasants alone constituted more than 70 per cent of the total. The official estimate was, therefore, an underestimation as far as these units in Lien-chiang were concerned.

Political importance of the poor and lower-middle peasants. The poor and the lower-middle peasants are not only the preponderant classes in Chinese rural society, as has been the case for centuries past, but they have now replaced the landed interest as the most powerful classes in the countryside.

There is fragmentary information showing the position poor and lower-middle peasants occupied in the various power centers in the Ch'ang-sha brigade of the P'u-k'ou commune.[107]

---

[105] The Four Classes were subsequently expanded to five by the inclusion of the "rightists."

[106] "Decisions on . . . Rural Districts."

[107] The data following are from unpublished documents.

Table 17

SOCIAL CLASSES IN LIEN-CHIANG

Commune unit	Number of households	Landlords	Upper-middle households	Affluent-middle households	Lower-middle households	Poor households
Ch'ang-sha brigade, Pu-k'ou commune . .	153	-	6	-	34	113
Ch'en Ch'in-fu team, Ao-chiang commune. . .	20	-	-	-	4	16
Lien-hsing team, Liao-yen commune . .	11	1	3	1	-	6
Total	184	1	9	1	38	135
Per cent of total . . .	100	0.5	4.9	0.5	20.7	73.4

Source: Figures on the Ch'ang-sha brigade are from an unpublished document; those on the other two are from Document V. In Document XV, table 1, the number of poor and lower-middle households in the Ch'ang-sha brigade is given as 127. According to the table, the poor and lower-middle peasants comprised 94.1 per cent of the total, substantially higher than the official estimate of 60 to 70 per cent.

In the brigade there were thirteen Communist Party members. Of them, eleven were poor peasants and two middle peasants. As can be inferred from table 18, the middle peasants could belong either to the new upper- or the new lower-middle class.

Of the nine persons comprising the brigade's cadre, eight were poor peasants and one was a middle peasant.

Of the seven team chiefs in the brigade, six were poor peasants and one was a middle peasant.

Class Corps were organized in the countryside for the dual purpose of their serving as activists in political movements and assisting and supervising the work of communes, brigades, and teams.[108]

There was one Class Corps in each of the seven teams in the Ch'ang-sha brigade. Information concerning the Class Corps in the first team is missing. The total membership of the other six Class Corps was 62, giving an average of 10.2 members for each. As there were 192 adults[109] in the teams concerned, every third adult belonged to a corps.

[108] "Decisions on . . . Rural Districts."

[109] There were 224 adults in the 7 teams of the brigade (Document XV, table 11). On a prorata basis, the 6 teams here considered should have 192 adults.

The membership of the Class Corps in the six teams is analyzed in table 18.

The middle columns of the table show that 89 per cent of the membership of the Class Corps consisted of poor and new lower-middle peasants and 11 per cent of new upper-middle peasants.

Other features are evident from the table, as follows.

(1) Each Class Corps included one or two members of the Communist Party, but not more.

(2) Seven members (58 per cent) of the Class Corps in the third production team belonged to the Youth Corps. This appears to be an exceptional case; the proportion of Youth Corps members in other Class Corps was not unusually high.

(3) Although the Class Corps were organized at the team level, four out of six had also the participation of one or two members of the brigade cadre.

It may also be pointed out that, of the members of the Class Corps under consideration, 84 per cent were males and 16 per cent females.

Thus, all of the rural power centers examined above--the party, the brigade cadre, the team leadership, and the Class Corps--were dominated by poor peasants, new lower-middle peasants, and new upper-middle peasants. Since the new upper-middle peasants were mostly evolved from the old lower-middle peasants, it can be said that the rural seats of power are practically wholly in the hands of the poor and lower-middle peasants (both old and new).

Political and economic attitudes of the social classes. The poor and lower-middle peasants were expected to support the Communist regime politically and to toe its socialist line economically. The events of 1962-1963 provided an opportunity to gauge the political and economic attitudes of these two classes.

In June 1962, Nationalist Chinese guerrillas landed at several places along the coastal areas of the mainland, giving rise to rumors of an impending Nationalist invasion, and preparations were made to meet that eventuality. This was the "War Preparation period" referred to in the documents. During that time, the poor and lower-middle peasants, the anticounterrevolutionaries, and the old revolutionaries reportedly were solidly behind the Communist government, while the upper-middle peasants were sitting on the fence. "Red and white are the same, so it does not matter who comes," the upper-middle peasants are supposed to have said. As to the Four Class elements, it was reported that they entertained high hopes from the expected attack and that between 30 and 40 per cent of them adopted an arrogant attitude. [110] The Four Class elements, however, were too small in number to be reckoned as a political force on the mainland. In the Ch'ang-sha brigade only three persons were so classified. [111]

The attitude of the poor and lower-middle peasants toward the economic system was less sure. Household Contract Production was regarded as a manifestation of the capitalistic spirit contrary to the principles of socialism. In the Hua-wu brigade of Ao-chiang commune, for every 100 households, 18 were in favor of it, that is,

---

[110] Document V.

[111] Document XV, table 10.

Table 18

MEMBERSHIP OF CLASS CORPS, CH'ANG-SHA BRIGADE

Production team	Classification by sex			Classification by class status			Other classification			
	Male	Female	Total	New upper-middle peasant	New lower-middle peasant	Poor peasant	Party cadre member	Brigade cadre member	Youth Corps member	Other
2	9	2	11	–	5	6	2	1	1	7
3	11	1	12	1	2	9	1	2	7	2
4	8	2	10	1	1	8	1	–	–	9
5	8	1	9	–	1	8	1	–	2	6
6	9	2	11	4	1	6	1	1	1	8
7	7	2	9	1	5	3	2	1	2	4
Total	52	10	62	7	15	40	8	5	13	36
Percent of Total	84	16	100	11	24	65	13	8	21	58

Source: Unpublished document. Document XV, table 1, contains data relating to poor and lower-middle peasant groups which appear to be the predecessors of poor and lower-middle peasant Class Corps.

in favour of capitalism; 25 were opposed to it, that is, opposed to capitalism; and the remaining 57 were sitting on the fence.[112] If we further assume that households in Hua-wu were distributed as in table 17, meaning that for every 100 households, 73.4 were poor peasants, 20.7 lower-middle peasants, and 4.9 upper-middle peasants, then it can be inferred that at most 27 per cent ($=25/(73.4+20.7)$) of the poor and lower-middle peasants were opposed to capitalistic practice, while the rest were either fence-sitters or actually in favor of it.

In some other teams the poor peasants, if not the lower-middle peasants, were more socialistic in their attitude.

In the Wang-chuang team of the Tan-yang commune, among the total of 14 households, all four poor peasants (28.5 per cent of all households) were opposed to capitalism as manifested in Household Contract Production and all four affluent-middle households were in favor of it, while the rest (43 per cent) vacillated.[113]

In the Ch'en Chih-shan team of the Chang-ling commune, among a total of 15 households, eight poor and lower-middle households (53 per cent of the total) were opposed to Household Contract Production, and three affluent-middle peasants and "veteran" contract production households (20.4 per cent) were in favor, while the remaining four households were vacillating. The last four households had an abundance of labor power (six full-time workers); their class status was not specified.[114]

The poor and lower-middle peasants participated in the struggles and liquidations during the land reform period and the subsequent antirightist and similar movements. Fear of revenge alone would compel them to stand behind the Communist government. Yet their attitude toward socialism was, as the foregoing examples show, less firm than the government had assumed. To change the economic attitude of the peasants was the principal aim of the Socialist Education movement, to be discussed next.

---

[112] Document VIII. Farther on in the document exactly the same percentage distribution is given in relation to the Huang Tseng-hsia team of the brigade.

[113] Document V.

[114] Ibid.

VII

THE SOCIALIST EDUCATION MOVEMENT

In the summer of 1966, Communist China startled the world by initiating a nationwide Proletarian Cultural Revolution. An event with many facets, the Cultural Revolution was first launched as an ideological movement, in continuation of the Socialist Education movement[115] which forms the subject of this chapter and with which 17 of the 25 documents printed here are concerned.

PURPOSE OF THE SOCIALIST EDUCATION MOVEMENT

The "Three Evil Tendencies." The analysis offered in the preceding two sections indicates that while the agricultural economy had become collectivized, people's habits and ideas had not changed to conform to it. In the course of 1962 and 1963 two Socialist Education movements were launched for the purpose of re-educating the people so as to bring their ideology into line with the changed environment.

The habits and ideas which the Socialist Education movement attempted to alter fell into three groups: capitalism, feudalism, and extravagance. These were referred to as the Three Evil Tendencies. Unlawful practices such as embezzlement also came under attack.

Capitalistic practices included household contract production, speculation, abandoning agriculture for peddling, lending at high interest, and doing "rat work" or odd jobs for gain.

Feudalism included superstitious activities, religious activities, and marriage by sale (wherein the man has to buy his bride).

Extravagance referred mainly to the giving of parties to celebrate weddings, beam raisings, christenings, birthdays, and so on.

---

[115] Referring to the Proletariat Cultural Revolution, this editor stated in a letter published in the San Francisco Examiner on July 11, 1966: "This type of ideological purge is not a new phenomenon in Communist China. Back in 1962, a movement of the very same nature, called the Socialist Education movement, was launched in the rural areas for the purpose of purging the rural population of their capitalistic ideas and habits. Soon after the conclusion of the Socialist Education movement, the present Proletariat Cultural Revolution was started. The one movement is thus a continuation of the other."

In its issue of July 22, 1966, the Peking Review said: "The fifth stage of the struggle started with the socialist education movement initiated by the Party in 1963 and has continued into the great proletariat cultural revolution which was launched recently at the great call of the Party."

<u>Harmful effects of the Three Evil Tendencies.</u> Some of the practices mentioned above were considered harmful to the efficient operation of the commune system, while others were objectionable on ideological grounds.

Extravagance, implying overconsumption and undersaving, was inimical to investment and economic expansion.

Marriage by sale interfered with collective production. In the Hua-wu brigade, a girl sold, on the average, for 750 yüan. In other instances a bride could cost up to 2,000 yüan. Either price was clearly beyond the ability of a man with an average annual income (some 88 to 142 yüan)[116] if he had to rely solely on his earnings from agriculture, especially the collective sector of agriculture. There was, therefore, every motive for him to neglect his work in the collective system in order to concentrate on private activities, both inside and outside the commune, so as to be able to earn enough money to pay for his bride.

Superstition and religion were considered undesirable because they would perpetuate a sense of fatalism. With a fatalistic habit of mind, peasants would submit meekly to droughts and floods as inevitable, whereas it was Communist policy to change nature, to combat droughts, and to control floods.

Peddling and performing odd jobs had the undesirable effect of draining labor power from the collectives. As was noted earlier, 50 per cent of the labor force of the Lien-teng brigade in the Ao-chiang commune worked outside the brigade. In the Li Tai-an team of the Lien-tang brigade, 19 members of its labor force of 23 quit the team, leaving insufficient hands for collective production.

Among the ideological issues were lending at interest, the hiring of workers, and the renting of land. These were regarded as forms of exploitation of man by man in violation of the principles of socialism.

Household Contract Production had even more serious implications. As stated earlier, the accounting unit of the commune system was first shifted from the commune to the brigade and then from the brigade to the team. Household Contract Production represented, in effect, a further shift of the accounting unit from the team to the household. This last shift would be tantamount to a breakdown of the collective system and a return to private enterprise.[117]

<u>Purposes of the Socialist Education movement.</u> To preserve the collective nature of the commune system and to enhance its efficiency, the drift toward capitalism, feudalism, and extravagance had to be combated. Unlawful practices had also to be stopped. The instrument used by the Chinese Communist Party for this purpose was the Socialist Education movement.

The first movement, launched near the end of 1962, had as its principal task the combating of capitalistic trends. Although the same theme was reiterated in the second movement, its main attack was directed against feudalism and extravagance.

THE THREE STAGES OF THE SOCIALIST EDUCATION MOVEMENT

Each movement was conducted in three stages. The following description is

---

[116] See p. 37, above.

[117] "Household Contract Production is not a problem of method in business management, but rather one of direction, the problem of the struggle between the two courses of socialism and capitalism in the villages." Document VI.

based upon what transpired in the Hua-wu brigade during the first Socialist Education movement, launched in November 1962.[118]

First stage. During the first stage of the movement, members of the public were alerted to the continued existence of classes and the class struggle. The classes were the proletariat and the bourgeoisie, and the struggle was between the socialism of the one and the capitalism of the other.

At this stage, the main effort of the Socialist Education movement was directed at convincing the masses of people of the superiority of the socialist system over individual enterprise. The normal method used to achieve this end was not violence but persuasion. People were reminded of the improvements in their economic condition under the collective system ("condition education"). They were encouraged to recall the hardship of the past ("recollection"), to compare the present with the past ("contrast"), and to balance the gains and losses under individual enterprise ("reckoning of accounts"). By these and other means the attempt was made to induce the people to embrace the socialist ideology and to rid themselves of their capitalistic habits and thought.

Second stage. While the first stage of the movement was concerned with general problems, the second stage dealt with specific issues such as Household Contract Production, excessive size of private plots, illegal occupation of collective land for private use, work quotas, the distribution of human rations, and so forth. Issues such as these were all dealt with in accordance with the "Revised Draft Regulations Governing Rural People's Communes."

Third stage. The third stage of the movement was devoted to strengthening the personnel and organization of local party units, the Youth Corps, and the Women's Associations, and to strengthening the management and operation of the production teams. Production plans were drawn up during the stage, toward the end of which mass meetings were held to announce the conclusion of the movement and to "inspire the masses to attain a high tide of production." In other words, at its conclusion, the Socialist Education movement was usually transformed into a movement for the promotion of agricultural production for the coming year.

The first two stages were essentially mass movements. Preceding the mass movements, expanded cadre meetings were held to rectify the ideology and malpractice of the cadre members and to train them for leadership in the subsequent mass movements. Participants in the expanded cadre meetings included cadres of the local party units, brigades, teams, the militia, the Women's Associations, and the Youth Corps. Also included were the so-called positive elements, elementary-school teachers, and cadres sent down from higher levels.[119]

MORAL HEALTH OF THE RURAL POPULATION AS REVEALED IN THE SOCIALIST EDUCATION MOVEMENT

In the course of the two Socialist Education movements, errors and aberrations were uncovered among the cadres and the public.

Evil tendencies in the cadres. In the Shang-shan brigade of the Ao-chiang commune, 113 members of the cadre (48 per cent of total cadre members) were found

---

[118] Document VIII.

[119] See, for example, Document XXI, p. 220 and Document XV, table 3.

to have committed errors of capitalism, feudalism, and extravagance and to have followed unlawful practices. Of the total, 33 were Communist Party members, amounting to 51 per cent of the party members in the brigade.

In 1962 the Ch'ang-sha brigade had 9 brigade cadres, 39 team cadres, and 27 other cadres, among whom 8 brigade cadres, 22 team cadres, and 15 other cadres were "guilty" of the Three Evil Tendencies.[120] In Document XV their misconduct is set out in detail in table 1 and presented in summary form, together with similar data relating to the Shang-shan brigade and to the same Ch'ang-sha brigade a year later, in table 19.

From the table, it can be seen that the most common Evil Tendencies among the cadres were: excessive consumption and purchase, excessive opening of un-cultivated land and usurpation of public land, unauthorized borrowing of public funds or food, favoring individual enterprise, speculation, abandoning agriculture for peddling, and gambling.

The Shang-shan data provide a measure of the magnitude of the acts of mis-conduct by the cadre. The profits from peddling and the unauthorized borrowing of public funds averaged about 80 yüan (US$33) per case. The opening of uNculti-vated land averaged 0.26 mou per case. The private plots were excessive by no more than 0.10 mou per case. Cases like these would come under the jurisdiction of the small courts in the U.S.A.; they may be regarded as greater offenses relative to conditions in China.

Evil tendencies in the public. The Evil Tendencies uncovered among the masses in the Chu-ch'i brigade of the Kuan-t'ou commune and in the Ch'ang-sha brigade of the P'u-k'ou commune are listed in table 20.

In 1962, the Ch'ang-sha brigade had 153 households, including six classified as affluent middle peasants. Of these, 80 (including three affluent middle house-holds) were free from the Three Evil Tendencies, while 73 (also including three affluent middle households) had them to a minor degree.[121]

As shown in table 20 (ignoring the figures in parentheses) the most prevalent abuses among the public were failing to fulfill fertilizer quotas, abandoning agriculture for peddling, cutting down trees, usurping collective land, participating in marriage by sale, failing to fulfill labor quotas, doing "rat work," gambling, and engaging in superstitious activities. The existence of these abuses indicates that many of the old social "evils" had persisted under Communist rule. Though it is not known whether they had become more prevalent in 1962 than in olden times, the Communist policy of periodically ferreting out the abuses and correcting them had most likely led to their reduction.

The "rectification" of abuses. The abuses were generally dealt with leniently. For example, in the Shang-shan brigade, restitution was required of cadre members who misappropriated public funds or food. Public land usurped was required to be returned to the collectives. Back taxes had to be paid on pigs privately slaughtered. As to the other offenses (abandoning agriculture for peddling, gambling, excess pur-chases, etc.), most of the offenders were pardoned after they gave a pledge of re-form. Although violence and deaths occurred during the movements, these were officially disapproved.[122]

---

[120] Document XV, table 4.

[121] Document XV, table 8.

[122] See Document XIV.

Table 19

THREE EVIL TENDENCIES AMONG THE CADRES

Type of tendency	Shang-shan brigade, number of cases and amounts involved, 1963	Ch'ang-sha brigade, number of cases	
		1962	1963
Capitalism:			
Favoring individual enterprise and household contract production	–	10	5
Abandoning agriculture for peddling . . .	11 (total profit, 870 yüan)	–	1
Emigrating or doing "rat work"	–	2	1
Excessive opening of uncultivated land and usurpation of public land	41 (10.8 mou)	11	2
Excessive size of private plots	4 (0.42 mou)	–	–
Benefiting oneself at expense of public . .	1 (150 yüan)	–	4
Lending money at high interest	–	11	–
Feudalism:			
Bridegroom married into the home of the bride	–	1	–
Gambling	12	–	–
Extravagance:			
Unauthorized slaughtering of pigs	6 (6 hogs)	–	–
Graft	1 (12 yüan)	–	–
Misappropriation of public food or funds .	9 (1,786 catties)	6	1
Unauthorized borrowing of public funds . .	42 (3,412 yüan)	–	–
Theft	–	–	4
Speculation	–	5	9
Decadent behavior	–	1	1
Refusal to serve as cadres	–	12	12
Bad work attitude	–	4	1
Excess purchase and consumption	47 (221 catties of food, etc.)	11	11

Source: Data for the Shang-shan brigade are from Document XXIV; 1962 data for the Ch'ang-sha brigade from Document XV, table 4; and 1963 data for the Ch'ang-sha brigade from Document XVI, table 2. The 1963 data for the Ch'ang-sha brigade represent the combined totals for party members, brigade cadres, team cadres, and the Seven Personnel. As a party member could at the same time be a member of the cadre or of the Seven Personnel, and vice versa, some double counting may (or may not) be involved here.

Table 20

THREE EVIL TENDENCIES AMONG THE MASSES

Type of tendency	Chu-ch'i brigade, 1963	Ch'ang-sha brigade	
		1962	1963
Capitalism:			
Favoring individual enterprise	–	9 (8)	1
Abandoning agriculture for peddling . . .	25	9 (2)	16
Arranging labor contracts	–	–	2
Doing "rat work"	11	7 (2)	–
Failure to fulfill fertilizer quota	–	153	2
Emigrating to work elsewhere	–	–	13
Failure to fulfill labor quotas	–	19	–
Usurping collective land	–	(15)	24
Hiring labor	3	–	–
Lending money at high interest	1	–	–
Speculation	–	(11)	9
Feudalism:			
Participating in marriage by sale	–	11	9
Number of geomancers	–	10 (1)	–
Number of marriage go-betweens	–	2 (1)	1
Superstitious activities	12	1	–
Gambling	16	–	–
Witchcraft and religious swindling	2	–	–
Speculation	–	–	?
Other feudalistic activities	–	3 (1)	–
Extravagance:			
Feast to celebrate new buildings	–	1	–
Feast to celebrate birth	–	1 (?)	–
Unlawful activities:			
Theft	–	– (35)	6
Cutting down trees	30	–	4
Slandering the government	–	–	8
Beating cadre members	–	– (5)	1

Source: Data for the Chu-ch'i brigade are from Document XXI; 1962 data for the Ch'ang-sha brigade from Document XV, table 7; and 1963 data for the Ch'ang-sha brigade from Document XVI, table 1. There are two sets of 1962 figures for the Ch'ang-sha brigade. The one in parenthesis is from table 8 and the other is from table 7, Document XV. The two tables probably relate to different months in 1962.

PART TWO
DOCUMENTS

Group I
Policy Statements and Production Plans

I

REGULATIONS GOVERNING BRIGADE-CONTRACT PRODUCTION FOR THE SHAN-K'ANG BRIGADE OF THE P'U-K'OU COMMUNE

The Shan-k'ang brigade was originally under the control of the Che-wei brigade. After the implementation of the Chinese Communist Party's "Sixty Draft Regulations Governing Agricultural People's Communes," it was established as a brigade in its own right. In the brigade there is only one natural village, made up of 138 households and having a total population of 552 persons. The region is purely agricultural. The brigade now has six production teams, the largest made up of 26 households and the smallest of 19 households. There are 409.65 mou of cultivated land. Of this, 325.85 mou are paddy fields, and 83.80 mou are dry fields. The total labor force of 215 persons comprises 93 full-time and 122 part-time workers. Each worker is responsible for 2.67 mou. There are 30 head of oxen.

Since January 5 our brigade has, under the correct leadership of the Commune Party Committee, launched a propaganda campaign concerning the advantages and policies of brigade contract production. The campaign had production as its central concern and socialist education as its motive force. Through education, the brigade cadres raised their level of ideological awareness, having come to realize that brigade contract production can stimulate production, increase the income of the commune members, and bring about the early fulfillment of food production quotas. For this reason, they have in general heeded the call of the Party Committee. The following resolutions have been made concerning the problems in brigade contract production.

I. SIZE OF PRODUCTION TEAMS

After cadre discussion, it was recognized that the number of households in the six production teams is adequate to supply labor power. For this reason, further transfers will not be made. Adjustments may be made in one or two teams, but the rest need not be changed.

II. PROBLEMS OF LAND, OXEN, AND FARM TOOLS

(1) Land. --The original division of land among the teams was considered suitable, and the labor force and the land were in balance. The masses had not been critical of the original "four-fixed" system, and therefore no changes were made.

(2) Plow cattle. --The original distribution of farm animals on the basis of land was suitably balanced. Plow oxen were sold to the teams by the brigade, and the rights of ownership belonged to the teams. Bonuses based on part of the average of the original and present prices were to be given to those with good records in raising the cattle.

(3) Farm tools. --The management and use of the original number of farm tools given to the production teams by the brigade was transferred to the teams.

III. PROBLEMS OF THREE FIXED PRODUCTION AND FOOD

(1) The problem of Three Fixed production was discussed by the commune members, and on the basis of production over the past several years it was recognized that the Three Fixed production of 1961 was reasonable. As a consequence, annual production was set on the 1961 basis at 829 catties per mou of paddy land, and 400 catties per mou of dry land.

(2) Distribution of levy-purchase obligations. --There will be no change in the quotas to be purchased by the brigades from the teams. Moreover, after deducting the levy and purchases and the seeds and feed from the quota output, 10 per cent of the remainder will be set aside as the work ration and the rest as the basic ration.

(3) The basic ration for the production teams will be determined according to two classes. Those aged one to thirteen years make up one class, and those of fourteen years and above make up the other. Each person receives an average of 18.4 catties a month, or 218.4 catties a year.

(4) Methods of distributing rations for the production teams and commune members:

(a) The basic rations will be linked to the basic working days. When the basic working days have been completed, full basic rations will be issued. A deduction in the basic ration will be made for those who do not complete the basic working days.

(b) The basic rations will be linked to the collection of fertilizer. Quotas for fertilizer collection will be set for the commune members by the brigade. When the quotas have been supplied, the basic rations will be issued in full. Deductions will be made from the basic food ration for those not fulfilling their fertilizer quotas.

(c) The work ration will be linked to the work-points, with variations on a seasonal basis. The work ration will be calculated and distributed monthly, guaranteeing greater gains for greater labor, and no gain if there is no labor.

(d) The excess-quota output will be distributed quarterly in accordance with the total number of work-points. Greater gains will be guaranteed to greater labor, and there will be no gain if there is no labor.

(e) Methods of reward and punishment for excesses and deficiencies in work performance. --Fifty per cent more work-points, which will entitle the worker to share in the excess-quota output, will be awarded for work in excess of the labor quota. Conversely, those who do not fulfill the labor quota will have 50 per cent of the work-points of the deficient portion deducted. Participation in the excess-quota output will be in proportion to the remaining work-points.

IV. HANDLING OF ECONOMIC CROPS

Economic crops are handled according to directives to the brigades from higher levels. The brigades distribute the obligation to meet purchase requirements among the teams. Fulfillment must be guaranteed, and fluctuations will be rewarded or punished for different crops as follows:

(1) Those not fulfilling the goal in hemp and peanuts will make up each 100-catty deficiency with 450 catties of food. Those who exceed their quotas can freely dispose of the surplus themselves.

(2) Vegetable quotas will be according to the varieties set for the brigade. Each team should complete its obligation to sell by quarters. Those who fail to fulfill it must provide 12 catties of food for every 100-catty deficiency in vegetables.

V. THE PROBLEM OF SUBSIDIARY AGRICULTURAL PRODUCTS

The higher levels will assign the purchase goal for subsidiary agricultural products among the brigades. The brigade will determine the varieties and schedules for each team. Each production team should strictly observe the time schedule and resolve to fulfill the quotas.

VI. THE PROBLEM OF HANDLING MOUNTAIN FORESTS

Mountain forests originally belonging to the brigades will not change ownership now, and all rights of ownership will remain with the brigades. They are to be divided into sections to be distributed among the production teams for management. From their total income, 70 per cent will be given to the teams as rewards for management and as wages. The remaining 30 per cent will be surrendered to the brigade. Income from pine trees will be surrendered to the higher levels at a ratio of two to eight. The brigade will receive 20 per cent as repayment for purchases from the brigade.

VII. THE THREE FUNDS PROBLEM

(1) The reserve fund, based on 5 per cent of the total income, will be used to expand reproduction. Three per cent will be surrendered to the brigade.

(2) The welfare fund, based on 5 per cent of the total income, will be used for welfare activities. One per cent will be surrendered to the brigade for use in welfare activities and as relief for the Five Guaranteed households. The two per cent remaining to the teams will be allocated to households in distress.

(3) Administrative expenses take 2 per cent of total income. Of this, 1.5 per cent is surrendered to the brigade for its management expenses and cadre wages. The 0.5 per cent remaining to the production team is for use in its management expenditures.

VIII. PROBLEMS OF HANDLING BRIGADE ENTERPRISES

(1) The labor force required by brigade factories and plants will be drawn from the production teams on the basis of 5 per cent of the total labor force.

(2) Staff and workmen in brigade factories and plants will be paid monthly on the basis of the quota output. The wages will be referred to the production teams for evaluation, and the workers will share in the work rations and in the excess-output rations.

(3) The brigade will use a method of total reward or total indemnity as rewards and punishments to workmen on their production quotas.

The above points have been decided by mass discussion and by a meeting of representatives.

Reported to the Party Committee for examination and approval.

SHAN-K'ANG BRANCH, CHINESE COMMUNIST PARTY

SHAN-K'ANG BRIGADE

February 1, 1962

APPENDIX TO DOCUMENT I: STATISTICAL TABLES RELATING TO THE SHAN-K'ANG BRIGADE

NOTE: The dash (-) in the columns of these and all other tables is to be understood as indicating that the item was blank in the original.

Table I-1

ALLOCATION OF CULTIVATED LAND, SHAN-K'ANG BRIGADE, 1962
(Area in mou, output in catties)

Team	Allocation of paddy fields					Allocation of dry fields				Tract I			Tract 2			Tract 3			Tract 4		
	Total area	Double cropping	Single cropping	Jute	Vegetable	Total area	Potato	Peanut	Private plots	Area	Output per mou	Total output	Area	Output per mou	Total output	Area	Output per mou	Total output	Area	Output per mou	Total output
Yun-chu	55.23	53.28	—	1.00	0.85	26.95	14.05	2.00	10.90	10.35	—	9,419	10.32	870	8,978	27.23	830	22,601	5.38	610	3,282
Szu-shih	53.00	51.48	—	1.00	0.85	26.00	13.30	2.00	10.70	10.35	—	9,419	10.31	870	8,978	25.43	830	21,115	5.38	610	3,282
Chin-chai	50.17	52.37	—	1.00	0.80	26.32	14.52	2.00	9.80	10.48	—	9,537	8.35	870	7,265	27.11	830	22,501	6.43	610	3,922
Neng-fa	54.17	52.37	—	1.00	0.80	26.33	14.63	2.00	9.70	10.47	—	9,528	8.35	870	7,265	27.12	830	22,510	6.42	610	3,916
Fu-hsing	59.55	57.70	—	1.00	0.85	27.55	15.65	2.00	9.90	9.25	—	8,418	13.26	870	11,362	29.96	830	24,867	5.43	610	3,312
Hua-mei	60.50	58.65	—	1.00	0.85	26.95	11.45	2.00	13.50	10.50	—	—	10.36	870	9,013	32.76	830	27,191	5.03	610	3,068
Total	336.85	325.85	—	6.00	5.00	160.10	83.60	12.00	64.50	61.40	—	55,876	60.75	870	52,861	169.61	830	140,785	34.07	610	20,782

Table I-2

PRODUCTION AND DISTRIBUTION OF FOOD, SHAN-K'ANG BRIGADE, 1962

(Area in mou; other figures, except for persons, in catties)

Team	Production quota						Total Area	Total output	Levies and Purchases			Retained portions						Basic ration				Classification of persons	
	Paddy Fields			Dry Fields															Ration per person			1-13 (16 catties per month)	Over 14 (20 catties per month)
	Area	Output per mou	Total output	Area	Output per mou	Total output			Levies	Purchases	Subtotal	Seeds	Feed	Work ration	Reserve	Total	Number of persons	month	year	Total ration	number	number
Yun-chu	53.28	–	44,280	–	40	5,620	67.33	49,900	2,546	21,354	23,900	1,457	981	2,480		28,828	94	–	–	21,072	31	63
Szu-shih	51.48	–	42,786	13.30	–	5,320	64.78	48,106	2,530	20,070	22,600	1,423	1,019	2,419	53	27,514	91	–	–	20,592	26	65
Chin-chai	52.37	–	43,225	14.02	–	6,808	66.89	49,033	2,538	23,262	25,800	1,455	1,000	2,322	34	30,601	82	–	–	18,433	26	56
Neng-fa	52.37	–	43,219	14.64	–	5,852	67.00	49,071	2,546	23,254	25,800	1,455	1,000	2,332	40	30,591	82	–	–	18,480	25	57
Fu-hsing	57.70	–	47,919	15.65	–	6,260	73.35	54,219	2,808	25,652	28,460	1,590	1,000	2,467	1,838	35,355	84	–	–	18,864	27	57
Hua-mei	58.65	–	48,837	11.45	–	4,580	70.10	53,407	2,767	18,673	21,440	1,610	1,000	2,861	0	26,911	119	–	–	26,496	43	76
Total	325.85	829	270,296	83.60	400	33,440	409.45	303,736	15,735	132,265	148,000	9,000	6,000	14,881	1,919	179,800	552	18.11	224.57	123,936	178	374

Table I-3

PRODUCTION QUOTAS OF SUBSIDIARY AGRICULTURAL PRODUCTS, SHAN-K'ANG BRIGADE, 1962

Team	Jute			Peanuts			Vegetables			Hay		Domestic animals and fowls				Clams and other shells			Shrimps (tan)
	Area (mou)	Output per mou (catties)	Total output (catties)	Area (mou)	Output per mou (?)	Total output (?)	Area (mou)	Output per mou (tan)	Total output (tan)	Area (?)	Output per mou (tan)	Pigs	Goats (number)	Fowls	Eggs (catties)	Area (mou)	Output per mou (?)	Total output (?)	
Yan-chu	1	200	200	2	120	80	0.85	60	51	53.25	96	1	1	23	23	17	22	340	220
Szu-shih	1	200	200	2	120	80	0.85	—	50	51.48	92	1	1	24	24	17	—	340	220
Chin-chai	1	200	200	2	120	80	0.80	—	48	52.37	94	1	1	23	23	16	—	320	210
Neng-fa	1	200	200	2	120	80	0.80	—	50	52.37	94	1	1	19	19	16	—	320	210
Fu-hsing	1	200	200	2	120	80	0.85	—	50	57.70	104	1	1	23	23	17	—	340	220
Hua-mei	1	200	200	2	120	80	0.85	—	51	58.65	105	1	1	26	26	17	—	340	220
Total	6	—	1,200	12.00	—	480	5.00	—	300	325.82	585	6	6	138	138	100	—	2,000	1,300

Note: The "?" indicates that the unit of area or quantity was not evident in the original.

II

PRELIMINARY OPINIONS ON THE SENDING DOWN OF THE ACCOUNTING UNIT AND BRIGADE CONTRACT PRODUCTION POLICIES OF THE HUNG-T'ANG BRIGADE OF THE P'U-K'OU COMMUNE

I. THE PRODUCTION TEAM SYSTEM

After a thorough discussion and study of our present production team system, we believe that it is basically consistent with the spirit of the Party Central Committee in its proposal that the optimum size for teams in plains regions be from 20 to 30 households. Of the brigade's twelve production teams, the largest comprises 31 households and the smallest, 26 households, with an average of 27 households. We have, therefore, decided not to alter the system. Any further subdivision of the teams must first be approved by a higher-level party committee before it is effected.

II. MEANS OF PRODUCTION

(1) Ownership of the land rests with the production brigade and is given permanently to the production teams for their use, generally on the basis of the Four Fixed system. Basically, this is not subject to change, and individual cases are to be adjusted on their own merits. [To determine] the scope of the adjustment, calculate the balance between land and labor. Land in excess of four mou will be adjusted suitably, but there will be no change in land under four mou. We cannot, however, be sticklers about details in the adjustment. Methods of adjustment:

(a) To balance land in exess of four mou, a labor force may be suitably sent down from the factories and plants.

(b) For medium-class land, or land that is not uniform in soil quality, amount of work required, difficulty of plowing, and level of production, adjustment should be carried out through democratic deliberation and in a spirit of allowing land in an area to go to those in its vicinity.

Method of handling:--Due consideration should be given to the teams when setting production and fertilizer quotas. In the adjustment of land area, if the land has already been worked and fertilized, an equal exchange in value should be made. Some have raised the question of the size of the land area, but this has been mentioned before and we have decided not to reopen the question here.

(2) Labor force. --Land and labor being in balance, the labor force will be attached to the production teams on a permanent basis. In case the brigade has a special need for laborers, the teams must agree upon their transfer.

(3) Plow oxen. --Ownership is sent down to the production teams. The governing principle is the Four Fixed system, which is not subject to change.

Individual cases should be adjusted individually. However, teams having a shortage of ox-power equivalent to that necessary for plowing fifteen or more mou should negotiate with other teams for hiring oxen at a price to be agreed upon. In general, the choosing of only the best oxen will not be allowed. Teams having less than a fifteen-mou shortage of ox power should strengthen the care and feeding of their plow oxen. Those who without reason bring about the death of plow oxen (by unlawful slaughter, unlawful injury, or poor care) must make compensation for the dead animals. Punishment will be made according to the severity of the circumstances.

After calving, an allowance of 10 catties of food grain per cow will be made. When the calves have been nourished for a full year, they should revert to the production team at a price, the money going as a reward to the household that cared for them.

In order to improve the care and feeding of plow oxen, the "six fixed" system should be adopted: fixed work load, fixed fodder, fixed body weight, fixed plowing, fixed fertilizer, fixed reward and punishment.

(4) Farm tools. --Ownership is sent down to the production teams on the basis of the Four Fixed system and is not subject to change. Tools are to be acquired, repaired, managed, and used by the production teams themselves. Large tools such as water pumps, double-blade plows, threshing machines, and potato choppers belong to the brigade.

III. FORESTS AND FRUIT TREES

Because this brigade is located on a plains region, there are no mountain plants and only a few large tracts of fruit trees. The brigade owns the fruit trees and lets them out on contract to the teams for management on a share-cropping basis or on a system whereby, when the production quota is exceeded, the excess portion may be kept and disposed of by the teams. The trees must be taken care of by the teams. Individual fruit trees at the back or in front of homes belong to the commune members. In order to encourage fruit production in the future, the harvest will always belong to the planter; however, collective land may not be used.

IV. BRIGADE CONTRACT PRODUCTION

(1) Fixed production. --This has been suitably adjusted on the basis of actual production during the last three years. As a result, production was set at 800 catties per mou for double-crop paddy fields, 525 catties for dry land, and 150 catties for autumn sweet potatoes.

(2) Fixed value. --This is the determination of the production team's total income from agriculture and subsidiary enterprises. It is the basis on which the brigade draws the Three Funds from the income. The value of agricultural production is generally calculated on the basis of the quota production multiplied by the respective prices of the crops concerned. For subsidiary production, it is based on the work-points. Except for the agricultural work-points, the remainder is calculated at 1.5 ytian for each 10 points.

(3) Food contract production. --On the basis of the principle of fixed production, total production is set at 8,413 tan. Of this, 3,720 tan, comprising 44.3 per cent of the total production, is transferred under state levy and purchase; 4,693 tan, which makes up 55.7 per cent of total production, will be set aside as the Three Retained Foods, comprising 295 tan for seed, 183 tan for feed, and 4,715 tan for human

rations, the latter making up 50 per cent of total production. Of the ration, 12 per cent (505 tan) will be for work rations, the remainder, making up 42.9 per cent of total production, is distributed individually on an average of 198 catties per person.

(4) Methods of calculating state levy and purchase. --In order to carry out the principles of the greater the labor the greater the gain, and the more acreage under one's responsibility the more his rations, the brigade, on the basis of fixed production and after deducting the Three Retained Foods, either surrenders the remaining provisions to the state or allows them to be purchased by the state according to planned proportions. The concrete method of calculation for the state levy is to apply a uniform ratio to the total fixed production, and the method for state purchases is to apply a uniform ratio to the fixed production after the deduction of the Three Retained Foods.

(5) Standards for the Three Retained Foods

Seeds. --For double-crop rice, 20 catties per mou are retained for the entire year, and for each mou of sweet potatoes three catties are retained.

Feed. --Forty catties are retained for each head of plow oxen, 200 catties per head for boars and sows, and 30 catties per head for pigs for meat (in that portion to be sold to the state). In order to guarantee the completion of the hog-sale obligation, feed provisions for two heads should be retained for each head allotted for purchase.

Rations. --This is a food-distribution relationship between the production team and the commune members. There are two methods of handling it: (a) fixed rations for children and old people, and variable rations for workers, whose shares depend on quantity of work performed, and (b) on a three-class division (children, old people, and workers), a food-distribution ratio of 70 per cent for workers and 30 per cent for nonworkers. Of these two methods, we have found the second to be preferable. The spread between the basic rations received by the different classes should, in general, be limited to three or four catties. Work rations in the amount of 14 per cent of the basic ration are given as supplements to commune members who work.

(6) Treatment of production excesses and deficiencies (or exceeding and falling short of quotas):

(a) Increased production. --In principle, the increased food production should be uniformly enjoyed by team members on the basis of their total work-points, with 30 per cent being set aside for distribution to nonworkers.

(b) Decreased production. --In principle, decreases in production brought about without sufficient reason must be completely compensated by the workers with work-points. If, however, the production decreases are brought about by unavoidable natural disasters, after a discussion of the disaster 70 per cent of the deficient portion will fall on the workers and 30 per cent on the nonworkers.

V. THE THREE FUNDS

Uniform proportions of the total income of the production teams are to be set aside for the use by various levels in the commune.

Reserve fund. --This takes up 4 per cent of total income, 60 to 70 per cent of which is surrendered to the brigade, and 30 to 40 per cent retained by the teams for use in expanding production.

Welfare fund. --This takes up 2 per cent of the total income. Thirty to 40 per cent of it is surrendered to the brigade, to provide social insurance for Five Guaranteed households, and 60 to 70 per cent is retained by the teams for allotment to households in distress.

Administrative expenses. --These take up 1.5 to 2.0 per cent of total income. Two-thirds of this is surrendered to the brigade for use in operating expenses and as wages for the cadres. One third is retained by the teams for expense payments. Two standards for selection are set here.

In the future, in disbursements of a nonproduction character the production team must strictly observe the following procedures: expenditures up to 3.00 yüan may be approved by the production-team chief; those from 3.01 to 10.0 yüan must be approved by the team committee; those from 10.1 to 20.0 yüan must be approved by a general meeting of the team members. Those above 20.0 yüan must be approved by a general meeting of the team members and be reported to the brigade for approval.

VI. CONTRACT PRODUCTION OF ECONOMIC CROPS AND SUBSIDIARY AGRICULTURAL PRODUCTS

(1) Production quotas for economic crops and subsidiary agricultural products are set according to the state's purchase plans. In order to guarantee the completion of the quotas, a food incentive method has been adopted (that is, for output exceeding the quotas, a reward in food, equal to 30 per cent of the excess output, will be awarded to the teams concerned).

Product	Production output (Catties)	Unit price (Yüan per tan)	Total value (Yüan)
Hemp	200	37	74.00
Peanuts	80	17	13.60
Taro	2,500	10	250.00
Eggplant	2,200	10	220.00
Ginger	1,500	10	150.00
Sweet potatoes	1,500	10	150.00
Melons	2,500	8	200.00

(2) Poultry-purchase obligation. --This year the purchase quotas are to be set all at one time, but they are to be completed in separate stages. The brigade specifies the amount of purchase to the production team, and the latter selects the household from which to make the purchase by democratic deliberation.

VII. METHODS OF DISTRIBUTION APPLICABLE TO BRIGADE ENTERPRISES

(1) The professional fishing team and the lime plant under the brigade belong, as before, to the brigade. After costs, expenses, and accumulations, 40 to 50 per cent of the remaining income will be uniformly distributed to the production teams on the basis of land area and 50 to 60 per cent kept as brigade income for expanding reproduction, for increasing reserves, and for basic construction on farms.

(2) Rations and wages of the brigade factory and plant workers. --The lime plants adopt the Three Fixed system, with rewards for output that exceeds the fixed quotas and penalties for output that falls behind. Wages have been set at 1.75 yüan for each ten work-points. Rations will not, in general, exceed 34 catties. For the rations for fishing teams, a supplement system has been adopted. For

open-sea fishing, this will not exceed 63 catties; for inland-water fishing, it will not exceed 45 catties. As for the wages of fishermen, after deducting costs, depreciation, and the Three Funds from the total income, 50 per cent of the remaining income is divided in the proportions of 65 per cent to the fishermen and 35 per cent to the brigade.

VIII. SOME CONCRETE POLICIES

(1) Labor force. --All male commune members between the ages of 16 and 60, and all female commune members between the ages 16 and 50, except those who are ill and who have completely lost their capacity to work, will bear a responsibility for production. Male commune members are required to work 26 days a month. Those between the ages of 51 and 55 are given 6 days' exemption from work, and those between the ages of 56 and 60, 13 days. Female commune members are required to work 22 days a month. Those between the ages of 41 and 45 receive a four-day exemption, and those between 46 and 60, a seven-day exemption. A two-month exemption is given for childbirth.

As exemption for women involved in household duties and the care of children, those with one child under five years of age receive an exemption of four days; those with two children, six days, and those with three children, ten days.

In order to expand hog production, women workers raising either boars or sows will receive a five-day excuse from work per head and those raising pigs for meat, three days per head. (There will be a ten-day exemption from work for those who have sows having litters.)

In summary, there are two methods of linking the basic work-points with the basic ration. One method is, regardless of the sex of the commune member, to pay a penalty of two catties of grain for each ten work-points short of the quota for labor. The other is to take rations in proportion to the work-points earned.

Approval must be obtained for sick leave. First, two days are subtracted from outside the quota, and then the work-points are subtracted from within the quota.

The basic rations of idlers, petty thieves, and drifters should be suspended. The basic rations for all household members of peddlers and those who blindly reclaim wasteland should be suspended. They should be required to buy their food at 150 yüan for each 100 catties.

(2) The quantity of fertilizer to be collected will be set individually. The total amount collected by a household will be given a value according to its quality and will be counted as part of the household's investment. As for the method of determining the amount of fertilizer (except for those from one to six years of age, who do not have a duty to hand over fertilizer), those from 7 to 10 years will hand over 20 catties; those from 11 to 16 years, 40 catties; male laborers over 17 years, 50 catties; female workers, 70 catties; and nonworkers, 90 catties. Treatment of collections exceeding and falling short of quotas: For each 100 catties in excess of the quota, a reward of 50 per cent of the value will be given. It will be purchased with cash, and will be credited with 10 nonwork-points. The individual will participate in excess-output rations and subsidiary agricultural products. For those who do not complete the assignments, 5 catties of that month's basic ration will be deducted for each 100 catties of fertilizer short of the quotas.

(1) Debts. --Except for debts owed by the brigade to the state, which will be uniformly repaid by the brigade, the remainder devolves upon the production teams.

(2) Credits. --Fixed assets such as waterwheels, plow oxen, and farm tools will be owed by the production team to the brigade.

(3) Production costs. --Costs are approved once a year, and the fund appropriated periodically. The approved amounts will be distributed by each production team to the households under it in proportion to the area of land held by the households.

X. PROBLEMS OF WATER-CONSERVATION CONSTRUCTION AND VOLUNTEER WORK

(1) Water drains are under the management of the production teams. We have adopted the three guarantee method--the guarantee of management, the guarantee of repair, and the guarantee of irrigation.

(2) Water-conservation volunteer work is apportioned on the basis of the area receiving its benefit.

(3) Basic construction belongs in the category of entire brigade construction, but work-points should be distributed according to the labor-force ratio.

Chinese Communist Party, Hung-t'ang Branch

March 24, 1963

III

[STATISTICAL TABLES RELATING TO THE HU-LI BRIGADE OF THE P'U-K'OU COMMUNE]

1 - Basic Statistics, Hu-li Brigade

2 - Labor Force and Domestic Animal Quotas, Hu-li Brigade

3 - Classification of Cultivated Land

4 - Allocation of Cultivated Land by Crops

5 - Production Quotas for Food Crops

6 - Distribution of Food Crop

7 - Production and Distribution of Economic Crops and Fruits

8 - Agricultural Implements and Plow Cattle "Sent Down" to the Teams

9 - Plow Cattle "Sent Down" to the Teams

10 - Income from Various Operations

11 - Appropriation for the Three Retained Funds

12 - Production Quotas for Vegetables

Table III-1

BASIC STATISTICS, HU-LI BRIGADE

Team	Number of households	Population			Labor force					Cultivated area (in mou)								
						Male		Female			Paddy fields				Dry fields			
		Total	Male	Female	Total	Full time	Part time	Full time	Part time	Total	Subtotal	Double cropping	Single cropping	Private plots	Subtotal	Fields	Under fruit trees	Private plots
Ting-chang	18	72	37	35	33	14	5	2	12	70.59	49.63	43.42	1.90	4.31	20.96	15.32	1.80	3.84
Pi kuei	14	71	39	32	25	10	5	–	10	71.68	50.58	44.64	1.90	4.04	21.10	15.70	1.80	3.60
Pi-fa	15	59	33	26	23	9	4	2	8	71.22	50.52	45.36	1.90	3.26	20.70	15.96	1.80	2.94
Yi-shao	25	96	53	43	43	15	10	3	15	102.29	69.85	62.05	2.50	5.30	32.44	25.19	2.65	4.60
Heng-tai	26	108	53	55	42	16	9	7	10	103.41	70.21	61.76	2.50	5.95	33.20	25.38	2.65	5.17
Pi-ch'eng	21	97	55	42	29	11	6	2	10	113.88	81.70	73.66	2.55	5.49	32.18	24.82	2.65	4.71
Shui-kuan-ti	22	87	44	43	33	15	6	5	7	113.20	81.48	73.92	2.55	5.01	31.72	24.77	2.65	4.30
Neng-chih	29	128	58	70	42	10	4	–	28	114.07	82.14	72.30	2.60	7.24	31.93	22.71	2.87	6.35
Tseng-pao	25	106	53	53	41	19	5	12	5	119.91	88.84	80.11	2.60	6.13	31.07	22.81	2.87	5.39
Ting-hsieh	28	117	59	58	48	19	6	14	9	124.80	91.37	83.56	1.17	6.64	33.43	25.04	2.87	5.52
Shan-chün	32	123	64	59	46	17	10	5	14	111.31	81.75	70.82	4.03	6.90	29.56	20.92	2.87	5.77
Ch'ang-mu	26	103	53	50	44	19	4	–	21	95.06	67.39	59.32	2.23	5.84	27.67	20.34	2.30	5.03
Ting-tuan	24	85	41	44	41	18	7	–	16	96.15	69.53	62.27	2.23	5.03	26.62	20.81	2.50	4.31
Chi-kuang	24	100	50	50	32	20	2	–	10	90.68	63.87	55.94	2.24	5.69	26.81	19.61	2.30	4.90
Hua-cheng	22	101	51	50	37	14	4	10	9	93.35	64.23	56.09	2.39	5.75	29.12	24.24	–	4.88
Cheng-tseng	20	84	49	35	32	14	3	–	15	92.97	64.04	57.41	1.83	4.80	28.93	24.86	–	4.07
Cheng-t'ung	20	104	51	53	39	17	6	–	16	94.21	62.87	54.98	2.15	5.74	31.34	26.45	–	4.89
Chen-te	20	111	52	59	45	15	5	7	18	91.28	62.37	54.87	1.43	6.07	28.91	23.86	–	5.05
Other		7	7															
Total . .	411	1,759	902	857	675	272	101	69	233	1,770.06	1,252.37	1,112.48	40.70	99.19	517.69	398.79	[34.58]	85.32

Table III-2

LABOR FORCE AND DOMESTIC ANIMAL QUOTAS, HU-LI BRIGADE

Team	Number of households	Population			Labor force			Total		Basic work-points						Domestic Animal Quotas (Annual)		
										Male			Female					
		Total	Male	Female	Total	Male	Female	Annual	Monthly	Persons in 1st class (8 pts. ea.)	Persons in 2d class (7 pts. ea.)	Persons in 3d class (6 pts. ea.)	Persons in 1st class (6 pts. ea.)	Persons in 2d class (5 pts. ea.)	Persons in 3d class (4 pts. ea.)	Pigs (head)	Poultry (head)	Eggs (catties)
Ting-chang	18	72	37	35	25	13	12	48,048	4,004	8	5	–	7	3	2	1	18	18
Pi-kuei	14	71	39	32	21	12	9	40,104	3,342	9	3	–	2	2	5	1	14	14
Pi-fa	15	59	33	26	23	12	11	43,488	3,624	9	2	1	3	6	2	1	15	15
Yi-shao	25	96	53	43	42	23	19	75,864	6,322	12	5	6	4	6	9	1.5	25	25
Heng-tai	26	108	53	55	42	25	17	75,120	6,260	12	5	8	1	3	13	1.5	26	26
Pi-ch'eng	21	97	55	42	33	18	15	60,336	5,028	12	3	3	2	5	8	1	21	21
Shui-kuan-ti	22	87	44	43	34	20	14	59,256	4,938	5	10	5	–	3	11	1	22	22
Neng-chih	29	128	58	70	43	18	25	73,608	6,134	8	7	3	7	10	8	1.5	29	29
Tseng-pao	25	106	53	53	34	20	14	68,448	5,704	14	2	4	12	2	–	1	25	25
Ting-hsieh	28	117	59	58	48	23	25	88,992	7,416	21	2	–	7	8	10	1.5	28	28
Shan-chün	32	123	64	59	47	28	19	88,968	7,414	19	3	6	–	14	5	1.5	32	32
Ch'ang-mu	26	103	53	50	42	20	22	78,480	6,540	12	6	2	15	2	5	1.5	26	26
Ting-tuan	24	85	41	44	42	24	18	82,008	6,834	18	5	1	7	6	5	1	24	24
Chi-kuang	24	100	50	50	41	22	19	74,784	6,232	12	5	5	6	5	8	1	24	24
Hua-cheng	22	101	51	50	33	18	15	61,992	5,166	9	5	4	9	2	4	1	22	22
Cheng-tseng	20	84	49	35	34	19	15	64,704	5,392	10	4	5	7	8	–	1	20	20
Cheng-t'ung	20	104	51	53	40	23	17	70,560	5,880	6	11	6	1	7	9	1	20	20
Chen-te	20	111	52	59	38	23	15	72,768	6,064	16	4	3	–	10	5	1	20	20
Other		7	7															
Total	411	1,759	902	857	662	361	301	1,227,528	102,294	222	87	62	90	102	109	21	411	411

Table III-3

CLASSIFICATION OF CULTIVATED LAND

(Area in mou; output in catties)

Team	Total planned production of collective land	Collective land — Paddy fields: Double-cropping fields Area	Output per mou	Total output	Single-cropping fields Area	Output per mou	Total output	Total Area	Output	Dry fields: Potato fields Area	Output per mou	Total output	Land under fruit trees Area	Output per mou	Total output	Total Area	Output	Private plots — Paddy fields Area	Output per mou	Total output	Dry fields Area	Output per mou	Total output
Ting-chang	45,040	43.42	793	34,432	1.90	300	570	45.32	35,002	15.32	620	9,498	1.80	300	540	17.12	10,038	4.31	793	3,418	3.84	620	2,381
Pi-kuei	46,244	44.64	793	35,400	1.90	—	570	46.64	35,970	15.70	620	9,734	1.80	—	540	17.50	10,274	4.04	793	3,204	3.60	620	2,232
Pi-fa	46,975	45.36	793	35,970	1.90	—	570	47.26	36,540	15.96	620	9,895	1.80	—	540	17.76	10,435	3.26	793	2,585	2.94	620	1,823
Yi-shao	67,057	62.05	798	49,516	2.50	—	750	64.55	50,266	25.19	635	15,996	2.65	—	795	27.84	16,791	5.30	798	4,229	4.60	635	2,921
Heng-tai	66,935	61.76	798	49,284	2.50	—	750	64.06	50,034	25.38	635	16,116	2.65	—	795	28.03	16,911	5.95	798	4,748	5.17	635	3,283
Pi-ch'eng	75,733	73.66	793	58,412	2.55	—	765	76.21	59,177	24.82	635	15,761	2.65	—	795	27.47	16,556	5.49	793	4,354	4.71	635	2,991
Shui-kuan-ti	75,908	73.92	793	58,619	2.55	—	765	76.47	59,384	24.77	635	15,729	2.65	—	795	27.42	16,524	5.01	793	3,973	4.30	635	2,731
Neng-chih	73,031	72.30	790	57,117	2.60	—	780	74.90	57,897	22.71	612	13,853	2.87	—	861	25.58	14,714	7.24	790	5,720	6.35	610	3,874
Tseng-pao	78,834	80.11	790	63,287	2.60	—	780	82.71	64,067	22.81	610	13,914	2.87	—	861	25.68	14,775	6.13	790	4,843	5.39	610	3,288
Ting-hsieh	82,749	83.56	790	66,012	1.17	—	351	84.73	66,363	25.04	620	15,525	2.87	—	861	27.91	16,386	6.64	790	5,246	5.52	620	3,422
Shan-chün	70,988	70.82	790	55,948	4.03	—	1,209	74.55	57,157	20.92	620	12,970	2.87	—	861	23.79	13,831	6.90	790	5,451	5.77	620	3,577
Ch'ang-mu	61,222	59.32	800	47,486	2.23	—	669	61.55	48,125	20.34	610	12,407	2.30	—	690	22.64	13,097	5.84	800	4,672	5.03	610	3,068
Ting-tuan	63,381	62.27	800	49,816	2.23	—	669	64.50	50,485	20.01	610	12,206	2.30	—	690	22.31	12,896	5.03	800	4,024	4.31	610	2,629
Chi-kuang	58,076	55.94	800	44,752	2.24	—	672	58.18	45,424	19.61	610	11,962	2.30	—	690	21.91	12,652	5.69	800	4,552	4.90	610	2,989
Hua-cheng	63,940	56.09	832	46,667	2.39	—	717	58.48	47,384	24.24	683	16,556	—	—	—	24.24	16,556	5.75	832	4,784	4.88	683	3,333
Cheng-tseng	65,567	57.41	832	47,765	1.83	—	549	59.24	48,314	24.86	694	17,253	—	—	—	24.86	17,253	4.80	832	3,994	4.07	694	2,825
Cheng-t'ung	64,824	54.98	832	45,743	2.15	—	645	57.13	46,388	26.45	697	18,436	—	—	—	26.45	18,436	5.74	832	4,776	4.99	697	3,478
Chen-te	62,091	54.87	832	45,652	1.43	—	429	56.30	46,081	23.86	671	16,010	—	—	—	23.86	16,012	6.07	832	5,050	5.05	670	3,384
Other	—	—	—	—	—	—	—	—	—	—	—	—	—	—	—	—	—	—	—	—	—	—	—
Total	1,168,193	112.48	—	891,848	40.70	—	12,210	1,153.18	904,058	397.99	—	253,821	34.38	—	10,314	432.37	264,135	99.19	—	79,623	85.42	—	54,229

71

Table III-4

ALLOCATION OF CULTIVATED LAND BY CROPS
(In mou)

Team	Allocation of paddy fields								Allocation of dry fields				
	Total area	Early rice	Late rice	Single-cropping rice	Rice seedlings	Jute	Vegetables	Private plots	Total area	Potato	Under fruit trees	Peanuts	Private plots
Ting-chang	49.65	38.11	40.12	1.90	2.01	1.90	1.42	4.31	20.92	13.92	1.80	1.40	3.84
Pi-kuei	50.58	39.16	41.32	1.90	2.16	1.90	1.42	4.04	21.10	14.30	1.80	1.40	3.60
Pi-fa	50.52	39.82	42.02	1.90	2.20	1.90	1.44	3.26	20.70	14.56	1.80	1.40	2.94
Yi-shao	69.85	54.45	57.45	2.50	3.00	2.60	2.00	5.30	32.44	22.89	2.65	2.30	4.60
Heng-tai	70.21	54.18	57.16	2.50	2.98	2.60	2.00	5.95	39.20	29.08	2.65	2.30	5.17
Pi-ch'eng	81.70	64.64	68.18	2.55	3.54	3.10	2.38	5.49	32.18	22.52	2.65	2.30	4.71
Shui-kuan-ti	81.48	64.89	68.44	2.55	3.55	3.10	2.38	5.01	31.72	22.47	2.65	2.30	4.30
Neng-chih	82.14	63.46	66.94	2.60	3.48	3.00	2.36	7.24	31.93	20.51	2.87	2.20	6.35
Tseng-pao	88.84	70.33	74.17	2.60	3.84	3.30	2.64	6.13	31.07	20.61	2.87	2.20	5.39
Ting-hsieh	91.37	73.54	77.47	1.17	3.93	3.40	2.69	6.64	33.43	22.84	2.87	2.20	5.52
Shan-chun	81.75	62.23	65.51	4.03	3.28	3.00	2.31	6.90	29.56	18.92	2.30	2.00	5.77
Ch'ang-mu	67.39	52.06	54.92	2.23	2.86	2.50	1.90	5.84	27.67	18.34	2.30	2.00	5.03
Ting-tuan	69.53	54.28	57.26	2.23	2.98	3.00	2.01	5.03	26.62	18.01	2.30	2.00	4.31
Chi-kuang	63.77	49.14	51.84	2.24	2.70	2.30	1.80	5.59	26.81	17.61	2.30	2.00	4.90
Hua-cheng	64.23	49.17	51.88	2.39	2.71	2.40	1.81	5.75	29.12	22.24	—	2.00	4.88
Cheng-tseng	64.04	50.39	53.14	1.83	2.75	2.40	1.87	4.80	28.93	22.86	—	2.00	4.07
Cheng-t'ung	62.87	48.25	50.90	2.15	2.65	2.30	1.78	5.74	31.84	24.45	—	2.50	4.89
Chen-te	62.37	48.15	50.76	1.43	2.61	2.30	1.81	6.07	28.91	21.86	—	2.00	5.05
Other	—	—	—	—	—	—	—	—	—	—	—	—	—
Total	1,252.27	976.25	1,029.48	40.70	53.23	47.00	36.00	99.09	517.69	361.99	34.38	36.00	85.32

Table III-5

PRODUCTION QUOTAS FOR FOOD CROPS

(Area in mou; output per mou in catties; total output in tan)

Team	Paddy fields							Dry fields							Total		
	Double cropping			Single cropping				Potato			Under fruit trees						
	Area	Output per mou	Total output	Area	Output per mou	Total output	Output Subtotal	Area	Output per mou	Total output	Area	Output per mou	Total output	Output Subtotal	Area	Output per mou	Total output
Ting-chang	40.12	793	318.15	1.90	300	5.70	323.85	13.92	620	86.30	1.80	300	5.40	91.70	57.74	725	415.55
Pi-kuei	41.32	793	327.67	1.90	300	5.70	333.37	14.30	620	88.66	1.80	300	5.40	94.06	59.32	725	427.43
Pi-fa	42.02	793	333.22	1.90	300	5.70	338.92	14.56	620	90.27	1.80	300	5.40	95.67	60.28	725	434.59
Yi-shao	57.45	798	458.45	2.50	300	7.50	465.95	22.89	635	145.55	2.65	300	7.95	153.30	85.49	725	619.25
Heng-tai	57.16	798	456.14	2.50	300	7.50	463.64	23.08	635	146.56	2.65	300	7.95	154.51	85.39	725	618.15
Pi-ch'eng	68.18	793	540.67	2.55	300	7.65	548.32	22.52	635	143.00	2.65	300	7.95	150.95	95.90	725	699.27
Shui-kuan-ti	68.44	793	542.73	2.55	300	7.65	550.38	22.47	635	142.68	2.65	300	7.95	150.63	96.11	725	701.01
Neng-chih	66.94	790	528.83	2.60	300	7.80	536.63	20.51	610	125.11	2.87	300	8.61	133.72	92.92	725	670.35
Tseng-pao	74.17	790	585.94	2.60	300	7.80	593.74	20.61	610	125.72	2.87	300	8.61	134.33	100.25	725	728.07
Ting-hsieh	77.47	790	612.01	1.17	300	3.51	615.52	22.84	620	141.61	2.87	300	8.61	150.22	104.35	725	765.74
Shan-chun	65.51	790	517.53	4.03	300	12.09	529.62	18.92	620	117.30	2.87	300	8.61	125.91	91.33	725	655.53
Ch'ang-mu	54.92	800	439.36	2.23	300	6.69	446.05	18.34	610	111.87	2.30	300	6.90	118.77	77.79	725	564.82
Ting-tuan	57.26	800	458.08	2.23	300	6.69	464.77	18.01	610	109.86	2.30	300	6.90	116.76	79.80	725	581.53
Chi-kuang	51.84	800	414.72	2.24	300	6.72	421.44	17.61	610	107.42	2.30	300	6.90	114.32	73.99	725	535.76
Hua-cheng	51.88	832	431.64	2.39	300	7.17	498.81	22.24	683	151.90	–	–	–	151.90	76.51	725	590.71
Cheng-tseng	53.14	832	442.13	1.83	300	5.49	447.62	22.86	694	158.60	–	–	–	158.65	77.83	725	606.27
Cheng-t'ung	50.90	832	423.49	2.15	300	6.45	429.94	24.45	697	170.42	–	–	–	170.42	77.50	725	600.36
Chen-te	50.76	832	422.32	1.43	300	4.29	426.61	21.86	671	146.68	–	–	–	146.68	74.05	725	573.29
Total	1,029.48	801	8,253.08	40.70	300	122.10	8,375.18	361.99	637	2,309.31	34.38	300	103.14	2,412.45	1,466.55	725	10,787.63

Table III-6

DISTRIBUTION OF FOOD CROP

Team	Total production (tan)	Quantities retained (QR) for seed							State levy and purchase (tan)	Quantities retained for feed													Quantities retained for human rations						Quantity to the brigade (tan)
		Paddy fields			Dry fields					Pigs			Ducks (for meat)			Ducks (for eggs)			Geese			Subtotal (tan)	Work ration (14%) (tan)	Basic ration			Ration for brigade enterprise personnel		
		Area (mou)	QR per mou (catties)	Total QR (tan)	Area (mou)	QR per mou (catties)	Total QR (catties)	Subtotal (tan)		Head	QR per head (catties)	Total QR (catties)	Head	QR per head (catties)	Total QR (tan)	Head	QR per head (catties)	Total QR (tan)	Head	QR per head (catties)	Total QR (tan)			Number of persons	Per person (catties)	Total (tan)	Number of persons	Total QR (tan)	
Ting-chang	415.55	45.32	20	9.10	17.13	4	69	9.79	201	1	40	40	–	–	–	–	–	–	–	–	–	–	–	27.47	72	234	165.48	–	–	8.24
Pi-kuei	427.43	46.34	20	9.30	17.50	4	70	10.00	213	1	40	40	–	–	–	–	–	–	–	–	–	–	–	28.18	71	–	166.14	–	–	9.71
Pi-fa	434.59	47.26	20	9.50	17.76	4	71	10.21	244	1	40	40	–	–	–	–	–	–	–	–	–	–	–	28.61	59	–	138.06	–	–	13.31
Yi-shao	619.25	64.55	20	12.90	27.84	4	111	14.01	320	1.5	40	60	–	–	–	–	–	–	–	–	–	–	–	40.65	96	–	224.64	–	–	15.25
Heng-tai	618.15	64.26	20	12.90	28.03	4	112	14.02	294	1.5	40	60	–	–	–	–	–	–	–	–	–	–	–	40.61	108	–	252.72	–	–	16.20
Pi-ch'eng	699.27	76.21	20	15.20	27.47	4	110	16.30	385	1	40	40	–	–	–	–	–	–	–	–	–	–	–	45.62	97	–	226.98	–	–	24.97
Shui-kuan-ti	701.01	76.47	20	15.30	27.42	4	110	16.40	408	1	40	40	–	–	–	–	–	–	–	–	–	–	–	45.71	87	–	203.58	–	–	26.92
Neng-chih	670.35	74.90	20	15.00	25.58	4	102	16.02	299	1.5	40	60	–	–	–	–	–	–	–	–	–	–	–	44.12	128	–	299.52	–	–	15.29
Tseng-pao	728.07	82.71	20	16.50	25.68	4	103	17.53	289	1	40	40	–	–	–	–	–	–	–	–	–	–	–	47.65	106	–	248.04	–	–	25.41
Ting-hsieh	765.74	84.73	20	17.00	27.91	4	112	18.12	394	1.5	40	60	–	–	–	–	–	–	–	–	–	–	–	49.56	117	–	273.78	–	–	30.60
Shan-chun	655.53	74.85	20	15.00	23.79	4	95	15.95	288	1.5	40	60	–	–	–	–	–	–	–	–	–	–	–	43.40	123	–	287.82	–	–	19.76
Ch'ang-mu	564.82	61.55	20	12.30	22.64	4	91	13.21	255	1.5	40	60	–	–	–	–	–	–	–	–	–	–	–	37.04	103	–	241.02	–	–	17.95
Ting-tuan	581.53	64.30	20	12.90	22.31	4	89	13.79	308	1	40	40	–	–	–	–	–	–	–	–	–	–	–	38.20	85	–	198.90	–	–	22.24
Chi-kuang	535.76	58.18	20	11.60	21.91	4	88	12.48	237	1	40	40	–	–	–	–	–	–	–	–	–	–	–	35.34	100	–	234.00	–	–	16.54
Hua-cheng	590.71	58.48	20	11.70	24.34	4	97	12.67	287	1	40	40	–	–	–	–	–	–	–	–	–	–	–	36.80	101	–	236.34	–	–	17.90
Cheng-tseng	606.27	59.24	20	11.90	24.86	4	99	12.90	336	1	40	40	–	–	–	–	–	–	–	–	–	–	–	37.62	84	–	196.56	–	–	23.21
Cheng-t'ung	600.36	57.33	20	11.50	26.45	4	106	12.56	*	1	40	40	–	–	–	–	–	–	–	–	–	–	–	35.70	104	–	243.36	–	–	18.10
Chen-te	573.29	56.50	20	11.30	23.75	4	95	12.25	*	1	40	40	–	–	–	–	–	–	–	–	–	–	–	35.27	111	–	259.7	–	–	15.63
Brigade	–	–	–	–	–	–	–	–	–	–	–	–	1,500	3	45	270	60	162	40	70	28	–	–	7	–	16.31	22	65.36	–
Total	10,787.63	1,153.18	20	230.64	432.37	4	1,730	247.94	5,309	21	40	840	1,500	3	45	270	60	162	40	70	28	243.40	697.55	1,759	–	4,116.06	22	65.36	320.94

*Figures illegible.

Table III-7

PRODUCTION AND DISTRIBUTION OF ECONOMIC CROPS AND FRUITS
(Production in mou; output in catties)

Team	Jute Area	Jute Output per mou	Jute Total output	Vegetable Area	Vegetable Output per mou	Vegetable Total output	Peanut Area	Peanut Output per mou	Peanut Total output	Strawberry First class	Strawberry Second class	Strawberry Third class	Strawberry Subtotal	Loquat	Peach	Pomegranate	Total	Population	QR per head	Total QR	State purchase
Ting-chang	1.90	250	475	1.40	3,500	4,900	1.40	100	140	1,133	1,608	1,407	4,148	—	528	240	4,916	72	30	2,160	2,756
Pi-kuei	1.90	250	475	1.42	3,500	4,970	1.40	100	140	1,133	1,608	1,407	4,148	—	528	240	4,916	71	30	2,130	2,786
Pi-fa	1.90	250	475	1.44	3,500	5,040	1.40	100	140	1,134	1,608	1,406	4,148	—	528	240	4,916	59	30	1,770	3,146
Yi-shao	2.60	250	650	2.00	3,500	7,000	2.30	100	230	1,712	2,692	1,992	6,396	—	32	—	6,428	96	30	2,880	3,548
Heng-tai	2.60	250	650	2.00	3,500	7,000	2.30	100	230	976	3,092	2,352	6,400	—	300	—	6,700	108	30	3,240	3,460
Pi-ch'eng	3.10	250	775	2.38	3,500	8,330	2.30	100	230	768	3,384	1,840	5,992	—	512	220	6,724	97	30	2,910	3,814
Shui-kuan-ti	3.10	250	775	2.38	3,500	8,320	2.30	100	230	828	3,448	2,032	6,308	—	352	520	7,180	87	30	2,610	4,570
Neng-chih	3.10	250	750	2.36	3,500	8,260	2.20	100	220	1,877	3,048	1,532	6,457	—	28	—	6,485	128	30	3,840	2,645
Tseng-pao	3.30	250	825	2.64	3,500	9,240	2.20	100	220	1,504	3,104	1,312	5,920	—	8	—	5,928	106	30	3,180	2,748
Ting-hsieh	3.40	250	850	2.69	3,500	9,415	2.20	100	220	1,688	2,736	1,475	5,899	—	—	—	5,899	117	30	3,510	2,389
Shan-chun	3.00	250	750	2.31	3,500	8,085	2.00	100	200	2,688	2,472	1,256	6,416	—	—	—	6,416	123	30	3,690	2,736
Ch'ang-mu	2.50	250	625	1.90	3,500	6,650	2.00	100	200	1,016	2,760	2,188	5,964	—	100	120	6,184	103	30	3,090	3,094
Ting-tuan	3.00	250	750	2.01	3,500	7,035	2.00	100	200	2,424	1,968	1,496	5,888	—	40	120	6,048	85	30	2,550	3,498
Chi-kuang	2.30	250	575	1.80	3,500	6,300	2.00	100	200	1,436	2,680	1,568	5,684	—	40	—	5,724	100	30	3,000	2,724
Hua-cheng	2.40	250	600	1.81	3,500	6,335	2.00	100	200	8,964	1,398	433	10,795	40	210	10	11,055	101	30	3,030	8,015
Cheng-tseng	2.40	250	600	1.87	3,500	6,545	2.00	100	200	9,338	841	568	10,747	34	30	220	11,031	84	30	2,520	8,511
Cheng-t'ung	2.30	250	575	1.78	3,500	6,230	2.00	100	200	9,004	1,578	628	11,210	40	60	—	11,310	104	30	3,120	8,190
Chen-te	2.30	250	575	1.81	3,500	6,335	2.00	100	200	8,839	1,151	598	10,588	33	—	150	10,771	111	30	3,330	7,441
Brigade	—	—	—	—	—	—	—	—	—	—	—	—	—	—	—	—	—	7	—	—	—
Total	47.00	250	11,750	36.00	3,500	126,000	36.00	100	3,600	56,462	41,156	25,490	123,108	147	3,296	2,080	128,631	1,759	30	52,560	76,071

Table III-8

AGRICULTURAL IMPLEMENTS AND PLOW CATTLE "SENT DOWN" TO THE TEAMS

(Values in yüan)

Team	Deep plow		Old-style plow		Large wheelbarrows		Small wheelbarrows		Hoes		Scuffle hoes		Wooden racks		Spray		Scale		Old-style rake		[Name illegible]		Plow cattle		Total value
	Quantity	Value	Quantity	Value	Quantity	Value	Quantity	Value	Quantity	Value	Quantity	Value	Quantity	Value	Quantity	Value	Quantity	Value	Quantity	Value	Quantity	Value	Head	Value	
Ting-chang	1	12.75	2	6.00	1	28.50	1	7.30	7	59.50	20	16.50	4	20.00	–	–	–	–	3	21.69	–	–	5	421.00	593.24
Pi-kuei	1	12.75	1	3.00	1	28.50	1	7.35	8	68.00	21	17.33	4	20.00	1	5.00	–	–	3	21.70	–	–	4	526.00	709.63
Pi-fa	–	–	2	6.00	–	–	1	7.30	8	68.00	21	17.33	4	20.00	–	–	–	–	4	28.92	1	34.76	6	704.00	886.31
Yi-shao	–	–	2	8.00	1	29.50	1	33.00	12	99.60	36	31.20	6	33.48	1	17.40	–	–	5	36.15	–	–	8	857.00	1,145.33
Heng-tai	–	–	2	8.00	1	29.50	–	11.50	12	99.60	36	31.20	6	33.48	–	–	–	–	5	36.15	1	34.76	8	919.00	1,191.69
Pi-ch'eng	–	–	3	8.00	1	29.50	1	11.50	9	89.10	25	42.20	6	32.50	1	18.90	–	–	5	35.00	–	–	11	1,239.00	1,505.70
Shui-kuan-ti	–	–	3	8.00	1	29.50	1	30.00	9	89.10	25	42.20	6	32.50	–	–	–	–	5	35.00	1	34.76	7	833.00	1,115.50
Neng-chih	1	13.80	3	12.00	1	83.34	2	30.00	16	93.40	111	89.20	6	27.94	–	–	–	–	5	31.50	–	–	10	1,115.00	1,496.18
Tseng-pao	1	13.70	3	12.00	3	83.34	3	30.00	17	93.40	111	89.20	5	27.94	–	–	–	–	4	31.50	1	34.76	9	1,197.00	1,612.84
Ting-hsieh	1	12.00	3	12.38	2	66.66	3	30.00	17	95.90	122	97.20	7	35.56	–	–	–	–	5	44.60	1	34.76	8	1,143.00	1,572.06
Shan-chun	1	12.00	3	12.37	2	66.66	2	16.00	17	95.90	121	97.20	7	35.56	–	–	1	10.00	5	44.60	–	–	9	1,352.00	1,756.29
Ch'ang-mu	1	12.27	1	4.00	2	40.00	2	16.00	10	65.40	59	61.33	6	29.00	–	–	1	7.00	4	40.33	–	–	7	1,038.00	1,313.33
Ting-tuan	1	12.27	1	4.00	1	40.00	2	16.00	10	65.40	59	61.33	5	29.00	–	–	–	–	5	40.34	–	–	7	1,164.00	1,432.34
Chi-kuang	1	12.26	1	4.00	1	40.00	2	10.00	10	65.40	60	61.34	5	29.00	1	9.00	–	–	4	40.33	1	34.76	6	990.50	1,302.09
Hua-cheng	–	–	2	6.75	1	35.00	1	10.00	8	72.83	45	59.10	5	29.12	–	–	–	–	1	9.00	–	–	5	1,104.50	826.90
Cheng-tseng	–	–	2	6.75	1	35.00	1	10.00	8	72.83	45	59.10	4	29.12	–	–	–	–	1	9.00	–	–	5	1,122.00	853.68
Cheng-t'ung	–	–	2	6.75	1	35.00	1	10.00	8	72.83	45	59.10	4	29.12	1	10.00	–	–	1	9.00	–	–	5	656.00	887.00
Chen-te	1	10.00	–	6.75	1	35.00	1	10.00	8	72.83	45	59.10	4	29.12	–	–	–	–	2	18.00	1	34.76	6	726.00	1,001.56
Total	10	123.80	36	134.75	22	735.00	26	285.95	194	1,439.02	1,007	991.16	94	522.44	5	60.30	2	17.00	67	532.81	7	243.32	126	16,111.00	21,202.53

Table III-9

PLOW CATTLE "SENT DOWN" TO THE TEAMS
(Amount in yüan)

Team	Ox — Class one Head	Quantity[1]	Unit price	Amount	Ox — Class two Head	Quantity[1]	Unit price	Amount	Ox — Class three Head	Quantity[1]	Unit price	Amount	Cow — Class one Head	Quantity[1]	Unit price	Amount	Cow — Class two Head	Quantity[1]	Unit price	Amount	Cow — Class three Head	Quantity[1]	Unit price	Amount	Total Head	Quantity[1]	Amount
Ting-chang	1	90	10	90	2	260	80	208	–	–	–	–	–	–	–	–	1	90	70	63	1	120	50	60	5	560	421
Pi-kuei	2	36	–	360	–	–	–	–	1	150	50	75	–	–	–	–	1	130	–	91	–	–	–	–	4	640	526
Pi-fa	2	400	–	400	1	160	–	128	–	–	–	–	1	120	80	96	–	–	–	–	2	160	–	80	6	840	704
Yi-shao	2	290	–	290	1	140	–	112	–	–	–	–	2	180	–	144	2	280	–	196	2	230	–	115	8	1,120	857
Heng-tai	1	170	–	175	1	190	–	152	–	–	–	–	4	510	–	408	2	270	–	189	–	–	–	–	8	1,140	919
Pi-ch'eng	2	280	–	280	2	390	–	312	–	–	–	–	6	740	–	592	–	–	–	–	1	110	–	55	11	1,420	1,239
Shui-kuan-ti	3	460	–	460	–	–	–	–	–	–	–	–	1	90	–	72	3	430	–	301	–	–	–	–	7	980	833
Neng-chih	1	200	–	200	1	190	–	152	–	–	–	–	6	700	–	560	2	290	–	203	–	–	–	–	10	1,380	1,115
Tseng-pao	6	930	–	930	–	–	–	–	–	–	–	–	2	220	–	176	1	130	–	91	–	–	–	–	9	1,280	1,197
Ting-hsieh	4	780	–	780	–	–	–	–	–	–	–	–	2	200	–	160	2	290	–	203	–	–	–	–	8	1,270	1,143
Shan-chun	5	1,000	–	1,000	1	80	–	64	–	–	–	–	3	360	–	288	–	–	–	–	–	–	–	–	9	1,440	1,352
Ch'ang-mu	5	790	–	790	1	210	–	168	–	–	–	–	1	100	–	80	–	–	–	–	–	–	–	–	7	1,100	1,038
Ting-tuan	5	940	–	940	–	–	–	–	–	–	–	–	2	280	–	224	–	–	–	–	–	–	–	–	7	1,220	1,164
Chi-kuang	4	820	–	820	–	–	–	–	–	–	–	–	1	90	–	72	1	140	–	98	–	–	–	–	6	1,050	990
Hua-cheng	1	180	–	180	1	220	–	176	–	–	–	–	2	230	–	184	–	–	–	–	1	130	–	65	5	760	605
Cheng-tseng	3	480	–	480	–	–	–	–	–	–	–	–	2	190	–	152	–	–	–	–	–	–	–	–	5	670	632
Cheng-t'ung	3	520	–	520	–	–	–	–	–	–	–	–	2	170	–	136	–	–	–	–	–	–	–	–	5	690	656
Chen-te	2	190	–	190	2	400	–	320	–	–	–	–	2	270	–	216	–	–	–	–	–	–	–	–	6	860	726
Total	52	8,556		8,556	13	2,240		1,792	1	150		75	39	4,450		3,560	15	2,050		1,435	7	750		375	126	18,420	16,117

[1] The unit and meaning of "Quantity" are not clear.

77

Table III-10

INCOME FROM VARIOUS OPERATIONS

(Quantity in "c" (catties) or "t" (tan = 100 catties); unit price in yüan per tan; amount in yüan)

Team	Food crops Quantity (t)	Food crops Unit price	Food crops Amount	Jute Quantity (c)	Jute Unit price	Jute Amount	Peanuts Quantity (c)	Peanuts Unit price	Peanuts Amount	Vegetables Quantity (t)	Vegetables Unit price	Vegetables Amount	Hay Quantity (t)	Hay Unit price	Hay Amount	Potato vines Quantity (c)	Potato vines Unit price	Potato vines Amount	Subtotal (amount)	Strawberries and peaches Quantity (c)	Strawberries and peaches Unit price	Strawberries and peaches Amount	Loquats & pomegranates Quantity (c)	Loquats & pomegranates Unit price	Loquats & pomegranates Amount	Subtotal (amount)	Income from brigade enterprises	Total amount
Ting-chang	415.55	8.60	3,574	475	30	143	140	17	24	49.00	7	343	84.04	2	168	1,572	2	31	709	4,676	15	701	240	15	36	737	–	5,020
Pi-kuei	427.43	–	3,676	475	–	143	140	–	24	49.70	–	348	86.40	–	173	1,610	–	32	720	4,676	–	701	240	–	36	737	–	5,133
Pi-fa	434.59	–	3,738	475	–	143	140	–	24	50.40	–	353	87.84	–	176	1,636	–	33	729	4,676	–	701	240	–	36	737	–	5,204
Yi-shao	619.25	–	5,326	650	–	195	230	–	39	70.00	–	490	119.90	–	240	2,554	–	51	1,015	6,428	–	964	–	–	–	964	–	7,305
Heng-tai	618.15	–	3,316	650	–	195	230	–	39	70.00	–	490	119.72	–	239	2,573	–	52	1,015	6,700	–	1,005	–	–	–	1,005	–	7,336
Pi-ch'eng	699.27	–	6,014	775	–	233	230	–	39	83.30	–	583	141.50	–	283	2,517	–	50	1,188	6,504	–	976	220	–	33	1,009	–	8,211
Shui-kuan-ti	701.04	–	6,029	775	–	233	230	–	39	83.30	–	583	141.98	–	284	2,575	–	52	1,109	6,660	–	999	520	–	78	1,077	–	8,295
Neng-chih	668.15	–	5,750	750	–	225	220	–	37	82.60	–	578	139.06	–	278	2,338	–	47	1,165	6,485	–	973	–	–	–	973	–	7,888
Tseng-pao	728.07	–	6,261	825	–	248	220	–	37	92.45	–	647	153.54	–	307	2,348	–	47	1,386	5,923	–	889	–	–	–	889	–	8,436
Ting-hsieh	765.74	–	6,585	850	–	255	220	–	37	94.15	–	659	157.28	–	315	2,571	–	51	1,317	5,899	–	885	–	–	–	885	–	8,787
Shan-chun	655.53	–	5,638	750	–	225	200	–	34	80.85	–	566	139.08	–	278	2,179	–	44	1,147	6,416	–	962	–	–	–	962	–	7,747
Ch'ang-mu	564.82	–	4,858	625	–	188	200	–	34	66.57	–	466	114.30	–	229	2,064	–	41	958	6,064	–	910	120	–	18	928	–	6,744
Ting-tuan	581.53	–	5,001	750	–	223	200	–	34	70.35	–	493	118.99	–	238	2,011	–	40	1,030	5,928	–	889	120	–	18	907	–	6,938
Chi-kuang	535.76	–	4,608	575	–	173	200	–	34	63.00	–	441	108.16	–	216	1,991	–	40	904	5,724	–	859	–	–	–	859	–	6,371
Hua-cheng	590.71	–	5,080	600	–	180	200	–	34	63.35	–	444	108.54	–	217	2,224	–	45	920	11,005	–	1,651	50	–	8	1,659	–	7,659
Cheng-tseng	606.27	–	5,214	600	–	180	200	–	34	65.45	–	458	109.94	–	220	2,286	–	46	938	10,777	–	1,617	254	–	38	1,655	–	7,807
Cheng-t'ung	600.76	–	5,167	575	–	173	200	–	34	62.30	–	436	106.10	–	212	2,445	–	49	904	11,270	–	1,691	40	–	6	1,697	–	7,764
Chen-te	573.29	–	4,930	575	–	173	200	–	34	63.35	–	444	104.70	–	209	2,186	–	44	904	0,588	–	1,588	183	–	28	1,616	–	7,450
–	–	–	–	–	–	–	–	–	–	–	–	–	–	–	–	–	–	–	–	–	–	–	–	–	–	–	18,200[1]	18,200
Total	10,785.88	–	92,761	11,750	–	3,530	3,600	–	611	1,260.00	–	8,822	2,140.70	–	4,282	39,677	–	793	18,078	126,007	–	18,901	2,227	–	335	19,296	–	148,295

[1] See Table III-11, "team" column, last six rows.

Table III-11

APPROPRIATION FOR THE THREE RETAINED FUNDS

(Amounts in yüan)

Team	Total income	Appropriation for the reserve fund						Appropriation for the welfare fund						Appropriation for the administrative fund							
		Per cent of total income	Amount	To brigade		To team		Per cent of total income	Amount	To brigade		To team		Per cent of total income	Amount	To brigade & team		To brigade		To team	
				Amount	Per cent	Amount	Per cent			Amount	Per cent	Amount	Per cent			Administrative expenses	Cadre wages	Administrative expenses	Cadre wages	Administrative expenses	Cadre wages
Ting-chang	5,020	3	150	75	1.5	75	1.5	2	100	50	1	50	1	2	100	26	74	10	30	16	44
Pi-kuei	5,133	3	154	77	1.5	77	—	—	102	51	—	51	—	—	102	26	76	10	30	16	46
Pi-fa	5,204	3	156	78	1.5	78	—	—	104	52	—	52	—	—	104	26	78	10	31	16	47
Yi-shao	7,305	3	218	109	1.5	109	—	—	146	73	—	73	—	—	146	36	110	14	44	22	66
Heng-tai	7,336	3	220	110	1.5	110	—	—	146	73	—	73	—	—	146	36	110	14	44	22	66
Pi-ch'eng	8,211	3	246	123	1.5	123	—	—	164	82	—	82	—	—	164	40	124	16	50	24	74
Shui-kuan-ti	8,295	3	248	124	1.5	124	—	—	166	83	—	83	—	—	166	42	124	17	50	25	74
Neng-chih	7,888	3	236	118	1.5	118	—	—	158	79	—	79	—	—	158	40	118	16	47	24	71
Tseng-pao	8,436	3	254	127	1.5	127	—	—	168	84	—	84	—	—	168	43	126	17	50	25	76
Ting-hsieh	8,787	3	264	132	1.5	132	—	—	176	88	—	88	—	—	176	44	132	18	53	26	79
Shan-chun	7,747	3	232	116	1.5	116	—	—	154	77	—	77	—	—	154	38	116	15	46	23	70
Ch'ang-mu	6,744	3	202	101	1.5	101	—	—	134	67	—	67	—	—	134	34	100	13	40	21	60
Ting-tuan	6,938	3	208	104	1.5	104	—	—	138	69	—	69	—	—	138	34	104	13	42	21	62
Chi-kuang	6,371	3	190	95	1.5	95	—	—	128	64	—	64	—	—	128	32	96	12	38	20	58
Hua-cheng	7,659	3	230	115	1.5	115	—	—	154	77	—	77	—	—	154	38	116	15	46	23	70
Cheng-tseng	7,807	3	234	117	1.5	117	—	—	156	78	—	78	—	—	156	38	118	15	47	23	71
Cheng-t'ung	7,764	3	234	117	1.5	117	—	—	156	78	—	78	—	—	156	38	118	15	47	23	71
Chen-te	7,450	3	224	112	1.5	112	—	—	150	75	—	75	—	—	150	38	112	15	45	23	67
Hilly-land-cultivation teams	750	3	22	112	1.5	112	—	—	16	8	—	8	—	—	16	4	12	2	4	2	8
Rice mill	3,000	3	90	45	1.5	45	—	—	60	30	—	30	—	—	60	15	45	6	18	9	27
Brick and the workshop	4,000	3	120	60	1.5	60	—	—	80	40	—	40	—	—	80	20	60	8	24	12	36
Ducks (for eggs)	5,500	3	170	85	1.5	85	—	—	110	55	—	55	—	—	110	28	82	11	33	17	49
Geese	1,200	3	36	18	1.5	18	—	—	24	12	—	12	—	—	24	6	18	2	7	4	11
Ducks (for meat)	3,750	3	120	60	1.5	60	—	—	96	48	—	48	—	—	96	24	72	10	29	14	43
	148,295	3	4,458	2,229	1.5	2,229	1.5	2	2,986	1,493	1	1,493	1	2	2,986	745	2,241	298	896	447	1,345

Table III-12

PRODUCTION QUOTAS FOR VEGETABLES
(Area in mou. Output per mou in tan [?].)

First half of year:

Team	Labor force (number of full-time workers)	Taro Area	Taro Output/mou (35)	Ginger Area	Ginger Output/mou (15)	Eggplants Area	Eggplants Output/mou (22)	Wax gourds Area	Wax gourds Output/mou (50)	Cucumbers Area	Cucumbers Output/mou (20)	(?) Melons Area	(?) Melons Output/mou (30)	Loutahs Area	Loutahs Output/mou (25)	Leeks & garlic Area	Leeks & garlic Output/mou (25)	Total area
Ting-chang	24	0.46	—	.18	—	1.29	—	1.14	—	.41	—	.41	—	.23	—	.18	—	4.10
Pi-kuei	20	0.38	—	.15	—	.91	—	.95	—	.34	—	.34	—	.19	—	.15	—	3.41
Pi-fa	18	0.34	—	.14	—	.82	—	.85	—	.30	—	.30	—	.17	—	.14	—	3.06
Yi-shao	32	0.60	—	.24	—	1.47	—	1.52	—	.54	—	.54	—	.30	—	.24	—	5.45
Heng-tai	34	0.66	—	.26	—	1.55	—	1.61	—	.60	—	.60	—	.33	—	.26	—	5.87
Pi-ch'eng	26	0.48	—	.11	—	1.17	—	1.23	—	.43	—	.43	—	.24	—	.19	—	4.36
Shui-kuan-ti	27	0.50	—	.20	—	1.22	—	1.28	—	.45	—	.45	—	.25	—	.20	—	4.55
Neng-chih	31	0.58	—	.23	—	1.41	—	1.47	—	.52	—	.52	—	.29	—	.23	—	5.25
Tseng-pao	29	0.54	—	.20	—	1.32	—	1.37	—	.49	—	.49	—	.27	—	.22	—	4.92
Ting-hsieh	37	0.70	—	.28	—	1.68	—	1.76	—	.63	—	.63	—	.35	—	.28	—	6.31
Shan-chun	38	0.72	—	.29	—	1.73	—	1.80	—	.65	—	.65	—	.36	—	.29	—	6.49
Ch'ang-mu	31	0.60	—	.24	—	1.41	—	1.47	—	.54	—	.54	—	.30	—	.24	—	5.34
Ting-tuan	33	0.64	—	.26	—	1.50	—	1.56	—	.58	—	.58	—	.32	—	.26	—	5.70
Chi-kuang	32	0.62	—	.25	—	1.46	—	1.52	—	.56	—	.56	—	.31	—	.25	—	5.53
Hua-cheng	27	0.52	—	.31	—	1.23	—	1.28	—	.47	—	.47	—	.26	—	.21	—	4.65
Cheng-tseng	27	0.52	—	.21	—	1.23	—	1.28	—	.47	—	.47	—	.26	—	.21	—	4.65
Cheng-t'ung	31	0.56	—	.23	—	1.40	—	1.45	—	.51	—	.51	—	.28	—	.23	—	5.17
Chen-te	31	0.88	—	.22	—	1.40	—	1.46	—	.51	—	.51	—	.29	—	.22	—	5.19
Total	528	10.00	35	4.00	15	24.20	22	25.00	50	9.00	20	9.00	30	5.00	25	4.00	25	90.00

Second half of year:

Team	Cabbages Area	Cabbages Output/mou (40)	Carrots Area	Carrots Output/mou (50)	Turnips Area	Turnips Output/mou (30)	Celery Area	Celery Output/mou (50)	Mustard Area	Mustard Output/mou (45)	Leeks & garlic Area	Leeks & garlic Output/mou (25)	Radishes Area	Radishes Output/mou (40)	Total Area
Ting-chang	.41	—	.46	—	2.02	—	.82	—	.92	—	.41	—	.92	—	5.96
Pi-kuei	.34	—	.38	—	1.67	—	.68	—	.76	—	.34	—	.76	—	4.93
Pi-fa	.30	—	.34	—	1.50	—	.60	—	.68	—	.30	—	.68	—	4.40
Yi-shao	.54	—	.60	—	2.64	—	1.08	—	1.20	—	.54	—	1.20	—	7.80
Heng-tai	.60	—	.66	—	2.10	—	1.20	—	1.32	—	.60	—	1.32	—	8.60
Pi-ch'eng	.43	—	.48	—	2.32	—	0.86	—	.96	—	.43	—	.96	—	6.44
Shui-kuan-ti	.45	—	.50	—	2.90	—	.90	—	1.00	—	.45	—	1.00	—	6.40
Neng-chih	.52	—	.58	—	2.55	—	1.04	—	1.16	—	.52	—	1.16	—	7.53
Tseng-pao	.49	—	.54	—	2.30	—	.98	—	1.08	—	.49	—	1.08	—	6.96
Ting-hsieh	.63	—	.70	—	3.08	—	1.26	—	1.40	—	.63	—	1.40	—	9.10
Shan-chun	.65	—	.72	—	3.17	—	1.30	—	1.44	—	.65	—	1.44	—	9.37
Ch'ang-mu	.54	—	.60	—	2.64	—	1.08	—	1.20	—	.54	—	1.20	—	7.80
Ting-tuan	.58	—	.64	—	2.82	—	1.16	—	1.28	—	.58	—	1.28	—	8.34
Chi-kuang	.56	—	.62	—	2.73	—	1.12	—	1.24	—	.56	—	1.24	—	8.07
Hua-cheng	.47	—	.52	—	2.29	—	.94	—	1.04	—	.47	—	1.04	—	6.77
Cheng-tseng	.47	—	.52	—	2.29	—	.94	—	1.04	—	.47	—	1.04	—	6.77
Cheng-t'ung	.51	—	.56	—	2.64	—	1.02	—	1.12	—	.51	—	1.12	—	7.48
Chen-te	.51	—	.58	—	2.64	—	1.02	—	1.16	—	.51	—	1.16	—	7.58
Total	9.00	40	10.00	50	44.30	30	18.00	50	20.00	45	9.00	25	20.00	40	130.30

IV

RESOLUTIONS ON THE FURTHER STRENGTHENING OF THE COLLECTIVE ECONOMY OF THE PEOPLE'S COMMUNES AND EXPANDING AGRICULTURAL PRODUCTION

(Adopted by the Tenth Plenum of the Eighth Central Committee

of the Chinese Communist Party, September 27, 1962)

SECRET DOCUMENT

In order to strengthen further the collective economy of the people's communes and to expand agricultural production, the Central Committee of the Chinese Communist Party has made the following decisions.

I. After completing the antifeudal land reform, the party's basic line on the agricultural problem was, first, the collectivization of agriculture and, second, its mechanization and electrification. Comrade Mao Tse-tung, in his July 1955 report on the problem of organizing agriculture on a cooperative basis, made on behalf of the party Central Committee, fully explained the party's basic line on the agricultural problem. In the Two Road struggle in the villages, this is the basic line that will lend firm support to socialism and ensure the defeat of capitalism. Following this fundamental line, the party adopted various flexible, transitional formulas to achieve collectivization within a comparatively short period of time. Later, the people's communes were organized from the agricultural collectives. Because the party Central Committee at all times used actual experiences to establish appropriate policies and measures, the people's communes are already on the road to healthy expansion. In short, the nation's socialist agricultural industry is moving ahead.

At the same time that we encourage the peasants to increase production, we must ask ourselves to concentrate and mobilize the forces of the party and the nation to give positive support to agriculture and to the collective economy of the people's communes in material, technical, financial, and organizational leadership and personnel so that we may thoroughly develop the economic policy advocated by the Central Committee and Comrade Mao Tse-tung. To develop the national economy with agriculture as its foundation, we must help strengthen the collective economy further, expand agricultural production, and create more favorable conditions for the mechanization of agriculture.

As Comrade Mao Tse-tung correctly pointed out in his report on the problem of organizing agricultural production on a cooperative basis:

> Because of the economic conditions of our nation, a longer
> period of time will be required for technical reform than

for social reform. It is estimated that for the nation as a whole the basic completion of technical reform in agriculture will probably require from four to five five-year plans, that is, a period of twenty to twenty-five years. The entire Party must struggle for the realization of this great mission.

This great mission advocated by Comrade Mao Tse-tung is becoming the major order of the day in the nation's economic construction for the entire party and the whole people. Although we have been somewhat slow in assuming this mission, if from this time forward we manage it correctly, in a spirit of practicality (rather than one of subjectivity), with flexibility (rather than inflexible uniformity), with dispatch (rather than protraction), with concentration (rather than diffusion of our strength), and with care (rather than rashness), after another twenty to twenty-five years of effort, we will be sure to succeed in the basic realization of the goal foreseen by the party Central Committee--the modernization of agriculture so long desired by both the peasants and the popular masses of the entire country. With the gradual realization of agricultural modernization, we will stimulate the nation's industry and the entire national economy to achieve an even more rapid expansion and abundance.

II. For this purpose, the Central Committee believes that the unified plan for the national economy must take the expansion of agriculture as its starting point. The order of priority of the economic plan is, first, agriculture, then light industry, and finally heavy industry. That is to say, we must begin our socialist construction with the expansion of agriculture. It is an error to disregard the extremely important position of agriculture in socialist construction. The state must draft long-term plans for the support of agriculture by all sectors of the national economy. The plans set up and the measures adopted by the state planning sectors--economic, industrial (both heavy and light), and handicraft, communications and transportation, commercial, fiscal and financial, and the scientific and cultural--must acknowledge agriculture as their foundation, direct their attention to the villages and put the support of agriculture and the collective economy in first place. The agricultural, heavy industrial, and scientific and technical sectors must draft reliable plans for the progressive realization of technological reforms in agriculture, according to the varying natural and farming conditions of each region of the nation. Each sector, however, when making its plans to support agriculture and adopt the necessary technical measures, must consult with the masses and cooperate in a comradely spirit with technicians, specialists, and concerned scientists. Agricultural techniques should be gradually extended through demonstrations. All Communist Party members bearing leadership and administrative responsibilities must respect the directives of the Central Committee and avoid being dogmatic. They should not be self-opinionated, nor should they trifle with the procedures of executive orders. They must not curry favor with the masses or with their superiors, but work hard in harmony and cooperation, learning how to make precise economic calculations, measuring advantage against disadvantage and differentiating between the primary and secondary, so that all work may have a firm footing, all plans may truly conform to actuality, and all measures may be effectively carried out.

III. What is the present course of our nation's industrial development? Comrade Mao Tse-tung early stated:

Our nation is a great agricultural country, with the population of the villages making up more than eighty per cent of the total population. Agriculture and industry must develop simultaneously so that there will be raw materials and markets for industry, and so that it will be possible to accumulate the large amounts of capital needed to establish a strong heavy industry. As everyone knows, light industry and agriculture are very closely related. Without agriculture, there can be no light industry. In the past it was not clearly understood that agriculture is an important market for heavy industry. However, the progressive modernization of agriculture, the gradual development of technical reform in agriculture, and the resulting growth in the machinery, fertilizer, irrigation, electric-power, transportation, fuel, and construction-material industries that serve agriculture will make it easier for people to understand the place of agriculture as the major market for heavy industry.

In other words, in our country the five hundred million or more people in villages make up the principal market for both light and heavy industry. This is a domestic market vaster than that of any other country in the world. This domestic market has a great potential to absorb an ever growing quantity of goods produced by light and heavy industry. It is here that the key problem in the establishment of our socialist economy lies. Consequently, all industrial sectors must resolve to base their work on agriculture. We must gradually establish a complete industrial system in the service of agricultural production. In addition to the necessity for light industry to utilize the raw materials of agriculture in the production of goods to supply the needs of urban and rural people, heavy industry must conduct painstaking research and experimentation, doing everything in its power to provide for agriculture such means of production as machinery, chemical fertilizers, agricultural chemicals, construction materials, fuels, and power and transportation tools suitable to the time and place. Heavy industry must further strive to provide equipment and raw materials for light industry in order to facilitate the increase of consumer goods.

IV. We must redetermine the ratio of investment for each sector of the national economy in conformity with the planning and economic sectors' policy of designating agriculture as the foundation for industry. The Central Committee believes that investment in agriculture, including investments in industry, transportation, and scientific research which directly serve agriculture, should be systematically raised in proportion to the gross investment for economic construction. Within a given period of time, investment in this sector should occupy a more important position than that in other sectors. The nation's agricultural investment should be appropriately used and not squandered, and money must not be spent arbitrarily. All of our financial and material resources must be used in the proper areas for us to achieve the best economic results.

Under certain conditions, the state can provide the required financial assistance for businesses and enterprises directly serving agriculture.

V. In order to stimulate agricultural production and provide the requirements for industrial expansion, and also to maintain a suitable ratio between the urban and agricultural populations, the agricultural taxes which the state levies and the quantity of food which it purchases must be stabilized at an appropriate level and within a definite period. Aside from the formally established state taxes (including regular taxes and surtaxes), no government agencies are authorized to add further taxes or to make assessments independently. When the state's requirements exceed the purchase and levy quotas, purchase should be made through

83

the commercial sector and principally through the supply and sales cooperatives, with agreement on price arranged by discussions with units of the collective economy. The state farms should strive to increase the productivity of labor, reduce costs, and increase the volume of production in order to facilitate the provision of more food and economic crops for the nation.

VI. Learning how to conduct and manage socialist business in order to stimulate the expansion of socialist industrial production remains one of our major tasks. We must improve our present business system, eliminate internal trade barriers, and organize a unified socialist domestic market. In addition to the effective operation of state trading enterprises, we must expand and strengthen cooperative business. Under the leadership of state trading enterprises and with the positive participation of cooperative business, we can correctly promote the function of the free markets. In the commercial sphere we must deal correctly with the relationships between industry and agriculture and between urban and rural districts. We should obtain agricultural products by economic rather than by administrative means, that is, through purchase by discussion and agreement, in order to expand the exchange of products between urban and rural areas. In this, the problem of price is especially important. In order to bring about the socialist industrialization of the nation, to transform it from an agricultural into a modern, industrial nation, and to enable socialist agriculture gradually to arm itself with modern techniques, the working classes must establish a deep and comradely friendship with the peasants and work in mutual assistance and understanding. At the same time, the real interest of the peasants should be given due consideration when considering price problems, and suitable prices should gradually be established for industrial and agricultural products on the principle of equal exchange for value. Moreover, appropriate differentials in price, owing to differences in region, quality, variety, and season, should be conscientiously put into effect. The nation must, to the greatest extent possible, provide ever-increasing amounts of the means of production and livelihood required by the peasants in exchange for agricultural products. The more agricultural products a region sells to the state, the more industrial products it should receive. Correct policies for price and for the exchange of industrial products are extremely important for the gradual strengthening of the alliance between industry and agriculture, the more rapid stimulation of socialist industrial production, the expansion of socialist agricultural production, and the strengthening of the collective economy of the people's communes. This is not only an economic problem, but also a problem of great political significance. The Central Committee requests that each sector concerned continually and earnestly study this problem and draft suitable measures based on Party policy.

VII. The Central Committee's "Draft Regulations Governing People's Communes in Rural Areas" and its directive on taking the production team as the basic accounting unit have stimulated the positive spirit of the peasants and have created new conditions for the strengthening of the collective economy and for the expansion of agricultural production. The above policies concerning the support of agriculture, the direction of industrial development, the increase of agricultural investment, purchase and levy, and prices all have as their purpose the further stimulation of a positive spirit of production among the collective body of the peasants and the further strengthening of the collective economy of the people's communes. These policies, which are concerned with the relationship between the state and the collective economy of the people's communes, are those which the party wishes to put into lasting effect.

The Central Committee has now, on the basis of more than a year's experience, made a revision of the "Draft Regulations Governing People's Communes in Rural Areas." On the basis of these revised regulations, the people's communes should continue to implement the socialist principle of "from each according to his ability, to each according to his work" and at the same time carry out the resolution to take the production team as the basic accounting unit. With the exception of a minority of regions in which the brigade continues to be the basic accounting unit, the production teams should undertake independent accounting, bear the responsibility for profit and loss, directly organize production, and organize the distribution of their output. According to the Draft Regulations, once the basic accounting system has been determined, there should be no change for at least thirty years. The organization and scale of various levels of the people's communes, and the major provisions laid down in the Draft Regulations, having been determined after mass discussion, should not be changed for long periods either. The policies concerned with the collective economic system of the people's communes are intended by the party to remain in force for a long time throughout the entire socialist society.

The Draft Regulations permit and encourage commune members to operate subsidiary domestic enterprises to supplement the collective economy. This is for the purpose of strengthening the collective economy and expanding agricultural production and is, as well, a policy that the party wishes to put into effect on a long-term basis. The commune members should have suitable private plots of land. At the same time, in regions with certain requirements and conditions the production teams may, on the basis of land conditions and with the approval of the commune through member discussion, set aside an appropriate amount of land for the commune members to plant in feed so that they may raise hogs and thereby provide fertilizer for the collective economy. Idle land and fragments of uncultivated land should be planted in feed to the greatest possible extent consistent with the conservation of water, forests, and grassland.

In these matters, the Central Committee reminds the comrades in each region to give attention to the following. As industry and other sectors strengthen their support of agriculture, the People's Communes must attend to the development of their own latent capacity. Of special importance is the protection and maintenance of animals and the making of all possible effort to increase the supply of organic fertilizer. Animal power must not be neglected, and the collection of organic fertilizer should not be slackened in anticipation of the mechanization of agriculture and the application of chemical fertilizers. Even when in the future we have chemical fertilizers and a largely mechanized agriculture, we still will not be able to do without animal power and organic fertilizer.

VIII. In their economic activities, the various organizational levels of the people's communes, and especially the production teams, must maintain the principles of voluntary action, instruction by example, mutual assistance, and mutual benefit. Operation and management must be perfected. We must conscientiously scrutinize the various experiences that have taken place since the "cooperativization" of agriculture and choose from among them those that can be accepted by the masses and can be easily put into effect to improve operation and management. We must establish a strict system of production responsibility in order to raise the collective spirit of the commune members to one of enthusiasm and to improve the quality of cultivation.

The various organizational levels of the people's communes, and especially the production teams, must practice democracy in their operations. Cadres at each level of the people's communes must learn how to follow the mass line. All cultivation, management, and distribution problems should first be thoroughly considered and discussed among the masses. It is especially important to seek advice from the older, experienced farmers. Cadre members should not act autocratically, either individually or in minority groups.

The various organizational levels of the people's communes, and especially the production teams, must manage their affairs frugally and conduct their finances openly. The state of affairs with regard to work-points, food and other materials, and funds must be made known periodically to the commune members and must be discussed among the masses. All working cadres must be sincerely and earnestly in the active service of the people, considering themselves as ordinary workers. They must not vie for special privilege, greedily seek their own self-interest, or take more than their share of food. The agencies of the county concerned with these matters should regularly assist, guide, and inspect all stages of commune accounting and financial work.

All organizational levels of the people's communes must vigorously effect simplification, decreasing as much as possible the number of cadres not involved in production and the number of work-points awarded to them. The number of such work-points must be determined through discussion and agreement among the masses.

In the villages, the party should strengthen its leadership at all organizational levels of the people's communes, and particularly at the level of the production teams. Party committee members and Party branches in the people's communes must learn how to handle business affairs effectively, as well as understand how to handle political and ideological work. Training in socialism, patriotism, and collectivism must regularly be carried out among the peasants and at all cadre levels. They must be educated so that they may better carry out the party's policies and the nation's laws with self-awareness and respect public property. We must raise the proletarian class-consciousness of party and Youth Corps members so that they may serve even further as models in the collective economic organization.

IX. Food is the basis of a diversified agricultural economy. The collective economy must conscientiously pursue a policy of equal support for both food and economic crops. At the same time that precedence is given to expanding food production, we must determine suitable production levels for all types of economic crops and strive to expand production of cotton, oil-bearing plants, vegetables, tobacco, hemp, sugar beets, silk, tea, fruits, medicinal plants, and other economic crops. The collective economy must give an important place to the livestock industry. The collective economy must strive to develop forestry, fishery, and all types of subsidiary production. All levels of the agricultural sector and all levels of the people's communes must organize a diversified agriculture on the basis of the traditional customs and according to the differing conditions of each region in order to facilitate the suitable use of the land, its resources, and the labor force, and also in order to increase production to meet the varied needs of urban and rural production, increase the incomes of the commune members, and strengthen the collective economy.

All levels of the agricultural sector must gradually extend, based on the willingness of the masses, the adoption of advanced knowledge and technical measures in production through repeated experimentation and demonstration. Experimentation and research in agriculture should be strengthened. Seeds of superior quality should be propagated and put into widespread use, and the production teams should be guided in selecting them. Agricultural chemicals of superior quality should be produced in order to control pests. The work of seed stations, technical extension stations, and veterinary stations should be improved and strengthened and their standards should be raised. Tractors and mechanical and electrical irrigation stations must be well managed in order to bring agricultural technical equipment to its full effectiveness.

We must, on the basis of the beneficial experiences and customs of a given region, put into effect a crop-rotation system in order to preserve the land and thereby increase production.

X. In order to strengthen the leadership in agricultural work, the collective economy of the people's communes, and the basic-level party work in villages, the Central Committee and the party committees of provinces, cities, and autonomous regions must select cadres who are loyal to the affairs of the people and who have a capacity for work, and who understand working along the mass line, to go out to districts, counties, and villages and participate in work for long periods of time. The Central Committee asks of these comrades that they truly become pupils of the masses, that they work together with their comrades who are native to a region, and that they come to a complete understanding of village conditions, effectively manage the collective economy, and accumulate agricultural knowledge. At all organizational levels of the communes, the cadres must be given training and assistance in raising their political level and their competence as workers. The Central Committee wishes all those comrades working in villages to understand that the work for which they bear responsibility is of the greatest importance to our nation and that they must conscientiously study the policies of the Central Committee concerning village work in order that this glorious mission which the party has given them may bear fruit.

XI. The progressive advancement of technical reform in agriculture, bringing about a gradual modernization in the techniques of collective agriculture, bears heavily upon the fate of our nation. This work must be completed through reliance on the affirmative spirit and the collective wisdom of the masses and, at the same time, through reliance on the centralized leadership of the Central Committee. As we all know, both the Party's statutes and the national constitution quite clearly prescribe a system of democratic centralism. Not long ago, in January 1962 at the Expanded Work Conference of the Central Committee, the leader of our party, Comrade Mao Tse-tung, and the Central Committee expressly requested all party comrades conscientiously to implement the system of democratic centralism in order to establish socialism. Comrade Mao Tse-tung said:

> If in our nation we do not fully extend the people's
> democracy and party democracy and do not fully effect a
> democratic system of the proletariat, then we cannot have
> a true system of proletarian centralism. Without a high
> level of democracy we cannot have a high level of centralism,
> and without the latter we cannot establish a socialist economy.

If we unceasingly strengthen the collective economy of the people's communes and fully exalt the superiority of the socialist collective agricultural economy, we will have observed this important directive of Comrade Mao Tse-tung. All levels of party committees and of the cadres of the people's communes should be attentive to the opinions of the masses, utilize the experiences of the masses, and, on this basis, establish a correct leadership.

XII. The party Central Committee has consistently maintained the principle of unifying the supreme authority in the Central Committee and of delegating lesser authority suitably. On this principle we are implementing a system of unified leadership and delegated management. The Central Committee realized that the development of local enthusiasm and of a flexible spirit of action best suited to a given region is especially important in agricultural work. Neglect of the principle of action suited to the needs of the region and the application of unvarying measures to all regions will harm agricultural production and cannot be allowed. However, the policies of overall agricultural development, the technical reform of agriculture, and all phases of the state's assistance to agriculture must be under a uniform Central Committee policy and under uniform national planning. This policy will require that all sectors of the national economy work together closely under the unified leadership of the Central Committee and not engage in independent action. In all economic work, the disruptive tendency to resist the unified policies and plans of the Central Committee is harmful to the development of a socialist collective agricultural economy.

The foregoing twelve clauses represent the basic decisions of the party Central Committee on the strengthening of the collective economy of the people's communes and on the development of agricultural production. If these decisions are to be carried out accordingly, all sectors and districts will be required to review their experiences conscientiously and to issue even more specific regulations concerning policy.

All party comrades and all peasants of the nation! You must understand that the causes of the Party leaders can only be those of the people and that our work is only to serve the people and to establish our land as a glorious and prosperous socialist country. For these objectives our party, under the leadership of Comrade Mao Tse-tung, has carried on a long revolutionary struggle in the villages, enjoying successes and suffering hardships together with the masses of the peasants. After our victory in the People's Liberation War, the party led the peasants in overthrowing the feudal landlords, taking them gradually along the road to collectivization. The peasant masses have actively supported the collectivization of agriculture because it provides the greatest possibility both for the development of agriculture and for their common prosperity. To the questions as to whether individual enterprise or the collective economy is stronger, whether it is individual enterprise or the collective economy that can banish the poverty of the peasants, and whether it is individual enterprise or the collective economy that is best adapted to socialist industrialization, the true answers are provided by the fact that our nation's agriculture in the course of its collectivization has each year increased production to levels never before attained in history and has given immense support to the development of our nation's socialist industrialization. The decrease in agricultural production in the past few years has resulted from a series of severe natural disasters and from deficiencies and errors in our work. Peasant comrades! You know that our party, under the leadership of Comrade Mao Tse-tung and the Central Committee, has severely criticized and firmly corrected these deficiencies and errors; moreover, it has struggled together with the peasants against natural calamity. Since last year, village conditions have taken a sharp turn for the better. Moreover, there will be continual and even greater improvement. Agricultural production and the livelihood of the peasants have improved from year to year. The new atmosphere that is beginning to appear in agricultural production and in the entire national economy can already be felt. A new level in the high tide of agricultural production is about to be reached.

The correct policies of the party Central Committee on village work, on industrial adjustment, and on other aspects of the economy have strengthened the alliance between the party and the peasant masses, as well as that between the

Party and the entire people, producing as a consequence a great force that has strengthened the position of socialism in our country. Because of the direction of the Central Committee's correct policies, the collective economy of the villages is moving under new conditions toward a new strength. Although difficulties still face us, difficulties which cannot lightly be dismissed, for us to overcome the difficulties in the path of advancement quickly it is, nevertheless, necessary only for everyone to work hard and carry out the policies of the Central Committee conscientiously. In the past, our activities have gone forward through the overcoming of difficulties. It is very clear that these decisions which our party's Central Committee has now issued are completely in accord not only with the present best interests of the peasants but also with their long-term best interests. Let all the party comrades, peasants, workers, intellectuals, patriots, and nationalities of the nation unite and, under the leadership of Chairman Mao and the Central Committee, raise high the three red banners of the party's general line of socialist construction, the Great Leap Forward, and the people's communes and, following the party's line of socialist construction, struggle to fulfill completely these historically significant decisions.

(For distribution to the communes)

V

IMPLEMENTATION OF THE RESOLUTIONS OF THE TENTH PLENUM OF THE EIGHTH CENTRAL COMMITTEE ON STRENGTHENING THE COLLECTIVE ECONOMY AND EXPANDING AGRICULTURAL PRODUCTION, BY WANG HUNG-CHIH

(Conference documents should be kept secret)

COMRADES:

The major issue of this meeting is the implementation of the spirit of the Provincial Committee's Expanded Conference and the propagation and implementation of the spirit of the Tenth Plenum of the Eighth Central Committee.

The content of the Tenth Plenum has already been given in the communiqué. Of greatest importance was the passing of resolutions on the problems of further strengthening the collective economy and of expanding agricultural production. In addition there were decisions on trade problems, on the problems of the planned exchange of principal leadership cadres at all party and governmental levels, and on the problem of strengthening supervisory committee members at all levels of the party. At the Tenth Plenum it was pointed out that the most urgent task in the strengthening of the collective economy of the people's communes is that of carrying out Comrade Mao Tse-tung's policy of designating agriculture as the foundation and industry as the leading factor for the expansion of the national economy, putting the expansion of agriculture first, correctly handling the relationship between industry and agriculture, and resolutely basing the industrial sector on agriculture.

Since October our country has begun the initial implementation of the essence of the Tenth Plenum. Within the county we held meetings of cadres above the team level and through them have launched propaganda education for the masses in which, for the most part, we have used the methods of recollection, contrast, airing complaints, and reckoning of accounts as [means of] criticism of the error of the Spirit of Individual Enterprise. The purpose was to bring those who pursue it to the understanding that there is a struggle between the two roads of socialism and capitalism and that this is, therefore, a class struggle, and to make them aware that only through reliance on the collective economy can agricultural production be increased. The spread and growth of the spirit of individual enterprise was effectively halted. All Household Contract Production land in the county, with the exception of that used for sweet potatoes not yet harvested, has reverted to the collective. The majority of those who drifted to the cities have returned to the villages, and the peddlers and speculators have sharply decreased in numbers. All these events have had a great effect in promoting the autumn harvest and the winter planting. But this is only a beginning. It must be pointed out that the previous stage of propaganda education was not sufficiently penetrating, and that many people do not have a clear understanding of the harmfulness of the Spirit of Individual

Enterprise. Superficially, it appears that individual contracting has been stopped, but we have not yet solved the fundamental ideological problem. The general attitude is one of waiting to see what happens. In a minority of teams, individual enterprise recurred while reform was under way. It was discovered during the winter planting that individual teams were engaging in Household Contract Production. For this reason, the task of this meeting is to resolve ideological problems conscientiously and to establish belief in the strengthening of the collective economy in order to expand agricultural production further.

I now pass on the following report based on the spirit of the Provincial Committee's Expanded Conference. I have prepared my report in two sections. Today I will discuss the three problems of conditions, class, and contradictions. The next time I will discuss how we can further strengthen the collective economy and expand agricultural production.

I. THE PROBLEM OF CONDITIONS

A thorough analysis of domestic and foreign conditions has already been made in the communiqué. Here our chief concern is a discussion of conditions in our county.

Although we, like the entire nation, have continually suffered the most severe natural disasters during the past three years, the general condition of the people's economy has improved over the past two years. After the autumn harvest, conditions throughout the county were even further improved, and the future is exceedingly bright. Speaking concretely, the present excellent conditions are principally manifested as follows.

First, there has been a recovery and an expansion in all phases of production, in agriculture, fishing, forestry, animal husbandry, and subsidiary enterprises. As preliminary estimates show, this year's total food production may reach 130 million catties, which is 86.7 per cent of the yearly average of 150 million catties. Of this, the collective accounts for 111 million catties. The area occupied by the collectives has decreased by more than 20,000 mou since last year, principally because of an increase in private plots and vegetable farming; however production in the collectives has increased over last year's 109 million catties. The increase in unit area production has been even more marked. The average yield of double-crop rice fields was 695 catties per mou, an increase of 14.7 per cent over last year. Nine teams produced 1,000 catties per mou, and nine brigades and eighty-eight teams produced more than 900 catties per mou. Viewed from the standpoint of volume of production, the total collective production of four brigades reached the 1957 level, the total collective production of sixty-five brigades reached the 1957 level, and the collective unit area production of fifty-six brigades also reached the 1957 level. Production in the fishing industry was even better. Up to the end of November, the total production volume of the county's fishing industry was 717,000 tan (of this, 113,000 tan was seaweed), exceeding last year's total annual production (700,000 tan) by 2.4 per cent and representing an increase of 13.4 per cent over last year's production for the same period (632,000 tan). The gross income of the county's fishing industry may reach 30.08 million yüan. In this industry there were eleven brigades with incomes of more than one million yüan. A great recovery in the animal husbandry industry has also taken place. There are now 15,600 pigs, an increase of 44.5 per cent over the number at the end of last year (10,790 head). Some teams had an even greater increase. In the Hua-wu team at Ao-chiang, the number of pigs reached 254, an increase of 2.9 times the number at the end of last year (64 head). Of these, the number of sows more than doubled. After policy implementation, the decrease in plow oxen ended, and in the entire county there are now 12,338 head, a 3 per cent increase over last year. There has also been a large expansion in poultry (chickens, ducks, and geese) and in rabbits, whose number may reach 400,000 and make an increase of 33 per cent over last year's 300,000.

Second, there has been an increase in the standard of living of the masses. The level of their food rations was better this year than last. According to statistics, the average basic ration last year (except that for the nonagricultural population) was 23 catties per person per month. Although the amount of state levies and purchases has increased over last year, the net ration from the collective, together with that from private plots, may reach 29 catties, an increase of 26 per cent. If supplements from the private plots are added, there will be quite a number of production teams that will have enough food. The masses say: "Life is better from year to year. The year before last we ate the 'three heads' (of betel nuts, bananas, and the sago palm); last year was the melon and vegetable era; and this year we eat as we please." In addition, income in money has increased. On the basis of statistics from seventy-one brigades, this year's collective total income is 8.78 million yüan, an increase of 3.7 per cent over last year. The total income of the fishing regions shows an increase of 3.68 million yüan over that for the same period last year. Because of these increases in production and income last year, the people are in better health. There is no more dropsy. The improvement in the life of the masses can be seen, further, in the fact that the villages have the "three many's"--many houses being built, many marriages taking place, and many children being born. In the entire county, this year there were 4,576 households (6.5 per cent of the total number) either building new homes or making repairs on their old ones totaling 8,747 rooms [built or repaired]. There were more marriages, and even more children were born. Many mountain districts that had no increase in population for many years have had a great increase this year. According to statistics up to the end of October for the entire county, 10,480 children were born, comprising 3.45 per cent of the total population.

Third, there has been brisk activity in the market. Commodities in the community increased, and industrial goods and supplementary foodstuff supplied by the state increased 26.7 per cent over last year (amounting in value this year from January through October to 1,032 million yüan and last year for the same period to 839 million yüan). For some major goods there was an even greater increase over last year. Alcoholic beverages increased 60 per cent over the same period last year (20,419 tan as against 12,797 tan). Production of cotton cloth (including the portions to be sold) increased 37.1 per cent over the same period last year (590,000 meters as against 430,000 meters). The supply of implements for the farming and fishing industries increased 12.35 per cent over last year (to a value of 692 million yüan as against 614 million yüan). Not only did the quantity of the tools used in agricultural and fishing production increase; they also improved in quality and decreased in price. As to the supply of industrial goods, this year there are twenty-five kinds of goods for which purchase permits are no longer required--such as wash basins and thermos bottles.

This year the agricultural market has been extremely active. In the distribution centers, sundries, mountain products, fruits, food products, and marine products could be bought as desired. According to statistics for October, agricultural trade reached 320,000 yüan. The opening of the agricultural market has, in effect, fulfilled the functions of a state trading enterprise; that is to say, the exchange of materials has been guaranteed, and the market has also been stabilized gradually.

Fourth, the social order has become more stable. Petty thieves are noticeably absent. This is reflected in the popular saying: "Last year we had to compete with thieves in gathering the sweet potatoes. This year we can leave them in the open, and no one will steal them." Furthermore, there has been a sharp decrease over last year in fighting and disorder among the masses.

In addition, conditions in our county on the battle lines of industry, finance, education, and sanitation are excellent. These facts indicate that conditions are improving from day to day, whether in the villages or in the cities.

What caused these favorable conditions? We believe that there are three major factors. First, party leadership has been correct, as have the Three Red Banners. For three years, continual natural disasters have brought us severe difficulties. However, because the people of the nation united closely around the Central Committee and Chairman Mao, because the masses firmly upheld the Three Red Banners of the General Line, the Great Leap Forward, and the People's Communes and came to grips with adversity in a constructive way, and, because they worked for the establishment of the nation and for the growth of its strength, in little more than a year there has been a change in conditions. Furthermore, all the accomplishments since the Great Leap Forward have gradually made themselves felt.

Second, the thorough implementation of a series of party policies has stimulated the enthusiasm of the masses. The implementation of the Twelve Articles, the rectification of the communistic spirit at the end of 1960, and the implementation last year of the Sixty Draft Regulations gave the commune members private plots and gave individuals permission to reclaim barren land on a limited basis. This year, provisions for lowering the administrative level of the basic accounting units (hsia-fang) and for allowing brigade-contract production were put into effect. In addition, we have implemented the Eight Character policy and also the Seventy Articles for industry and Forty Articles for business [not identifiable from available sources] which have as their central concern the adjustment of the national economy, including the opening of the agricultural markets. These policies have stimulated an active spirit of production among the commune members. This year, after the implementation of brigade-contract production, there was a general increase in the number of days worked and in the effectiveness of the commune members' labor, so that preparations for this year's spring plowing, such as collecting fertilizer, digging out pond mud, and burning over fields, were of a kind rarely seen before in history. The earth dug out by the Ch'ing-t'ang team came to 79 per cent of its total land area, and in Tan-yang and Liao-yen the burning over of fields reached the greatest height in several years. These are the major causes of this year's increase in production.

Third, the strong support given to agriculture by the state, the support of agriculture by industry, and the support of the villages by the cities were further causes of improvement. The party policy of taking agriculture as the foundation, together with the two times that the number of workers and crowded urban populations have been reduced, strengthened the first line of agriculture. This year, loans for agriculture and fishing for the entire county are 1.70 million yüan (of this amount, the portion for agriculture is 730,000 yüan), and the investment in basic construction and water conservation was 600,000 yüan, making a total of 2.3 million yüan. The supply of chemical fertilizer was 33,000 tan, an increase of 30 per cent over last year, allowing 16.5 catties of chemical fertilizer to be spread on each mou of cultivated land. The supply of lime, marine fertilizer, granulated fertilizer, and ammonia water was more than 100,000 tan, and of sheep manure was 17,000 tan. The supply of farm tools reached 450,000 pieces (an increase of 130 per cent over last year's 195,000 pieces). The supply of all types of fishing implements was 3.38 million yüan (an increase of 62.3 per cent over last year). We believe that these three points are the basic reasons for the improvement in conditions this year.

Two different points of view exist concerning the reason for these improved conditions. The majority of the people believe that the improvement is due to party leadership, the strength of policies, and state support. Some, however, are confused in their ideology and say that these favorable conditions have resulted from the "small freedoms"; others say that these conditions result from the use of private plots, reclaimed land, and free markets. These problems of ideology are also problems of viewpoint concerning party leadership and must be clarified. We know that the small freedoms are also a policy determined by the party to supplement the collectives. Speaking for the entire county, the volume of production of the county collectives may reach 111 million catties, whereas that of the private plots, reclaimed land, and household contract production for one crop came to no more than 20 million catties. Without the collective economy, could we have attained good conditions by relying solely on these 20 million catties? (There are some regions where the small freedoms ratio is too great. As a result, this ratio has influenced the collective economy and is an error.) Again, seen from the standpoint of this year's collective production, in certain critical seasons we took measures to assure an increase in agricultural production. If it were not for the implementation of the Sixty Draft Regulations and the Brigade Contract Production policy, could this year's preparations for plowing have been handled so quickly and so well? After the disaster this summer, had it not been for the plentiful supply of state fertilizer and funds, where would the rich autumn harvest have come from? Could the rich harvest in fishery production have been obtained without the state's supplying the means of production, which accounted for more than 75 per cent of the total requirement? We can say with assurance that this would not have been possible. Therefore, the view that these favorable conditions have been brought on by the small freedoms is one-sided and incorrect. One can only say that the collectives are good, and that small freedoms are also good and that they supplemented the collective economy.

Naturally, under these generally favorable conditions, some temporary difficulties still exist. Compared with the last two years, the extent of these difficulties have greatly decreased. The difficulties are of a twofold nature, the first being those brought about by the continual and severe natural disasters, which are now being overcome. Secondly, in a country as large as China, where "for each poor person, there are two who are naked," and which lacks experience in building socialism, how can goals be attained without going through difficulties? Therefore, it is only natural, and not to be feared, that some difficulties exist.

Our major difficulty at present is that food production has not yet completely regained the highest post-liberation level. Our best food year was 1959, when the total volume of production of the county was 160 million catties. We have not reached this level this year, nor have we reached the "One Five"[1] average level. For these reasons, there are still some among the masses for whom food rations are somewhat restricted. In many kinds of economic crops, the recovery will require great effort. Agriculture has not been able to provide a sufficient supply of commodities--food and raw materials for industry--and the amount of cotton clothing will still be somewhat restricted. In addition, the current spirit of individual enterprise is still widespread and intense, and in the villages a tendency toward low production still exists. Because of the influence of the spirit of

---

[1]This refers to the figure of 150 million.

individual enterprise, market management is also in disorder, and varying degrees of ideological confusion exist among some of the masses and cadres. However, these are all temporary phenomena, and it is only necessary for us to carry out the spirit of the Eighth Session of the Tenth Plenum conscientiously, unifying our thought and our awareness and continually laboring and striving to strengthen the collective economy, for these difficulties to be overcome quickly and for our future course to be endlessly glorious.

How should we deal with these difficulties? We should have a correct attitude. That is to say, we as a party should unite our hearts and our strength to overcome difficulty. As for party members, national difficulties are everyone's responsibilities, and one must never adopt attitudes of watching from the sidelines or taking pleasure in the misfortunes of others. In the face of temporary difficulties, moreover, party leadership and the Three Red Banners must not falter. Without the correct leadership of the party, these temporary difficulties could not have been fundamentally reversed in little more than a year. Nor could we have accomplished so much under conditions of continual and severe natural disaster without the correctness of the Three Red Banners. Since the Great Leap Forward, throughout the county new industry has begun to develop. The accomplishments in basic agricultural construction are even more marked. Construction for water conservation took place in 222 places in the county, increasing the area under irrigation and flood control by more than 110,000 mou--more than twice as much as under the first five-year plan. More than 40,000 mou of land was reclaimed. There were 11 more tractors. In addition, the fishing industry now operates 77 motorized fishing boats. More than 83 kilometers of roads have been built, and 720,000 mou have been afforested. In the future, these accomplishments will have an even greater effect in expanding production. A still more important point is that through the Great Leap Forward we gained direct experience in building socialism, a gain which cannot be expressed in figures. Therefore, we say that the policy of the Three Red Banners is correct, that we have made fundamental accomplishments in our work since the Great Leap Forward, and that errors and deficiencies have been secondary. These so-called errors and deficiencies were of two kinds, errors in command, and excessive levy and purchase. The former was corrected last year, and the latter has been corrected this year. In the past, some people have expressed their opinions about errors and deficiencies in actual work. One may express opinions, but it must be clearly understood that an expression of opinion has solidarity as its purpose, not simply the expression of grievances and insults. Especially now that the party has led the way in correcting errors and deficiencies, we must unite our hearts and our strength with the party. We cannot have further differences of opinion, nor can we disavow party leadership or the policy of the Three Red Banners merely because temporary difficulties still exist. To disavow them is to commit an error.

Attitudes toward difficulty are also problems of class feeling. Different attitudes also reflect different kinds of class consciousness. Thus, this is also class struggle. In short, there are three attitudes. The first is that of resoluteness, in which there is no vacillation even in the face of hardship, and in which the Three Red Banners are firmly upheld. The second is that of vacillation, in which there is a desire to turn from the road of socialism to that of capitalism, to turn from the collective economy to capitalism, and to promote individual enterprise. The third is that of hostility. All reactionaries and the unreformed Four Class elements like this. They make use of difficulties in order to carry on destructive acts, to attack us, and to plan their own restoration. Therefore, the first is the correct attitude; it is the attitude which every Communist Party member and revolutionary cadre should have.

Class is a basic problem. Our analyses of conditions and contradictions and our discussions of work must all contain class analysis. Therefore, the Eighth Session of the Tenth Central Committee Plenum gave an affirmative answer to the question whether classes and class struggle now exist. Classes still exist. This is because (1) the capitalist class is still receiving fixed-interest incomes, (2) the exploitative class-consciousness still exists, although landlords and rich peasants were eliminated from the economy, and (3) the petty bourgeoisie is extremely widespread. Among these, in part of the prosperous strata, a spontaneous tendency toward capitalism exists. In addition, the old customs are still powerful. All these contribute to class struggle. Therefore, the communiqué of the Eighth Session of the Tenth Central Committee Plenum stated that "During the entire historical period of transition from capitalism to communism, a period that will require several decades or even longer, the class struggle between the proletariat and the capitalist class and the Two Road struggle between socialism and capitalism will continue to exist." This is to say, class struggle exists and will continue to exist for several decades, if not longer.

We are raising this question because some people do not hold this view, and they say that there is no longer a class struggle. This is the viewpoint of international revisionism. This kind of confused thought exists even among cadres who bury themselves in production and who do not have a keen sense of class struggle. The system for the control of the Four Classes has become a mere formality. The cadres have not conscientiously dealt with the counterattack, the reactionary plotting of landlords and rich farmers, and the destructive activity of counterrevolutionary elements as problems of class struggle. Moreover, they were deficient in class analysis in their investigation and research and in their reflection of conditions. In everything it has been "the demands of the masses." Therefore, the Eighth Session raised this problem, which is of deep educational significance to the entire party.

Seen from the situation in our county, is it true that a class struggle no longer exists? It is only necessary for everyone to recall the situation during the last few years for the answer to be very clear. After the high tide of cooperativization in 1956, the socialist revolution scored a decisive victory on the economic battle-front. But the class struggle still existed on the battle line of ideology, and during the following spring there occurred the attack by the right-wing elements, to which the affluent middle peasants in the villages immediately responded in a slashing condemnation of cooperativization and controlled purchase and sale. A turmoil arose over food, there was a clamor to withdraw from the communes, and members of the cadres were reviled and beaten. If the plots of the right-wing elements had succeeded, we would have left the stage, the bourgeoisie would have taken it, and the landlords and rich peasants would have been restored to the same position of domination they held before liberation. Is this not an acute class struggle? In the last three years, because of continual natural disasters and errors and deficiencies in our work, all sectors have encountered certain temporary difficulties. Beginning last autumn, class enemies have greatly increased, and up to the spring of this year some landlords and rich peasants would not participate in collective labor and openly took away collective farm tools and plow oxen. They raised a commotion over Household Contract Production. When the war-preparation period came, they completely revealed themselves as class enemies. The slightest rumor made them think that the world had changed. Since this year, Hsü I-sung, a landlord of Ts'ai-ch'i in Ao-chiang, has not participated in collective labor, and during the War Preparation period he twice held family meetings, saying, "First we want to settle accounts with the cadre, and second we want the return of our land and eighteen houses." Hsü's son, taking advantage of the fear psychology of the masses during the War Preparation period, came out to tell people's fortunes, saying that the cadre was on the way out and that fate had condemned the poor farmers to a life of hard work. For the bad elements and the false Pao-chia chiefs he predicted, "First hardship, later pleasure." He thus made everyone afraid. In the Shan-t'ang brigade there is a bad element by the name of Cheng Huo-ch'üan who in the past never spoke a great deal, but during the War Preparation period read the newspapers every day, talked about the situation, and acted in and watched plays. He purposely went to the city gates to buy tobacco and tea, and invited bad elements to eat and drink together. To everyone he said, "My day has come." This kind of incident became very frequent at that time, and in the June statistics, thirty to forty per cent of the Four Classes arrogantly disobeyed the cadre. This is also an acute class struggle. Comrades, in the mere six years from the time agriculture was organized in cooperatives until the present, we have twice encountered difficulties, and class enemies have twice challenged us. On the road ahead, we will of necessity encounter some difficulties. Who can guarantee that class enemies will not again raise a challenge? Therefore, we say that the class struggle will be of long duration, complex, repetitive, and alternately resurgent and recessive. When our work is proceeding favorably, the class struggle will lay low, but whenever we encounter difficulties, it will suddenly appear again. This will continue during the entire period of transition from socialism to communism, which will require several decades or more.

The class struggle is therefore of long duration, complex, repetitive, alternately resurgent and recessive, and sometimes acute. The reasons are as follows.

First, there is the power of old customs. The peasants have gone through several thousand years of feudal control and more than a hundred years of semifeudal-semicolonial control. Feudal, semifeudal, and semicolonial thought is deep-rooted and cannot be corrected overnight. Although they have received ten years of education in socialist ideology since the liberation, the peasants fall back on the old customs when the opportunity occurs, thereby producing class struggle on the battle fronts of politics and ideology. For example, since the liberation by consistently opposing superstition and marriage by sale, we were able to correct these old patterns of thought to some extent. Last year, however, when we encountered difficulties, marriage by sale began to reappear, and the masses once again began to engage in activities inspired by superstition, such as worshiping Bodhisattvas, divination, and fortunetelling. The commotion over individual enterprise is also of this kind. The peasants had followed a course of individual enterprise for several thousand years. Although after the liberation they were gradually collectivized, the influence of the spirit of individual enterprise is still deeply rooted among some of the rich peasants and arises when opportunity permits. In 1957 there was agitation in the villages for withdrawal from, and further subdivision of, the cooperatives. This year the prevalence of the spirit of individual enterprise is even more evident. In the past, when we were proceeding with cooperativization, we learned that the small peasant economy was at a crossroad and was vacillating on the course of socialism. There was no Communist Party leadership and the farm economy could have gone the way of capitalism. As we have already demonstrated countless times in practice, this year, when the free markets were opened, and [state] control could not keep pace, speculation immediately appeared and there were people who abandoned farming for commerce. This indicates that the reform of old customs is not easy.

The force of old customs not only exerts itself among the masses, but also within the party as well. We repeatedly carry on class education among party members, but it cannot be said that there are none within the party who hold to the ideology of the bourgeoisie. Now, as the nation is passing through a state of temporary difficulty, the great majority of party members is good; nevertheless there is a minority among whom old ideas predominate. Take the problem of superstition, for instance, Communist Party members are fundamentally atheists. Yet a minority of members are inclined toward superstition. The party has consistently taught party members that they must be honest in public business and work for the common good and not for their own selfish interests. Yet, as soon as we encounter difficulty, a number of party members among whom there is a deep bourgeois influence become greedy, misappropriate funds, and engage in illegal and disorderly conduct such as excessive consumption, decadence, and corruption. This indicates that the Two Road struggle also exists within the party.

Second, the overthrown classes do not willingly die out, and they come to life when opportunity permits. We are located on the coast and daily wage battle with the enemy. This is a violent class struggle--the highest form of class struggle. Furthermore, although the landlords and rich peasants in the economy have been overthrown, these people are still present. And, although counterrevolutionary elements in politics have been deposed, they have not yet been reformed. On the international scene, imperialism still exists, and yet-to-be-liberated Matsu and Taiwan are still under the sway of Chiang Kai-shek and his bandits. These imperialistic and reactionary groups are always conspiring from afar with the class enemies and would utilize every opportunity to stage a comeback. This was seen most clearly this year during war-preparation period. To understand this, it is only necessary for everyone to recall the various attitudes existing at the time. The positive elements among the masses of poor peasants, the lower-middle peasants, the land reformers, the counter-revolutionists, and the old revolutionaries have the best attitude. Many ask for assignments of duty and express a determination to annihilate possible invaders. The upper-middle peasants, however, are irresolute and most of them are apathetic. Some say, "Red and white are all alike, so it doesn't matter who comes." There are some party cadres of upper-middle peasant background who also exhibit an attitude of vacillation and compromise (to the extent that some cadres went to fortunetellers, and some asked counterrevolutionary elements, "What should I do?") Among the Four Class elements, an overwhelming majority cherish great hopes for the "counterattack." They became arrogant in their attitude. Some spread rumors and engage in destructive conduct, and others secretly applaud; things have reached the point where cadres have been beaten in public. These incidents show that the class enemy cannot be reconciled to its death.

Third, in addition to classes, there are class strata. Lenin said, "Small producers are at each instant giving rise to capitalism and the bourgeoisie." Our China is a large country, a nation with a vast number of small producers. For this reason, it is difficult to avoid the continual production of a bourgeoisie. What are small producers? Individual producers and handicraft industries are examples. Although we have collectivized, domestic industries and private plots still exist. These are all instances of small-scale production. They are supplements to the collective economy, required by the collectives, which we cannot do away with. However, they are also capable, at each instant, of giving rise to capitalism and bringing about the struggle between the Two Roads.

As to the peasants, there are affluent middle peasants, middle peasants, and poor peasants. As to the middle peasants, there are distinctions between new and old, and upper and lower. There are some among the affluent middle and upper-middle peasants who have strong spontaneous capitalist tendencies. Which groups responded positively to the rightists' attack in 1957 and to the Spirit of Individual

Enterprise instigated this year by the Four Class elements? For the most part they were upper-middle peasants (especially the old ones) and the affluent middle peasants. The class strata will in time become classes in their own right.

Fourth, each class stratum has its own characteristic tenacity. Our working class is tenacious in its desire to realize socialism and communism in China. The landlord class is tenacious in its desire to restore feudal society, and the bourgeoisie is tenacious in its desire to continue to exploit the working classes and to obstruct the revolution and socialist construction. These are the so-called class characteristics. They are tenacious, and the resultant class struggle is a protracted one. Therefore, we say that classes are tenacious, and that we must understand and analyze them from every angle if we are not to be paralyzed.

Therefore, the class struggle is protracted, complex, repetitive, alternately resurgent and recessive, and sometimes acute. Our attitude regarding this question is one of serious consideration and continual surveillance. We will conduct education throughout the party and among the people so that everyone may come to understand the laws of class struggle. Young people under twenty years of age now understand only that there are workers and peasants, but they do not realize that there once was a landlord class. For this reason, universities and middle and elementary schools should all conduct class education, and it should continually be conducted among the masses as well. Discussions of class struggle in meetings and descriptions of it in textbooks will prevent us from becoming paralyzed.

Now we will discuss the problem of the Spirit of Individual Enterprise. This is the principal manifestation of the struggle between the two classes and the Two Roads. It can be divided into three questions.

(1) Circumstances Surrounding the Spirit of Individual Enterprise

The Spirit of Individual Enterprise in our county has begun to develop gradually since spring of this year. At the time of spring planting, Household Contract Production was being practised by only a few teams (according to statistics at that time, only in seventy-seven teams). After a while its spread was reversed. After the summer harvest, however, because of the urgent requirements of war preparation, we relaxed our ideological leadership in this regard and, as a consequence, a Spirit of Individual Enterprise calling for Household Contract Production on part of the land arose in the villages. Although this is not widespread in our county, and individual enterprise itself is not general, this type of thought is widespread, and if it is not stopped in time many more teams will most certainly take up Household Contract Production and embark upon individual enterprise.

According to the statistics through October, 768 teams had taken up private contracting (26.5 per cent of the total number of teams in the county). Altogether there are 7,178 mou of land under private contract. This amounts to 2.05 per cent of the total area of the county and includes 395 mou of land for paddy rice (0.28 per cent of the total rice-paddy area), 3,783 mou of land for sweet potatoes (8.2 per cent of the total sweet-potato area), and 326 mou of land for economic crops (3.0 per cent of the total economic crop area). Basically, there are three forms of private contracting. The first is the allotment of bad fields and remote land to the households in proportion to the private plots they hold. The output from these fields will not be used to offset the basic ration and is not counted as part of the output used in calculating state levies and purchases. Fourteen teams in the county handle it in this way. They have 23 mou--all bad fields. This is a permanent distribution of land. The second form is Household Contract Production, which makes up the greatest proportion, there being 747 teams in all (98 per cent of the total production teams engaged in private contracting), with a land area of 4,089 mou (of these, 306 mou are double-crop land and 3,783 mou are sweet-potato land). The conditions obtaining with regard to Household Contract Production are not entirely similar. (There are, in all, four kinds: in the first, the paddy is a collective, but all dry fields are contracted to the households; in the second, the paddy is a collective and part of the dry fields is contracted to the households; in the third, part of the paddy and part of the dry fields are contracted to the households; in the fourth, part of the economic crops is contracted to the households. Among these teams, the major part of Household Contract Production is for a one-year period. Only in a minority is it for long periods. According to statistics on 130 teams in the Ao-chiang commune practicing Household Contract Production, there are five teams practicing it for long periods, 19 teams waiting to see which way the wind blows, and 106 teams which followed the practice only until autumn. The third form of private contracting is that practiced in a few hilly regions. There, commune members having the labor power are given the freedom to cultivate the early rice crop for themselves, while the autumn harvest belongs to the collective. There are seven teams of this kind. Their single-crop rice fields amount to 66 mou. Once Household Contract Production is begun, farm tools and privies follow the same course. According to the statistics for the entire county, 1,197 private privies and 1,988 small farm tools are privately owned.

Another manifestation of the Spirit of Individual Enterprise is emphasis on the individual and neglect of the collective, as when commune members do not hand over fertilizer to the collective and when they fail to participate in collective labor; and when a large amount of uncultivated land is reclaimed for private planting. According to an investigation of the twelve model teams at Shan-pien, there was a 50.2 per cent decrease in the quantity of fertilizer handed over this year from January to September, compared with last year for the same period. On the average, only 13.8 days of labor power per month were devoted to work for the collective, and for the third team in Shan-pien only 8.0 days. Where does the labor force go if it does not work on the collective? It engages in subsidiary production, miscellaneous work, and peddling. In the Lien-teng brigade of the Ao-chiang commune, after the summer harvest 96 workers out of 190 drifted outside (50 per cent). Moreover, some devote all their efforts to the individual reclamation of barren land. According to preliminary statistics, about 40,000 mou of barren land were reclaimed in the entire county. Small Freedoms land (including private plots) makes up, on the average, more than 30 per cent of the county collective area. In a minority of teams, it has reached more than 50 per cent.

In addition, individuals have encroached upon the collective farms by usurping collective land for basic construction. They have "reclaimed" collective land. In household-contract production, the output quota is set too low. As regards fertilizer, they have reduced the share due the collectives, reducing thereby the superiority of the collectives. These are all manifestations of the Spirit of Individual Enterprise.

The Spirit of Individual Enterprise also exists in the fishing industry. There are five principal manifestations. First, in the offshore fisheries we discovered that five brigades and 56 boats were engaged in Household Contract Production. Secondly, in the offshore fisheries, boats were contracted out to the workers, some on a sharecropping system, and in other cases with the whole catch, after making payments for depreciation, belonging to the workers. There were twenty teams and 75 boats in this category. Third, there is individual enterprise in the hatcheries. The masses use state-owned oyster and clam beds for their own planting. Altogether, 22 mou have been so planted. And fourth, the workers combine to build boats and reserve all income therefrom for themselves. In one brigade it was discovered that twenty households built twelve small boats. Fifth, transport boats were contracted to the workers. There were five boats in one brigade. In addition, excessive distribution of profits also occurred in fishing regions, thereby decreasing the collective income. According to the investment regulations, if a commune member invests 100 yüan, he will receive a reward of 200 to 250 catties of the catch; in some cases, for each 100 yüan invested there is a monthly interest charge of five catties of dried shrimp, equivalent to a 20 per cent return.

Furthermore, in all aspects of industry, handicrafts, business, and culture and education the Spirit of Individual Enterprise is manifested. The workers' clamor to quit working in the factories and individual enterprise on the part of handicraft workers and doctors are manifestations of this spirit.

The facts prove that the Spirit of Individual Enterprise need not be long in evidence before it produces evil results.

In the first place, there is serious polarization. The phenomenon of exploitation of man by man has again appeared in the villages. Households with plentiful labor would go the way of landlords and rich farmers, exploiting others. Households having many members but few workers, patriot families, military families, worker families, and Five Guaranteed households may expect to encounter even greater difficulties. This is the present situation. In the half year since the Spirit of Individual Enterprise has appeared, hired labor and high-interest loans have arisen, and such phenomena as labor-deficient households renting out land and letting land lie waste have begun to appear. On the basis of incomplete statistics for the period, cadre families had 184 mou of land lying waste, 118 labor-deficient households hired labor, and nine households rented out land. In Hsiao-ao a cadre family contracted for half a mou of farm land for 100 catties and, because it did not have any labor, rented the land out and paid only 54 catties in rent. On the other hand, according to statistics from the Ao-chiang, Kuan-t'ou, and Huang-ch'i communes, 384 households have been discovered hiring out high-interest loans amounting to 72,440 yüan and 14 tan of food. The ordinary monthly interest is from 1.0 to 1.5 per cent. Li Chao-fang, an upper-middle peasant of the Lien-teng brigade in the Ao-chiang commune, working as a labor contractor, extorted more than 7,500 yüan. This year he lent out 4,200 yüan at a monthly interest of 1.5 per cent. Most recently, he built a new house, bought a plow ox, a watch, silk, and gold bars. To his wife he said, "Why should we go out to work when the weather is this hot! We would not have to worry even if there should be a three-year drought." This household has been named as new rich peasant by the masses. We can see from this example that class differentiation is still marked. If Household Contract Production continues, people like Li Chao-fang will be appearing everywhere in a few more years.

Next, the existence of "individual-enterprise households" has necessarily created a severe decrease in collective food production. Wherever the Spirit of Individual Enterprise is intense, production has decreased sharply, and where it is most prevalent, the decrease is the sharpest. This is plain fact. The Pei-men brigade and the Ts'ai-ch'iao brigade of the Ao-chiang commune are neighbors. The output of the double-cropping fields in the Pei-men brigade was only 635 catties per mou, and the total production was 1,323 tan less than the brigade's output quota (27.8 per cent), while the Ts'ai-ch'iao brigade, in spite of having land inferior in quality to that of Pei-men, had an output of 840 catties per mou, or 32 per cent more than Pei-men. Furthermore, the decrease in collective production had a bad effect on the ideology of the masses, giving them the distorted view that "the collectives have lost their superiority," when actually this was entirely the result of the Spirit of Individual Enterprise.

Third, the Spirit of Individual Enterprise has also affected the solidarity of socialism. Abandonment of farming and fishing by farmers and fishermen so as to enter business, cadre members' lack of interest in the revolution, military men's withdrawal from the ranks, students' lack of interest in their studies, private slaughtering of pigs, felling of forests, and speculation--all are the bad results of the Spirit of Individual Enterprise. According to the statistics for the period, 2,505 farmers and fishermen abandoned their work for business, 71 military men petitioned for discharge from the ranks, and many asked not to be members of cadres any longer. Among these were some whose families were in actual hardship and some who were attracted by the Small Freedoms.

(2) The Causes of the Spirit of Individual Enterprise

The data from many investigations indicate that the basic cause of the Spirit of Individual Enterprise is the disturbance created by landlords, rich peasants, counterrevolutionaries, and bad elements and the spontaneous tendency toward capitalism on the part of some affluent middle peasants. They make use of the temporary vacillation toward the collective economy by a minority of the poor and lower-middle peasants and the errors and deficiencies in our work as means of incitement. This is the essence of the problem. Therefore, the Spirit of Individual Enterprise and the struggle against it is a struggle between the proletariat and the bourgeoisie as well as a struggle between socialism and capitalism.

The former Kuomintang regional party secretary Ch'en P'in-kuan (a counterrevolutionary) instigated the ruin of the collective economy of the Ch'en Ch'in-fu production team in the Tung-men brigade of the Ao-chiang commune, which had twenty households (16 poor peasant and 4 middle peasant households). Ch'en P'in-kuan is an upper-middle peasant. Altogether there are seven people in his family, four of whom are workers. Although he himself was put under supervision after the liberation, he did not reform. Beginning with this spring, only his third son worked, in a brickyard, while the others acted as labor contractors or were engaged in speculation and profiteering. When the cadre called him to work, he said, "The cords of the collective are too tight." He even made fun of the cadre saying: "I see a lot of cadre members who can't stick to their jobs to the end. Can you?" During the War Preparation period he was even more insubordinate, openly saying, "When our day comes, we will reckon accounts with the cadres." He threatened the team chief, saying: "You should take a little care. When the time comes, there will be a good play to watch." It was at this time that he opened a stall to sell fried cakes. Because of a controversy over the exchange of grain, he took advantage of the team chief's not being at home to have his third son beat up the chief's wife. She was injured in seven places, one of which has not yet healed. When the complaint was taken to the court, it was settled by a 20-yüan compensation. Even more serious were his excessive provocations during the War Preparation period. To the wife of the middle peasant Ch'en Ts'ung-tien he said, "Since you're such a good worker, it doesn't pay for you to be tied up with everyone else." To the poor peasant Chuang I-hung he said: "You work hard but have so little food. If you go to work on your own, in one or two years you will be rich." For this reason, many people in the team have become irresolute. The wife of Ch'en Ts'ung-tien also raised a turmoil, demanding fields from the team. She made such a fuss that she obtained seven mou for sweet potatoes. When the time for autumn rice came, work was contracted out to individual households and a serious production decrease in the team resulted. There was a 40-tan production decrease in 57 mou of early rice, and a 45-tan decrease in the autumn crop. The monthly food ration per person was only a little more than 11 catties. The poor farmer Yü Ch'ang-chi (who has a family of three and no labor force) said: "When bad men raise the wind, poor men suffer. This year's Spirit of Individual Enterprise has brought hardship to my whole family."

The Lien-hsing production team in the Hsing-lin brigade of the Liao-yen commune comprises altogether ten households: one landlord, one rich peasant, two upper-middle peasant, and six poor peasant households. The team had been very good in the past and was regarded as a model. This year the rich peasant Chang Ch'i-ch'üan caused trouble in the team; he quit going out to work and refused to hand over fertilizer. At the time of War Preparation, he went to the team and took away two threshers, a plow, a harrow, and sixteen poles for sweet potato vines. Moreover, he stirred up trouble, saying: "Our team is too big. We want to elect a new team chief and split up the team. Otherwise we won't have any food to eat." In addition, this rich peasant engaged in speculation and profiteering and deceived the people with religion. The team chief consistently criticized him, but he paid no attention. When he took the farm tools, even after the team chief told him not to, he broke a "water stick,"[2] angering the team chief. There was nothing the team chief could do and no one supported him, so he timidly gave in and let Chang go.

Other causes of the Spirit of Individual Enterprise are confused ideology in the cadre, destructive behavior by the Four Classes, and spontaneous capitalism on the part of some affluent middle peasants. At this time, the attitude of the cadre members is crucial. If they are not resolute, and if they either tacitly consent to or promote Household Contract Production, then the Spirit of Individual Enterprise will grow. Conversely, if their attitude is resolute, the Spirit of Individual Enterprise will not grow. In the Yü-nai-ch'in production team of Hsi-men, Ao-chiang, seven cadre members are poor and lower-middle peasants. When the entire village of Mu-p'u was considering Household Contract Production, the cadre members were very vigilant except for one, who was the accountant and who vacillated. As a consequence, even though the commune members raised disturbances at each meeting that was held, the cadres were resolute and did not give in. At one meeting a middle-peasant commune member threatened: "Not to engage in household-contract production is all very well, but you cadres will be responsible for making good any deficiency in production." The cadres remained opposed and at last convinced the commune members that they should be obedient, with the result that the team increased production from year to year and had the highest volume of production in all Mu-p'u. The team's food production in 1961 was 790 catties per mou, and this year's production was 847 catties per mou, an increase of 7.2 per cent over last year and 8.0 per cent over the Three Fixed production quota. Total money income was 5,500 yüan, an increase of 17 per cent over last year.

According to our investigation, many factors cause cadre members to vacillate when faced by the Spirit of Individual Enterprise. One is that the cadre with an abundance of labor power represents affluent middle-peasant ideology. Another is that when the cadres do not participate in collective labor, commune members are critical. Another is the uncertainty that occurred during the War Preparation period. In addition, there are many cadre members who because of confused understanding and unclear conceptions of right and wrong have been taken in by others.

The Shan-t'ang [brigade] Ch'en Ping-yu production team of the P'u-k'ou commune has a seven-member cadre and five of the members are affluent middle peasants. Since the autumn of last year they have engaged in Household Contract Production. This summer the team committee resolved to let out contracts for sweet potatoes to the households. Since the poor peasants did not agree, the team cadre, in the name

---

[2] The precise meaning of the term "water stick" is not clear.

of "mobilization for guaranteed output," farmed out the work anyway. One poor peasant, Ch'en Shu-hsiu, would not agree, and the cadre chief threatened him, saying, "You do not have to accept if you do not want to, but later we will not give you any potato seed." Ch'en Shu-hsiu was forced to agree. The poor peasants said: "When you carry water in two bamboo baskets, both will be empty. Individual enterprise will starve us, but we will not be able to rely on the collective either."

In the Hsia-ch'i second team of the Kuan-t'ou commune the ideology of the masses was confused during the War Preparation period. They had not planted their sweet potatoes and were demanding Household Contract Production. The team chief was afraid of offending the masses and said: "When soldiers come, they break through bamboo fences. The important thing is to get the sweet potatoes in. I'll be a nice fellow so that even if the Kuomintang comes, they will not behead me." The result was that half the team engaged in Household Contract Production.

For a while after the summer harvest, the leadership of the County Committee did not understand that Household Contract Production was a form of class struggle. Consequently, its attitude toward handling the Spirit of Individual Enterprise was not sufficiently firm and some of the methods adopted by the interested departments were not entirely appropriate (such as free-market management and encouragement of sales), thereby confusing some comrades as well as abetting individual enterprise. Further, a minority of cadre members in the organizations, when they returned to their homes, began secretly to practice Small Freedoms and to open up uncultivated land. A few units stationed in villages took over collective land. All these practices had an extremely bad influence on the masses and abetted the development of the Spirit of Individual Enterprise.

In addition, some problems also exist in our work itself. These created a pretext for those promoting individual enterprise. These problems are principally manifested in two ways. First, because of the unlimited reclaiming of uncultivated land, a contradiction has arisen between the individual and the collective concerning the use of labor and fertilizer. In this situation, the cadres did not actively teach the commune members to adopt measures to protect the collective and, in a negative sense, allowed Household Contract Production. Second, many problems exist in the work of the production team itself, and these have not been well solved. For example, in the entire county, about 15 per cent of the teams are still third class. In these teams, the leaders are not able to fulfill their responsibilities and are team leaders in name only, and in some cases they have been replaced several times a year. Collective production has not been handled well and has not been welcomed by the masses. The attitude of some cadre members has not been democratic; financial transactions have not been open, and some members have indulged in excess consumption. Commune members have been critical. Some, because of the scarcity of food, have caused a minority of poor and lower-middle peasants to waver in their attitude toward the collective in the face of temporary difficulties. In some production teams, policies of "to each according to his work" were not completely carried out, special allowances were not given to those in need, and greater reward was not awarded for greater labor. There were also some production teams in which business management was poor, creating slowdown of work, waste, and low-quality farming. These deficiencies have all been used by those promoting individual enterprise.

Beginning with this year, many people have been influenced and misled because a number of incorrect ideas concerning the Spirit of Individual Enterprise have become widespread. It is therefore necessary to discuss and correct these ideas.

(a) Some say that Household Contract Production is a good method of business operation and management.

This idea, which has misled and confused many people, is actually a deceitful trick. Household Contract Production and business management do not, basically, have any points of similarity. Business management indicates the concrete management of collective production, while Household Contract Production is unadulterated each-for-himself, individual enterprise and does not basically have any collective flavor. Can that be called business management?

(b) Others say that Household Contract Production can increase production and that it is a good method for overcoming difficulties. Some people have been summarizing the "superiorities of individual enterprise" in order to persuade us of this. Recently, when we opposed the Spirit of Individual Enterprise, some persons said, sarcastically, "The government is afraid the masses will eat too well, and so they promote the collectives."

Many facts prove that this viewpoint is basically incorrect. It is principally a problem of outlook. These people see only their own private plots and reclaimed land, and not the greater collective land. The actual situation is that the keener the Spirit of Individual Enterprise, the greater the decrease in production. When the Chang-ho team in the Kuan-hsiang brigade of Ao-chiang commune reckoned accounts, although 48 more tan could be harvested from the reclaimed lands, and 12 more tan could be harvested from private contracting—making a total of 60 tan—it was found that the collective's double-crop rice harvest fell from 840 catties to 583 catties per mou, a loss of 111 tan to the team. The gain was thus not equal to the loss. In the Kuei-lin brigade of the Tan-yang commune there were two households with an equal number of persons and manpower (six persons and one-and-a-half workers each). One household was in a team maintaining collective production, the other in a team largely engaged in Small Freedoms. At the summer harvest, Lu Lien-hsing (on the predominantly Small Freedoms team) had a collective ration distribution of 176 catties. Although the free land produced 700 catties, each person had only 30 catties to eat a month. On the other hand, Ch'en I-feng (in the good team) had a collective distribution of 700 catties, an excess quota ration of 300 catties, and a work ration of 1,409 catties. Although he derived less from the Small Freedoms (300 catties), each member of his household had 70 catties a month. There are many more examples similar to these from every region. From this, can it be said that individual enterprise increases production?

(c) A third statement is that Household Contract Production is demanded by the masses.

This statement does not have a class basis, and investigations have found that this is not the essence of the situation. This spring, in our investigation of the fourth section of Wang-chung in Tan-yang, in which the most serious movement for individual enterprise occurred, we found that of the fourteen team households, only four households (28.5 per cent) of affluent middle peasants were actually resolutely advocating Household Contract Production, that there were six households (43 per cent) whose ideology was confused and who were at times irresolute, and that there were four households (28.5 per cent) of poor peasants who resolutely opposed private contracting. When we investigated the Ch'en Chih-shan production team of Chien village in the Ch'ang-lung commune, which was raising a serious disturbance over individual enterprise, we found three attitudes among the fifteen households of the team. Eight of the households (three poor peasant and five lower-middle peasant households), making up 53 per cent of the team, opposed individual enterprise. Four households (26.6 per cent) were irresolute. The labor force in these households was slightly larger (six workers in the four households), had considered engaging in Household Contract Production and Small Freedoms. On the other hand, they were afraid that with each person working for himself they could not surpass the affluent middle peasants. The affluent middle peasants held to the course of individual enterprise. There were three households of old families engaging in individual enterprise (20.4 per cent), with a total labor force of six, who were very dissatisfied with the collective when collectivization came in.

(d) The fourth viewpoint is that Household Contract Production can lead to greater gains from greater labor and can stimulate enthusiasm for labor. There was a cadre member who said this: "There is not one Chinese with an unselfish public spirit. Only under individual enterprise will he redouble his efforts." This way of thinking is strictly in terms of distribution according to labor and is one not wanting anything to do with communism. Actually, it is also a pretext on the part of the affluent peasants for squeezing out poor peasants who do not have any labor force. We must analyze this kind of thinking from a class outlook. The party's aim, by leading the peasants to organize, is to prevent class polarization and to ensure common prosperity for all. One must realize that in any society anyone may encounter natural disasters and personal misfortunes. Who can guarantee that a man will be able to work vigorously all his life or that he will not encounter times when his ability to work is lessened? Moreover, there must be a suitable division of labor in a society. We need workers, and we need the People's Liberation Army for national defense. In the past, we opposed egalitarianism in order to obtain a greater share for labor. If we now turn about and emphasize absolute distribution strictly according to labor, this will be regressive and reactionary. Furthermore, we must consider that in stimulating a positive spirit in labor, it is essential that we have, besides correct policy, ideological teachings. The statement "Only under individual enterprise will he redouble his efforts" is without basis. Did not our ancestors exert themselves during the thousands of years of individual enterprise before the liberation? Why didn't they get rich? They engaged in individual enterprise for thousands of years; why has there been such a tiny percentage of them who were landlords and rich peasants? Even affluent peasants have been few, and the masses of peasants are poor. Is this not the result of individual enterprise?

(e) Yet another view is that freedom of individual enterprise means less trouble for the cadres.

This is principally a problem of freedom. Collective labor is in fact very free. Each month there are several days of vacation to permit workers to attend to private matters, and leave may be had for illness. Those with heavy family responsibilities are given extra days off. What sort of lack of freedom is this? Before the liberation, all farmers were individual entrepreneurs and the masses of peasants were oppressed and exploited. They did not have enough to eat and wear. Can that be called freedom? Actually, when these people demand freedom, what they demand is freedom to engage in peddling, freedom to hire labor, and freedom to lend money at high interest--in short, a freedom allowing them to exploit others--and it is this kind of freedom that we will not allow and that we must firmly oppose. As far as being a cadre is concerned, this is a worthy thing. Engaging in socialism is troublesome, but what is there to fear?

When we compare these viewpoints with Tito's revisionism, is there any difference? I feel that they are the same.

III. CONTRADICTIONS

The Tenth Plenum of the Eighth Central Committee discussed the present major contradictions, of which there are seven: the contradiction between us and the enemy, which is that between the revolution and the counterrevolution; the contradiction of the two roads, which is that between socialism and capitalism; the contradiction between democracy and centralization; the contradiction between uniformity and diversity; the contradiction between saving and consumption; the contradiction between developing our own potential and imitating foreign countries; and the contradiction between the correct and the incorrect.

Why do I bring up these seven contradictions? The reason is that they now exist, are interfering with the progress of socialism, and were, therefore, brought up and resolved in the Tenth Plenum. The decisions made by the party Central Committee for strengthening the collective economy and the decisions on business are steps in the ultimate resolution of these contradictions.

In our county, these seven contradictions exist in our present work. Some of these I have already discussed. Here I will discuss two of them.

(1) The contradiction between democracy and centralization. --Democracy and centralization are antithetical. Which of the two is dominant? It is centralization that is the most important. However, some comrades do not see the problem in this way. This year, after implementing the system of democratic centralism, another extreme arose within the party--that of extreme democratization, or democracy without centralization. In all affairs, these people permit only themselves, not others, to talk; permit only the lower levels, not the upper levels, to talk; permit only the lower levels to criticize the upper, and not the upper to criticize the lower. It seems as if it were undemocratic to let others talk, undemocratic to let the upper levels talk; and undemocratic to criticize the cadres who leave their work posts. This condition exists at all levels. If the upper-level party directives suit the lower levels, then they obey them. If they do not suit them, they do not obey. It has reached the point where disorganization and disorder have already occurred among a minority of cadres. When the commune Party Committee called a meeting of branch secretaries, they could refuse to attend without sufficient cause. There was one brigade chief who refused to participate in a commune distribution meeting because he was building his house. Some commune Party Committee members have reported that most recently a very perverse spirit has developed, and that the more they oppose it, the further it develops. There are also some persons who have found a pretext for extreme democracy in what they call "the demands of the masses" and "general opinion," and on these pretexts have openly opposed the upper levels. This situation also exists among the masses. They do not obey the directions of the cadre, even going to the point where they beat the cadre without being punished.

There is a principle of democracy, stated in the Party Regulations, to the effect that the minority is subordinate to the majority, that the lower levels are subordinate to the upper levels, that the individual is subordinate to the organization, and that the party is subordinate to the Central Committee. If we contravene this principle, then the party is no longer the party of the working class. Comrades, think a moment. In our county there are more than 240 brigades and close to 3,000 teams. If these more than 200 brigades have two hundred minds, and the 3,000 teams have three thousand minds, what fighting strength can the party have? How can we guarantee that high-level directives will be carried out? This principle is also a discipline that every party member must respect. What the high levels decide must first be resolutely and unconditionally put into effect. You can express your disagreement, but you must not hinder implementation. Each Communist Party member must uphold the solidarity and the unity of the party at all times and in all places. This is the source of the party's strength. The Party Regulations also decree: "The party's principle of democracy cannot be separated from its principle of centralization. The party is a battle organization united by the observance of its discipline by all party members. Without discipline, the party could never lead the nation and the people to victory over their powerful enemies, nor bring about socialism and communism."

(2) The contradiction between uniformity and diversity.--Uniformity and diversity are antithetical. Total uniformity is not satisfactory. We must develop the best aspect of each level. However, total diversity without uniformity is also unsatisfactory, since the purpose of developing a positive spirit is uniformity. Therefore, uniformity is the most important, and it is especially at this time that we need a high degree of uniformity.

Our present trouble is the tendency to deemphasize uniformity and to strive for diversity. The current tendency toward low production is a manifestation of the doctrine of diversity. In addition, the subsidiary products of peasants and the marine products of fishermen are not being used to fulfill the sales obligations to the state, but are taken to the free markets and sold at high prices. There are also some cadre members who do the same. Until now, teams who were not fulfilling their levy-purchase obligations to the state and who had adopted stalling techniques were in the minority. In addition to this, in our county there were 277 tan of unfulfilled hemp quotas this year, and only 49.08 per cent of the pig purchase quota was fulfilled. In the fishing regions, there is a very serious situation because fish products are not being sold to the state.

While the nation is still in a condition of temporary difficulty, we should concentrate manpower, matériel, and financial capacity to a high degree in order that they be of the greatest possible use in quickly overcoming difficulties. If we practice diversity, with each individual region and sector dispersing manpower, matériel, and financial power, the time required to overcome difficulty will be prolonged. This will affect the speed of socialist construction throughout the entire nation. In addition, the doctrine of diversity and the tendency toward low production may affect the faith of some people in the development of collective enterprise (as manifested in low rations), and may furnish a pretext to those promoting individual enterprise, thereby affecting the strength of collective enterprise. This doctrine is not beneficial to the work of the party. Therefore, correct handling according to policy of the three important relationships-- between the state, the collective, and the individual--and rapid fulfillment of the levy-purchase obligations for each kind of agricultural and subsidiary product are, if the actual situation is correctly reflected, the correct behavior that every party member and cadre should display. The doctrine of diversity occurs at all levels. It is found in the economic sector, in the party, in the administrative sector, among the popular organizations, and in the collectives. We must resolve to correct it now. At the last Provincial Committee meeting we devoted time to an investigation of the problem of diversity, indicating that this problem has already received serious consideration at higher levels. In the past we did not recognize its harmfulness. We now understand this harmfulness and have resolved to correct it. If we do not do so, we will be making a mistake. In the future, the lower levels must not keep information from the higher levels. There must be a mutual interchange of intelligence, and when handling problems, a petition must be made before action is taken and a report must be made afterward. We cannot have independent "kingdoms" in operation.

(3) Finally, I wish to discuss the problem of attitudes among the cadre members. This problem is one of class (a concrete reflection of the class struggle), and it is also a problem of contradictions. The problem of attitude among cadres occurred principally after the rectification movement. There was no clear perception of the boundaries between right and wrong; there was the idea of trying to be a good fellow; there was a tendency to muddle through things; and when a tendency toward error was seen, the cadres did not dare to start criticism struggles. This failure allowed various bad tendencies to arise, such as disobedience to law and order, embezzlement and misappropriation of funds, excessive consumption, extravagance, superstition, and indiscriminate felling of trees. Some of these are relatively serious. Here we shall discuss some of the more prominent cases.

(a) The spread of house building among the cadre. --House building is a good activity which the state wishes to support. The present problem is that cadres are making use of their authority to build houses by every unscrupulous means. Wages of cadres are not high, and their labor power is not as strong as that of ordinary commune members. Moreover, with wood so scarce, where could the capital and materials have come from? This question aroused our suspicions. On the basis of preliminary investigations, it has been found that many used their authority to usurp collective land, dispatched the masses to work for them, and took materials from brick and tile factories and used wood intended for use in production to build their houses. Concerning wood, much misconduct has been discovered, such as the issue of false certifications and the misappropriation of materials for boat construction for private use.

(b) Extravagance. --Conspicuous at present are many instances of inviting guests to parties on numerous occasions such as beam raisings, first-month birthdays of babies and other birthdays, stove buildings, and wall raisings. According to incomplete statistics, during this year there have already been 1,409 parties, amounting to 6,987 tables. The majority of these involved cadres. This kind of party giving was quite widespread at P'an-tu. There are some cadres who make use of parties for extortion. It is said that when one brigade chief married off his daughter and built a house this year, he gave a thirty-four-table party. At the tables, presents were received from his guests, with the result that he made a profit of 1,600 ytian.

Extravagances in the collectives are also very serious. Cadres use the collective's money and food to hold feasts, to engage blindly in basic construction, to send presents, to put on operas, and to organize play companies. Some teams have spent huge sums on large-scale play companies and on buying ancient-style opera costumes. They have even taken young people to study acting. Some teams, in order to maintain play companies, have even asked counterrevolutionaries to direct them. Others have hired play companies from distant places and have continually put on performances. This practice has affected production. Even more serious is the fact that some people do not show any shame for their wasteful conduct. On the contrary, they feel that it is worthy, saying, "Since our income is so large, what does it matter if we use a little of it." As to the problem of sending gifts, they say: "Sending gifts is for work's sake," or "For the sake of cooperation, it pays to give a little." These views are all thoroughly wrong. When income is high, we should manage the communes frugally and save for a rainy day. Were there not some fishing brigades whose income was lower this year than last year? If one does not save during a year of rich harvests, what can one do if there is a decrease in production later? As far as cooperation is concerned, gifts should not be sent indiscriminately. Actually, the sending of presents and holding of banquets have opened a convenient door to corruption, misappropriation, and excess among cadre members, and this corrupts and destroys the cadre as a whole.

(c) Corruption and misappropriation. --This is very severe among a minority of cadre members. At present, we have discovered six cases of extensive corruption involving up to 3,445 yüan and more than 2,000 catties of food.

Misappropriation is quite widespread, and even money for distribution to the masses has been taken. There are some persons who work little and who have very low incomes, but who do not hesitate to borrow huge sums of public money. Evidently, they are not prepared to repay it.

In addition to this, there are other abuses such as the awarding of excess work-points as well as the excessive consumption of production-team materials and food.

(d) The indiscriminate felling of trees is also widespread. According to county statistics, 294,900 trees were felled, for the most part by cadres. Even more serious is that after felling the trees, they engage in speculation and sell them at high prices. There was one brigade chief who, with a group of "reform through labor" elements, cut down 22 camphor trees and 21 pine trees, selling them for 830 yüan. After expenses, 443 yüan remained to be divided among the five persons.

(e) Superstition is very conspicuous in coastal districts. According to an investigation made by the Huang-ch'i commune, 31 temples have been built and 11 have been repaired, and there are 67 temples that have idols. The total expenditure was 8,185 yüan. In addition, most recently, religious activity of Taoists and people who spread religion has been very extensive. If these activities are not handled properly, they will certainly be used by counter-revolutionary elements. Many cadre members do not dare to take any action against superstitious conduct, and some cadre members and their families have led the way in participating in superstition, crying "Freedom of Belief" and "Superstition is the Demand of the Masses." We of the Communist Party are atheists, and for us to participate in superstitious activity is a matter not of "freedom of belief," but of our attitude toward Marxism-Leninism. The practice of superstition is, in general, the exploitation of the backwardness of the masses by a minority. . . .[3]

1962

---

[3]About 400 characters follow, the text of which is illegible.

VI

PROPAGANDA OUTLINE FOR "THE FURTHER STRENGTHENING OF THE COLLECTIVE ECONOMY OF THE PEOPLE'S COMMUNES AND EXPANDING AGRICULTURAL PRODUCTION"

(For distribution to the branch sections for oral communication)

I. Come to a clear understanding of conditions, redouble effort, raise the Three Red Banners, and wrest a new victory for socialist construction.

At present, the people's economy of our nation has already taken a turn for the better. It has improved over the last two years in both villages and cities. We have already passed victoriously through our most difficult period, and our economy is growing better from day to day. This can be seen clearly by everyone in everyday life.

In the villages, because of the implementation of policies concerning the agricultural communes, the strengthening of the collective economy, and the stimulation of enthusiasm among the masses of peasants, conditions have markedly improved. The harvest from this year's summer crop showed an increase over that of last year, and it is estimated that the fall crop in most regions will show an increase over past years. We can already be assured of an increase in agricultural production throughout the nation as a whole. The villages present a picture of joyous revival, and the superiority of the collective economy in the village communes is continually becoming more apparent.

The improvement in agricultural production has had a stimulating effect on industrial production, and adjustments in basic construction and industrial production have also produced positive results. There has been a rather large increase in the means of agricultural production, such as chemical fertilizers, agricultural machinery, and trucks. Production of the major light and handicraft industries dependent on industry for materials has increased greatly over that for the same period last year. At present, production of some of the most urgently needed heavy industrial goods has, for the most part, increased over that for the same period last year. Among these, the chemical fertilizer industry has produced 330,000 more tons of chemical fertilizer and 2,900 more tons of major agricultural chemicals during the first eight months of this year than for the same period last year. Beginning this year, the steel industry has produced on a trial basis 119 kinds of new steel goods, involving about 180 specifications; more than half of these were produced for agriculture and light industry. This year the petroleum industry fulfilled 117.7 per cent of the planned quota of kerosene required in the villages. This is an increase of 1.3 times over the same period last year. There have also been improvements in the business management of many enterprises, increases in the varieties of goods, improvements in quality, decreases in costs, and an increase in the productivity of labor.

There have also been new improvements in trade. An improvement has already begun to appear in the state of the domestic markets, and the supply of goods needed for daily life in the cities and country is somewhat better than before.

Many accomplishments have also been made in scientific research, culture, and education.

The people's economy and the agricultural production that we have established in Fukien, like those of the nation as a whole, have grown better from year to year. This is manifested not only in agriculture and in the villages, but also in industry and in the cities. This year's plans for industrial production were quite well fulfilled, especially in such agricultural means of production as chemical fertilizer and small steel farm tools. There was also a continual and rapid increase in the commodities produced for daily use by the light and handicraft industries which are dependent on industry for materials. There was an increase in the total production of food crops in the province. Economic crops also increased in varying degrees. Accompanying the improvement in food production, animal-husbandry production also rose. There was a new expansion in trade as well as a progressive improvement in the market supply.

How were these improvements achieved? Clearly, they were achieved because of the enlightened leadership of the party Central Committee and Chairman Mao and because of the solidarity of the party and the people around the Central Committee and Chairman Mao, the upholding of the Three Red Banners of the General Line [of Socialist Construction], the Great Leap Forward, and the People's Communes, and the accomplishment of difficult work in all phases. These improvements resulted from the implementation of a series of policies and effective measures for the adjustment of the agricultural people's communes and of the people's economy and from the coming into effect of the material base forged since the establishment of socialism, particularly since the Great Leap Forward.

The development of these conditions fully demonstrates the great superiority of the systems of people's ownership and collective ownership under our nation's socialism, and demonstrates as well the great significance of the General Line of Socialist Construction, the Great Leap Forward, and the People's Communes, as well as the correctness of the policies set down by the Central Committee and Chairman Mao. There are people who say: "The improvement in village conditions is primarily due to the increase in Small Freedoms, and the improvement in the market is primarily due to 'free market activity.'" This viewpoint is wrong. It is wrong because the Small Freedoms and the free markets are, in the final analysis, only a minor sector. If the collective economy and the entire people's economy were managed poorly, then it would be absolutely impossible to improve the overall people's economy.

As an examination of the actual struggle indicates, we are worthy of being a great nation, our people are worthy of being a great people, our armies are worthy of being great armies, and our party is worthy of being a great party. There still are difficulties ahead of us, and at present some of these difficulties are quite severe. For example, industrial and agricultural production still cannot satisfy the needs of national construction and of the people. There still are large numbers of production teams, factories, and shops in which the work is not done well, and there still are deficiencies in attitudes in some sectors of leadership and among some cadres. These cannot be neglected, and must be dealt with conscientiously. We firmly believe, however, that these difficulties and deficiencies can gradually be overcome. This is because our leadership is enlightened, our economy is stable, our political authority is firm, and the people are united. Our course is correct, and the future is bright.

The urgent task of our people is "The full implementation of Chairman Mao's policy for expanding the people's economy with agriculture as its foundation and industry as its leading factor--which consists of placing the expansion of agriculture in the first place, handling the relationship between industry and agriculture correctly, firmly shifting industry to an agricultural base, striving for a rich agricultural harvest next year, striving for the expansion of the people's economy, and struggling for the new victory of our nation's socialism."

The entire party, the cadres, and the people of the province should further concentrate their forces in order to expand agricultural production, striving for a bigger harvest and an even greater increase in production over that of last year. This is not only the common hope of the people of the whole province; it also has a basis in our concrete preparations. This is to say, as the policy of treating agriculture as the foundation has become more clearly carried out, there has been a systematic increase in the support of agriculture on the material, technical, and financial planes and in terms of technical manpower. The series of policies for the agricultural people's communes has further gained in strength. The rice-paddy water conservation program that was initiated several years ago has grown in effectiveness. Through the practices of recent years, the cadres and the masses of people have accumulated many valuable experiences. The great ideology of self-sufficiency [tzu-li keng-sheng] in the struggle against hardships, and the establishment of the nation through diligence and thriftiness, must grow in the future. It is especially under the leadership and the call of the Tenth Plenum of the Eight Central Committee that there will be an even greater enthusiasm within the party and the cadres. Under the guidance of correct policies, they will unite the masses and advance relentlessly. We need only to see that all these beneficial conditions come about to be assured of better agricultural production next year!

In summary, conditions are very good, and the future is bright. It is only necessary for the party and the people to join together even more solidly under the leadership of the Central Committee and of Chairman Mao. If we join our minds and our strength, lifting ever higher the Three Red Banners and advancing bravely, we cannot fail to achieve a rich harvest in agricultural production next year, stimulate a new expansion of the nation's economy, and bring about an early victory for socialist construction.

II. Firmly maintain the basic line of agricultural collectivization and mechanization on the road to common prosperity.

After the series of concrete Central Committee policies--including the revised draft of the "Regulations Governing Rural People's Communes" and "The Production Team as the Basic Accounting Unit"--were carried out in the villages of our province, they aroused the enthusiasm of the masses of peasants and the agricultural people's communes proceeded on a course of healthy expansion with conditions improving from year to year. Now, overall village conditions are good, and the collective economy of the people's communes is, for the most part, strong. This is the principal and basic aspect, and it is the mainstream of conditions in the villages.

Even so, around the time of the summer harvest this year, the individualistic spirit of Household Contract Production arose and temporarily misled some people. How did this spirit arise? Principally, it was through the influence of the several thousands of years of the private-ownership system in the villages. The force of the customs of small producers and the concept of private ownership cannot be completely eliminated at once. Because of a spontaneous tendency toward capitalism among some affluent middle peasants, when the opportunity occurs they attempt to depart from the socialist road and follow that of capitalism. Furthermore, landlords, rich peasants, and remnant counterrevolutionary elements take advantage of opportunities to engage in destructive conduct; and, making use of our temporary difficulties and of certain deficiencies in our work, they promote Household Contract Production and fan the Spirit of Individual Enterprise. It is now clear that if Household Contract Production and the promotion of individual enterprise continue, it will not be long before a polarization occurs. It is especially large households with few workers, military and worker families, and Five Guaranteed households that may encounter great difficulties. Even households with workers may suffer sickness or misfortune and may thereby encounter great difficulties. Household Contract Production is not a problem of method in business management, but rather one of direction, the problem of the struggle between the Two Roads of socialism and capitalism in the villages. It should be clearly realized that classes and class struggle still exist in the villages. The viewpoint that there are no classes and no class struggle in the villages is incorrect and not consistent with reality.

There are people who ask, do we criticize individual enterprise because we want only the collective good, but do not want the individual good? We say, definitely not. Our emphasis on the collectives is for the purpose of further assuring and satisfying the good of each individual. The unity of the collective and the individual good should be the standard for our action and speech. This is the spirit of socialism, and it is the ideological and political guarantee for our transition from a dispersed, small-farm economy to a collective economy. Each peasant, regardless of how great his diligence, ability, or talents, can and should use them for the collectives. The collective will provide a suitable compensation on the basis of the principle of compensation according to labor and greater gains for greater labor. In this way the individual and the collective good are united.

There are also people who ask, when you criticize the incorrect conduct of the affluent middle peasants who take the road of capitalism, is it because you do not approve of prosperity among the farmers? We say, definitely not. The objective of the land reform and collectivization led by the Communist Party and Chairman Mao is prosperity among the masses of peasants. What we oppose is exploitation and opportunism. What we advocate is common prosperity and riches through labor. We oppose laziness and advocate diligence. We oppose waste and advocate frugal home management. We do this for the purpose of bringing prosperity to the entire body of peasants.

In order to clarify our thinking further, I offer the following discussion of three problems.

(1) What is the direction of agricultural production and the basic line for agriculture?

The party Central [Committee] early indicated clearly that the basic party line on agriculture is, first, to bring about the collectivization of agriculture and, second, on that foundation, to bring about its mechanization and electrification. This basic line, whether seen from the standpoint of the collective good or of the national good or from that of the present or long-term good of the peasant, is the only correct line.

The principles are very clear. Under the conditions existing in our nation, we must bring about collectivization before we can bring about mechanization, and only after collectivization, mechanization, and electrification have been realized can agriculture begin to expand to a high degree and agricultural goods increase in quantity. Then the industrialization of the nation can be quickly realized, the standard of living of the peasants can be greatly improved, and our sons and grandsons will be able always to enjoy a rich and happy life. If individual households continue to rely on human and animal power and on ancient and outmoded farm tools, as generation after generation did in the thousands of years before the liberation, then we can never escape a tragic destiny of hardship and bankruptcy. Then only a very small minority of our peasants can, through luck, grow rich and prosperous, while the overwhelming majority cannot escape from the "bitter sea and the deep abyss." As the saying goes, "A thousand families in hardship while only one gets rich." We cannot take this course. At the same time, agriculture is the basis of the nation's economy; and if agricultural expansion follows an incorrect course, the effects extend not only to agriculture itself, but to the economy of the entire nation. The problem of the direction of agriculture, therefore, is a problem related to the socialist construction of the entire nation.

Because of the past three years of continual natural disasters, our lack of experience in building socialism, and deficiencies and errors in our work, there have been great losses in agricultural production and great difficulties within the collective economy. But these are problems of natural disaster and work, and they have not occurred because the course of collectivization is incorrect and the system bad. There are some people who confuse the problems of disaster and direction, and those of work and of system, which is not correct. We must firmly uphold the line of collectivization not only in favorable periods, but in difficult periods as well. We have entrusted our hopes for overcoming difficulties in the collective economy, and being thus firmly resolved, we have already made evident accomplishments. We can imagine that after several years of severe natural disasters, without collectivization, we could not have reduced the losses which they entailed, and many farm families would have been ruined and made bankrupt. Now, agriculture has made a rather rapid recovery, and there has been a great improvement in the villages. These are clearly the manifestations of the great superiority of collectivization. Without collectivization, these accomplishments would have been unimaginable.

(2) Which is stronger, the strength of the individual or that of the collective?

Our ten years' experience of cooperativization tells us that organized strength is stronger than individual strength, and that collectivization is incomparably superior to individual enterprise. In the first place, in the collective economy the land can be devoted to the most suitable crops, so that it will "yield the greatest possible result." Second, division of labor can be instituted, so that "a man's capacities can be used to the greatest extent." Third, water, fertilizer, seeds, and animal power can be appropriately used, so that "materials are used to their greatest effect." Fourth, the collective strength can be relied upon, so as to prevent disasters. Fifth, manpower, material power, and financial power can be concentrated for water conservation and for basic construction on agricultural land, so as to stimulate agricultural production. There is evidence of all these from our history. After land reform, food production continually rose, and the standard of living continually improved as the organization of cooperatives proceeded. The masses of peasants, upon seeing with their own eyes that collective production was capable of increasing production and income, gradually were drawn into the organization of the collective economy. It must be realized that the villages in our province already have a ten-year history of being organized into cooperatives and that the present collective economy is, for the most part, strong. In the course of achieving the cooperative system, the organized peasants, under the leadership of the party and relying on collective strength, have already spurred the yearly growth of agricultural production, have accomplished the great feat of increasing yearly production, and have attained the highest level of output in history. These facts unequivocally prove the superiority of organizing agricultural production on a collective basis and the superiority of the socialist collective economy.

There is one further point in our statement that collective strength is stronger than individual strength, and it is that the collective economy is backed up by the state and by an economy owned by the people. It is only when the economies of collective ownership and of ownership by the people are closely united that an incomparable strength is revealed. If agricultural production is to expand greatly, it must mechanize, and if it is to mechanize, it must have the massive support of the manpower, the material power, the financial power, and the technology of the state. In recent years the state has supported the collective economy with large amounts of funds and has provided such means of production as superior seeds, chemical fertilizer, farm tools, and water pumps. It has established agricultural technology extension stations and has actively organized exchanges of experiences in production. When natural and personal calamities occurred, the state has dispensed large quantities of emergency rations and funds, organizing the collective strength to combat disaster, to tide over famine, and to recover production. At the same time, the collective economy has provided great amounts of food, industrial raw materials, and labor power for the nation, thereby stimulating the expansion of the nation's industrialization. The expansion of industrial production and of scientific techniques have, in turn, increased the strength by which the nation can help agriculture. In this manner, city and country have aided each other, and with the mutual support of industry and agriculture an inexhaustible force has been brought about that has stimulated a great expansion of the economy of the entire nation. However, this large-scale mutual assistance and stimulation could only have been brought about through the joining of the organized collective economy and the national economy owned by the people; it could never have been achieved through the efforts of individual families and households. From this it can be seen that the collective strength is great and that the future development of the collective economy is boundless.

(3) Is individual enterprise or agricultural collectivization best adapted to socialist industrialization?

As everyone knows, socialist industrialization is related to the future happiness and prosperity of the people of the entire nation. Without socialist industrialization, the modernization of agriculture cannot be brought about, and if agriculture is not collectivized, it cannot meet the needs of socialist industrialization. Consequently, the establishment of socialism in our nation has required the mutual coordination of agricultural collectivization and socialist industrialization.

The reason is very clear. First, it is only when we have agricultural collectivization that we can bring the individual, scattered, family, small-farm economy onto the planned course of socialist construction and proceed with planned economic construction. Second, it is only when we have agricultural collectivization and mechanization that we can release the large amounts of labor power required to meet the nation's large-scale industrial construction needs. Third, it is only when we have agricultural collectivization that we can provide large quantities of foodstuffs and industrial raw materials for the nation. If industry does not have sufficient materials and the workers do not have full rations, neither light nor heavy industry can expand rapidly. Our present level of agricultural production is still very low. This is an acute contradiction, which individual enterprise can only aggravate. Fourth, it is only when we have agricultural collectivization and mechanization that we can utilize agricultural machinery, chemical fertilizers, water pumps, generators, tractors, and trucks on a large scale. The villages not only make up a vast market for industry, but also accumulate large quantities of capital for the expansion of industry. None of these things can be brought about on the basis of a small-farm economy. Consequently, we should deepen our self-awareness and advance ever more resolutely on the course indicated for us by the Central Committee and by Chairman Mao in building a great, modernized, socialist agriculture.

The new socialist villages of our nation have a future of great and glorious development ahead of them. The peasants of the new China also have a glorious future. It is indeed glorious and worthy of the people's praise to be socialist peasants contributing their own strength to socialist construction on the agricultural front.

III. Resolutely implement all phases of party policy for villages, the strengthening of the collective economy, and the expansion of agricultural production.

(1) To carry out the general policy of agriculture as the foundation and industry as the leading factor for the expansion of the nation's economy, we have placed the expansion of agriculture in the first place and have resolutely shifted the industrial sector toward a course having agriculture as its foundation. This is to say that we will concentrate and mobilize the strength of the party and of the nation in support of agriculture and in support of the collective economy of the people's communes. This is also to say that in unifying national economic plans we will take the expansion of agriculture as our starting point, and that whenever we determine plans and adopt measures, whether in the planning, economic, heavy or light industrial, commercial, communications, financial, scientific, or cultural sectors, we must be steadfast in taking agriculture as our foundation. We will turn toward the villages and will place the support of agriculture and the support of the collective economy in the first place.

As for the course of industrial expansion, both light and heavy industry must adopt the villages as their principal markets. The industrial sector must conscientiously conduct research and experimentation, exhausting its utmost efforts to provide such means of production as heavy machinery, chemical fertilizers, chemicals, construction materials, fuels, power, and means of transportation for agriculture best suited to the time and the place. It must also exert every effort to produce light industrial goods and to increase consumers' goods for the urban and rural markets. The agricultural, heavy industrial, and scientific sectors must draw up dependable plans for the gradual realization of technological innovation in agriculture, based on the peculiarities of natural and farming conditions in each given area. Technological innovation in agriculture should be realized stage-by-stage, according to systems most beneficial to a given area.

The state has made planned increases in agricultural investment, and, within any fixed period, agricultural investment should occupy a more important position than investment in other sectors. The state will provide loans to production teams having difficulty in finding production funds. To be sure, the people's communes and the production teams must give their attention to developing their own latent potential, implementing the spirit of progress through their own effort and avoiding reliance solely on outside assistance. Of particular importance is the protection and propagation of livestock and the effort to increase all kinds of organic fertilizer. We cannot neglect animal power or relax in collecting fertilizer while waiting for agricultural mechanization and chemical fertilizers. This is because we shall not be able to do without animal power and organic fertilizer even when we have achieved mechanization and are using chemical fertilizer.

(2) The policy of conscientiously raising both food and economic crops in an overall expansion of the farm economy.--The people's communes and the production teams should actively expand production in agriculture, forestry, animal husbandry, subsidiary enterprises, and fisheries, and should actively develop and expand handicrafts and subsidiary products. This is an important policy for developing collective production and strengthening the collective economy.

Food production is the basis of the various kinds of agricultural operations. Consequently, production teams in general should emphasize the expansion of food production. This cannot be neglected. The production teams, however, at the same time that they give precedence to the expansion of food production must also energetically expand all types of activity. On the basis of conditions in a given region, we must energetically expand the production of cotton, oil-bearing crops, vegetables, tobacco, jute, sugar, silk, tea, fruits, medicinal plants, and other economic crops, as well as endeavor to expand production in forestry, animal husbandry, fishing, and other subsidiary industries. Production teams in regions where economic crops are concentrated should emphasize the planting of economic crops. In fishing regions they should specialize in fishing or treat fishing as their main occupation. In animal-husbandry regions they should devote themselves exclusively or mainly to animal husbandry. Production teams in mountainous and semimountainous regions should cultivate and protect trees, severely restricting the excessive cutting and destruction of trees for the purpose of opening up land. Moreover, they should actively engage in reforestation and, according to the best interests of the region, develop timber forests, bamboo forests, economic forests, firewood forests, mountain goods, and subsidiary forest products. Production teams in regions in which there is a concentration of bamboo and timber should focus on their management, combining production of bamboo and timber with food production.

The production teams should, according to the needs and conditions of their given regions, actively expand their workshops for the processing of subsidiary agricultural goods (grinding mills, flour mills, oil presses, and bean-curd shops), their handicraft industries (farm tools, kilns, paper, knitting), and their animal husbandry (the raising of sows, breeding livestock, duck and geese flocks, and keeping bees), as well as collecting, fishing, hunting, and short-haul transportation. These varied activities of the production teams may be based on different production content and may use different formulas. Some will make use of nonfarming seasons to organize their forces and engage in collecting, short-haul transportation, hunting, and fishing. Some will organize a portion of their commune members with technical training to carry on various kinds of processing work. Some will specialize in distributing materials to scattered commune members for further processing. The distribution of the income from the various activities of the production teams should be determined by discussion among the commune members.

The collective economy must expand the various activities of a region according to local conditions and traditional customs and in a manner best suited to the time and the place. In this way we can utilize land and other resources and our labor forces completely and suitably to effect a great increase in collective production, thereby meeting the productive demands of city and country and the daily requirements of the people, increasing the income of the commune members and strengthening the collective economy as well.

(3) The permitting and the encouragement among the commune members within the collective economy of the use of spare time and vacations in carrying on domestic subsidiary production as a supplement to the collective economy. --This is also for the purpose of strengthening the collective economy and expanding agricultural production. It is likewise a policy which the party wishes to effect over a long period.

Domestic subsidiary production among commune members. --This refers to permitting the commune members to till their private plots allocated by the collective, and to the encouragement of commune members to raise domestic animals and fowls. They may also raise sows and large livestock. In addition, they may engage in such domestic handicraft industries as knitting, sewing, and embroidery, or in such subsidiary production as hunting and fishing, silkworm raising, or beekeeping. The commune members may also attend to the fruit trees and bamboo groves allocated by the collective and permanently owned by the commune members. The income and products of the domestic subsidiary enterprises all remain in the possession of the commune members and are at their disposal. After fulfilling the purchase agreements entered into with the state, except in instances where there are special limitations, the remainder of the products may be sold on the market. At the same time, for the benefit of commune members keeping hogs and plowing cattle, and in order to provide fertilizer and animal power for the collective economy, the commune members may be permitted to reclaim mountain land and uncultivated land as grazing land--upon discussion by a commune-member meeting and approval of either the commune or the production brigade, under uniform regulations. The opening up of uncultivated land, however, must never be permitted to destroy land and water maintenance, forests, grassland, and water conservation projects; nor may it impede communications.

Under conditions that would better the collective economy, would not impede its expansion, and would assure its absolute superiority, permission may be given to the commune members to engage in subsidiary domestic enterprises to aid and supplement the collective economy and in order to increase the goods available to society, activate the village markets, and increase the incomes of the commune members, thereby benefiting production. At present, however, a number of improper manifestations has appeared in some places. For example, some commune members have become overenthusiastic about the Small Freedoms, have not participated actively in collective production, and have not been able to fulfill the number of working days set for collective production. They do not hand over the fertilizer they are required to sell to the collective. At busy seasons, they do not go out to work, but either till their private plots or engage in other subsidiary enterprises. Others have abandoned farming for commerce and are engaging in speculative buying and selling. All these phenomena, if allowed to continue developing, will have a severe effect on collective production and on the strength of the collective economy. Consequently, we must educate those commune members who have gone wholeheartedly into the Small Freedoms system of farming, in order to change their incorrect conduct and bring them to a correct handling of the relationship between the collective and the individual. Subsidiary domestic production by commune members should be carried on under the principles of "the collective first, and the Small Freedoms land second" and "the collective first, and the individual second."

In order to strengthen the collective economy, we must respect and protect the rights of the commune members and educate them to carry out their obligations with self-awareness. The members of the people's communes enjoy within the commune those political, economic, cultural, and welfare rights to which they are entitled. In matters of commune and team production, distribution, and welfare and financial disbursements, the commune members have the right to make suggestions, to participate in discussion and voting, to criticize, and to supervise. The commune members have the right to lodge charges against cadres for unlawful conduct. All means of livelihood and farm and work tools owned by the commune members remain in the perpetual ownership of the commune members and may not be usurped by anyone. The production teams must bring about a combination of labor and leisure and must assure the safety of the commune members in their work. The commune members must carry out their required obligations within the commune. Each commune member must respect the policies and laws of the nation and carry out the resolutions of the commune representatives' meetings and commune-membership meetings. They must preserve the collective, respect work regulations with self-awareness, and struggle against whatever harm is being done to the collective economy as well as against the breaking of regulations. They must fulfill the basic labor quotas and must supply the fertilizer quota. They must preserve the common property of the nation, the commune, and the teams so that damage will not be suffered. They must raise their revolutionary alertness and prevent destructive and restorative activities by feudalistic and counterrevolutionary elements.

(4) In order to cause the commune members to participate even more actively in collective production and in strengthening the collective economy, we must conscientiously carry out a policy of distribution according to labor and of greater gains for greater labor so that the income of the peasants will continually increase on a foundation of expanding production. It was, therefore, laid down in the Draft Regulations Governing Rural People's Communes that, first, a policy of reducing deductions and increasing distribution must be maintained. During the next few years the communes and brigades should, in general, not appropriate reserve and welfare funds from the production teams. The needs of the production teams themselves, on the basis of the harvest of a given year, should be held within five and eight per cent of the gross disposable income. (The reserve fund should be held within three to five per cent. Production teams in a small number of economic-crop regions, forest regions, and suburban regions which have a higher income level may retain somewhat more. Production teams that have sustained severe disasters may set aside little or no reserve at all. Two to three per cent may be retained as a welfare fund.) Second, we must decrease the burdens on the commune members in collective construction work. Production-team construction work should be limited to about three per cent of each commune member's annual number of basic working days. Production teams taking part in construction and the restoration of small-scale water conservation projects should be given work-points and participate in the distribution of the given year. Third, we must greatly decrease the number of cadres disassociated from production and reduce work-points given to cadres as bonuses. The work-point bonuses for brigade and production team cadres should in general be one per cent, and should not exceed two per cent, of the total work-points, and should moreover be awarded through mass discussion and agreement on the part of the commune members. Fourth, we must suitably distribute collective rations, with due regard to the basic ration and the number of work-points earned, or according to work-points plus special allowances, or other suitable methods that may also be used. Whatever methods are adopted should encourage the majority of the commune members and assure them that large households short of labor, military families, and worker families will all obtain standard rations.

(5) We must correctly carry out the state's policies on food purchase and prices. When the state is purchasing food, it must consider the best interests of the state, the collective, and the individual, and it must also guarantee that the more a production team produces, the more it may keep. The quantity of food that the state purchases should be stabilized at suitable levels and during fixed periods. In order to lighten the burden of the production teams and the commune members, no further imposition of food purchase would be permitted apart from the state purchases. Regions, communes, and production brigades will not be permitted to appropriate food for the reserves. The production team, through a decision by a meeting of its members, can retain a suitable quantity of food for storage in the event of famine. The quantity of food retained, however, should not in general exceed one per cent or, at the most, two per cent of the distributable quantity remaining after fulfillment of the state levy-purchase obligations. The remainder of the food should all be distributed to the commune members. Once distributed to the households, it should be at the free disposal of the commune members themselves.

When the state must exceed the purchase quotas, purchase should be made through the supply and sales cooperatives. Prices should be discussed with the peasants, or purchase should be made in the markets.

As to prices, we should consider the actual best interests of the collectives and of the peasants, and, to the greatest extent possible, supply continually increasing amounts of industrial goods in exchange for farm goods. Suitable ratios of exchange between industrial and farm goods should gradually be determined according to the principle of equal exchange of value. Furthermore, we should conscientiously carry out a system of differentiating prices according to regions, quality, variety of goods, and season. We should improve and adjust the methods for the purchase and exchange of subsidiary agricultural products so that regions selling greater quantities of subsidiary agricultural products will receive a greater amount of industrial products. The commercial and related sectors should continually and conscientiously conduct research and work out appropriate measures in order to handle correctly the relationships between agriculture and industry, and between city and country, and to strengthen further the alliance between industry and agriculture.

(6) We must continue to improve the operation and management of the collective economy and to maintain the policies of democratic and frugal commune management. All organizational levels of the communes, and especially those of the production teams, should carefully summarize their experiences since they were organized as cooperatives and, on the principles of free will, teaching through demonstration, mutual help, and mutual benefit, correctly establish a system of responsible production and efficient management.

Production teams must be managed democratically, and a positive spirit of the commune member as the master of his own house must be fully developed. The important affairs of the production team, that is, production operation, management, and distribution, should first be deliberated upon by the masses and finally resolved through discussion meetings of the commune membership. Neither the cadres nor any minorities should take it upon themselves to make the decisions. All levels of cadre members in the communes must learn how to follow the mass line, discuss all affairs with the masses, and especially respect the opinions of the older farmers.

The production teams must be frugally managed through precise and detailed calculations and opposition to waste. The production teams must establish sound financial-management systems. All disbursements must be made in accordance with established, approved procedures, and all revenue and expenditure accounts (including the state of work-points, food, and other materials, as well as the state of funds) must be made public to the commune members at fixed periods and be discussed by them. The production team should provide, through discussion and agreement in commune-member meetings, supplies or supplements to the weak, the orphaned, the widowed, the ill, and the disabled commune members who have no means of livelihood and also to commune members who have encountered misfortunes or who have had problems in maintaining their livelihood. All cadre members must earnestly serve the people and participate actively in collective labor. They are not to be permitted to clamor after special privileges, nor are they to engage in corrupt practices or excessive consumption.

IV. Strengthen party leadership and solidarity in the struggle to achieve a rich agricultural harvest next year.

In order to strengthen the party leadership of the collective economy of the people's communes, the Central Committee has decided to select a group of cadre members who are loyal to the affairs of the people, who possess satisfactory capacities, and who understand the work methods of the mass line, to be sent to regions, counties, communes, and teams for long-term participation in work in order to strengthen leadership of the lower strata. All cadres working in the villages are also asked to strengthen investigation and research, to discuss events with the masses, to follow the mass line, to enjoy the sweet and endure the bitter along with the masses, and to conscientiously put into effect the Eight Points to Observe and the Three Great Disciplines for party and government cadres.

The party organizations within the people's communes must complete ideological and political work, and, in various forms, regularly disseminate to commune members, party members, and the masses the thought of Marxism-Leninism and of Chairman Mao and the party's General Line of Socialist Construction. They must also carry on instruction concerning current events, socialism, patriotism, collectivism, and the alliance of industry and agriculture. We must teach the commune members how to handle the relationships between the state, the collective, and the individual correctly, thereby strengthening the people's communes and the collective economy both ideologically and politically.

In order to achieve an overall increase in the production of food and economic crops next year, the Provincial Committee has decided that during this winter and next spring a commune rectification movement will be conducted in all the villages of the province. Its content is a socialist education movement having as its central aim the strengthening of the collective economy. It is a movement intended to mobilize the people and the party of the province, to stimulate their efforts to strive for superiority, and to expand agricultural production. We should enter into this movement actively and enthusiastically.

We firmly believe that only if we have a full understanding of the present advantageous conditions, determine the correct direction, reaffirm our resolve, stimulate our diligence, unite the people and the party ever more closely around the Central Committee and Chairman Mao while raising ever higher the Three Red Banners, continue to carry out thoroughly all phases of the party's policies, reform our work attitudes, and perfect our work--then, after a period of effort, the collective economy of the people's communes will be further strengthened, agricultural production will be further developed, our nation's economy will reach a new high, and our socialist construction will obtain a new and even greater victory!

PROPAGANDA BUREAU, FUKIEN PROVINCIAL COMMITTEE,
CHINESE COMMUNIST PARTY

December 10, 1962

VII

CONCERNING THE PROBLEM OF WORK ARRANGEMENTS FOR THIS WINTER AND NEXT SPRING, BY CH'EN FU-LUNG

COMRADES!

Through several days of meetings we have come to a clear understanding of the problems of "conditions," "class," and "contradictions," and we have furthered our understanding of the Spirit of Individual Enterprise as a manifestation of class struggle and as a struggle between socialism and capitalism. The overwhelming majority of our comrades have resolved to oppose the course of individual enterprise. I would now like to present the following five opinions concerning work arrangements for this winter and next spring. I have based these on the Central Committee's resolutions to further strengthen the collective economy of the people's communes and to expand agricultural production and on the spirit of the Provincial Committee and Municipal Committee directives on carrying out these resolutions.

I

We should carry out a commune rectification movement which should be conducted in separate periods and groups throughout the entire county. It should have production as its central objective, and Socialist Education and the thorough implementation of the Revised Draft Regulations as its principal tasks.

(1) We should carry out a widespread and thorough-going program of Socialist Education as the ideological basis for the effective completion of the commune rectification movement. Therefore, after the conclusion of this meeting, we should carry out a program of education, proceeding from above to below and from the inside to the outside, for all cadre and party members of the communes, brigades, and production teams, in which the communiqué of the Tenth Plenum of the Eighth Central Committee and the related documents of the Central Committee and Provincial Committee will be presented. (Party members should also study basic party doctrines and educate themselves through party courses.) The purpose of this educational program is to clarify the understanding of conditions, unify ideology, inspire conviction, clarify direction, raise the policy level, strengthen solidarity, inculcate diligence, and perfect our work. On the basis of the increased understanding of the cadre and party members, we can conduct a program of widespread and thorough socialist education for the masses of commune members.

(a) The content of Socialist Education. --Its essence is education about conditions; the struggle between socialism and capitalism; patriotism; and education about policy with the Draft Regulations Governing the Rural People's Communes as its basis. Education concerning conditions will bring the masses to understand present conditions that have improved, and will increase their faith in the communes. Education concerning the Two Road struggle will make the masses realize that classes and the class struggle exist and that this struggle will be long and complex and, at times, violent. In addition, it will cause the masses to understand that socialism is the only means by which the peasants can first be liberated and then advance toward common prosperity, and that promotion of individual enterprise can only give rise to the polarization of classes and prevent the great majority of people from escaping the fate of poverty. Which is stronger, the collective or private enterprise? Is it private enterprise or the collective that can lead the peasants out of poverty? Is individual enterprise or the collective best suited to socialist industrialization? It is these questions that the movement is designed to answer. Through a program of education in patriotism, the relationships between the state, the collective, and the individual will be resolved, and the masses will be brought to understand their duty to subordinate themselves to the interest of the state, to understand the relationship between workers and peasants, and to realize the basic benefit to the peasants of socialist industrialization. From this, they will understand the great significance of strengthening the alliance between industry and agriculture, and of supporting cities and industry, and they will, with self-awareness, guarantee the fulfillment of the state's objectives in purchasing food and subsidiary agricultural products.

(b) The methods of Socialist Education.--recollection, contrast, the airing of complaints, and the reckoning of accounts--will, as usual, be applied. Education of the masses will also be carried out through such methods as presenting facts and arguments, utilizing the experiences of the masses themselves, and using living persons and events as examples. Demonstration with facts is a highly effective method. The more facts one can present, the more thoroughly can the principles be discussed and the deeper will the education be. Therefore, education should aim at clearing up misconceptions the masses have about conditions, the class struggle, and Household Contract Production. The masses should be assisted in attaining clarity of thought and better understanding through recollection and contrast, as well as through the statements of "model" persons.

Socialist Education must be comprehensive and profound. Therefore, its methods must be flexible, detailed, and varied. This will require the coordinated use of large and small gatherings and discussion groups, with small gatherings and discussion groups predominating. Different educational methods and different content should be adopted for different groups such as old people, young people, poor peasants, and middle peasants. Socialist Education must become familiar to every household and must enter everyone's mind.

(c) Socialist Education in brigades can generally be carried out in three steps.

The first step is to call meetings at each and every level, to arouse the masses, and thus to initiate Socialist Education. This step should lead from the inside to the outside. Meetings should be held, and education should be aimed at clarifying ideology and direction. As time progresses, Socialist Education should reach a profound solution of problems. This process should require about half a month.

The second step is the solution of problems related to policy. The Revised Draft Regulations should be emphasized and discussed among the masses. After that, there should be repeated study and resolution, in mass meetings and in commune representatives' meetings, of policies not consistent with the Revised Draft Regulations, so that the regulations will be thoroughly implemented.

The third step will be concerned with organizational problems and the initiation of a high tide of production. After the internal problems of the party, youth corps, militia, and women's organizations have been clarified by means of the movement, criticism and self-criticism can be initiated in the various organizations, primarily through meetings of party members. This will have the aim of correcting tendencies toward error, raising understanding, and completing production and work. In the course of the movement there should be an emphasis on making examples of good cadre members and good commune members. At the same time, positivist elements that emerge should be cultivated and eventually absorbed into the party and the Youth Corps.

Finally, mass meetings should be held to announce the conclusion of commune rectification, and mass emotions should be harnessed so that they will lead to a high tide of production. In this manner the Socialist Education movement may be completed in a brigade in about one month.

It should be emphasized here that production must be the core of the movement. That is, we must begin with production and seek to improve it. There should be no mechanical differentiation between stages, which should blend into each other. Ideological education, especially, must be thorough from beginning to end. At the same time, it should be emphasized that we do not want to hold struggle meetings or conduct key-point criticisms.

(2) The conscientious implementation of the Revised Draft Regulations. -- The Tenth Plenum of the Eighth Central Committee has supplemented and revised the draft regulations. On the basis of these revised regulations, we should conscientiously and systematically investigate the extent to which they have been carried out, and continue to carry them out in those areas in which they are found to be insufficiently applied.

These regulations stipulate that there will be one people's commune to a village and that in certain cases even a small village can organize a commune. The organization of the communes may be on two levels--that is, the commune and the production team; or it may be on three levels--the commune, the production brigade, and the production team. After the implementation of the draft regulations, the size of the production brigades and production teams should be adjusted. The commune is now on somewhat too large a scale, and suitable adjustments should be made in order to strengthen leadership. The size of the production brigades and production teams is basically suitable and will, in general, not be changed. It has, in fact, been stabilized, and will not be changed again. In the light of present conditions, and because of the influence of the Spirit of Individual Enterprise, some teams have asked to be subdivided further. As this subdivision would prevent the proper distribution of labor power, animal power, and farm tools, it would be harmful to the expansion of various activities, and no further subdivisions should be made. Extremely small production teams should be suitably adjusted through mass discussion. The facts have demonstrated that about twenty households is optimal for production teams in agricultural regions and that the number should be slightly higher in fishing regions. The concept that the best production team is the smallest is incorrect.

The regulations stipulate that the people's communes should permit and encourage commune members to carry on subsidiary domestic enterprises such as raising hogs and fowls and knitting to supplement collective enterprises. This is beneficial to the collective economy and to the expansion of agricultural production. It is a party policy and meant to be an enduring one. Commune members must, however, be taught to uphold the collective economy and to learn to think of the commune as their family. The stipulations of the regulations concerning domestic subsidiary enterprises are very clear--that is, such enterprises can be carried on only during spare time and on holidays and must not impede the expansion of the collective economy. The absolute superiority of the collective economy must be assured, as must the fulfillment of the daily work quotas and the maintenance of the quality of work in the production teams. The greater part of subsidiary enterprises, and those on a larger scale, should be handled by the production team and should not be given to individuals. Commune members must be taught that they cannot neglect collective production to take care of domestic subsidiary enterprises and that they must not harm the common good by abandoning farming for peddling and speculation.

The regulations stipulate that through discussion meetings of the production team, and with brigade approval, commune members may, under uniform regulations, reclaim uncultivated land for use in domestic subsidiary production and that this land may, in general, be equal in amount to the present private plots. The problem at hand is that the uncultivated land thus opened greatly exceeds the amount of private plots, to the point that it seriously affects collective production. Therefore we must reach a suitable solution of these problems through the commune rectification movement, so that the opening of uncultivated land by commune members will not be permitted to destroy soil and water conservation, forests, or grazing lands or to interfere with communications. All reclaimed land violating these conditions should be confiscated. Production-team land that has been "reclaimed" should also revert to the production teams and be cultivated by them.

The regulations stipulate that the production teams should organize all persons able to work for participation in labor. The number of basic working days that each male and female full- and part-time worker must fulfill should be determined through democratic discussion on the basis of collective production requirements and the varying circumstances of the individuals. When determining the basic labor quota for female commune members, consideration should be given to physiological conditions and the practical demands of their household duties. The production teams should also organize all those capable of supplementary work for participation in labor suited to their circumstances. They should be recompensed on the basis of work performed. We must correct the unsuitable method, used in the past, of mechanically dividing the participants in collective labor according to age.

II

The resolute rectification of the Spirit of Individual Enterprise on the basis of Socialist Education:--The rectification of the spirit of individual enterprise and Household Contract Production must begin with the party and the cadre. We know that the problem concerning the attitudes of party and cadre members toward the Spirit of Individual Enterprise has, for the most part, been caused by confusion in ideology and temporary loss of direction; it also consists of an insufficient understanding of the long duration and complexity of the class struggle. Through education, the majority of our comrades will be enlightened. We must, however, also raise the problem of the Spirit of Individual Enterprise, the crux of which lies in the attitudes of party and cadre members. If their attitudes are resolute, the problem is easily handled. The attitudes of party and cadre members should be especially resolute, and Communist Party members must resolve to follow the course of collectivization. This is a test for each party member. All who uphold the course of private enterprise and do not reform, in spite of successive instruction, should be disciplined.

In rectifying the Spirit of Individual Enterprise, however, we cannot adopt simple or harsh methods in dealing with the masses. We should repeatedly explain that there is no future for individual enterprise and that we do not approve of it. We should educate the masses to a conscious return to the course of collectivism. Now, after completion of the previous stage of our work, three conditions exist in our county. The first is the resolve to follow the collective course and return Household Contract Production land to the collective. This is the attitude of the majority. Another is that of still unsolved ideological problems, exemplified by vacillation, the following of prevailing tendencies, and a wait-and-see attitude. The third is the resolute maintenance of individual enterprise by a minority of affluent middle peasants. The events of the past several years tell us that affluent middle peasants vacillate on the road toward socialism. If, however, we can bring the general standard of living to a higher level than theirs, then they can be turned into supporters of socialism. They should be dealt with by the methods we use to resolve the contradictions existing among the people. We must adopt policies of patient waiting and persuasion through education. We must not oppress them or discriminate against them, but work actively among them, enlightening them through education and gradually turning them from their present course. Production teams engaging in Household Contract Production must regularly meet their responsibilities for the sale of crops and subsidiary agricultural products to the state. They must also bear their responsibilities for giving support to military persons and workers belonging to Five Guaranteed households. Means of production such as land, plowing oxen, farm tools, and fishing implements belonging to the collective may not be destroyed or sold. Private transactions in land and other means of production are against the law. Collective farm tools and fishing gear that have been sent down to the households should be taken back, and payment be made for those that have been damaged.

We must resolve to attack class enemies and the Four Class elements who engage in such activities as counterattacking, attempting to restore the old order, and destroying the collectives.

III

The concentration of our efforts to perfect the production team. --The production team is the basic accounting unit of the people's communes. As such, it carries on independent accounting, is responsible for its own profits and losses, organizes production, and distributes income. For this reason the quality of production-team management is directly related to the strength of the collective economy and is a crucial problem. We must resolve to manage these teams well. What are the standards of effective production-team management? The resolutions of the Provincial Committee set up a "five goods" standard. These are: first, good cadre members, with firm conviction, democratic work attitudes, and fairness in handling affairs; second, good operation and management, with increased production and income; third, good distribution and open finances; fourth, good performance in fulfilling obligations to the state; and, fifth, good solidarity and education.

Three types of conditions exist among our county production teams. Some production teams are well managed; some are in an intermediate stage; and a minority are poorly managed. In the latter, production and income have decreased while the Spirit of Individual Enterprise is relatively widespread. We must use techniques of leadership that will bring the backward teams up to standard. We must get a good hold on the work of the backward teams and

127

request all communes and brigades to provide one effectively managed production team to serve as a model for the rest to follow. Through the commune rectification movement, we should give special attention to raising the standards of poorly managed and backward teams. In our work of bringing about effective production-team management, it is important that we grasp the following points.

(1) The provision of good cadre members to strengthen leadership. --Many facts have shown that poor production-team management is directly related to the quality of the team committee leadership, and especially to that of the production-team chief. For this reason, conscientious selection must be made. For the purpose of commune rectification, a democratic election of production-team cadre members should be held. Production-team chiefs should be selected from among those who have the necessary qualifications, work well, have experience in agricultural production, understand how to deliberate with the masses, manage affairs impartially, and are capable of handling affairs for the commune members. The production-team leadership groups should be established on the basis that poor and lower-middle peasants hold absolute superiority. There are some affluent middle peasants holding authority in production teams. They should be replaced. Those whose ability is low, but who do not have problems in other respects, should be given further training.

(2) The improvement of business operation and management. --Business management in general has four major aspects, these being labor management, production management, financial management, and democratic management. This is a key problem in raising the quality of farm life and managing production effectively. At present, we still do not have enough experience. This means that we must further summarize and put to use the best part of our experience since the cooperatives were organized. We must maintain the principles of voluntary action, instruction by example, and mutual assistance and benefit, and must establish a sound system of production responsibility whose central objective will be to raise the standards of collective labor and improve the quality of farm work.

There are two major policies that must be carried out correctly in business operation and management. First, we must resolve to carry out a policy of democratic commune management and learn how to follow the mass line. All farming, business management, and distribution problems should be deliberated upon and discussed among the masses before action is taken, and may not be decided upon by any individual cadre or by a minority. Meetings of production-team commune personnel should be held periodically--at least once a month. Special meetings may also be held as the demands of production and distribution require. Second, we must resolve to carry out a policy of frugal commune management. All affairs must be managed after precise and detailed calculations have been made and their economic effectiveness has been investigated. All waste and extravagance must be firmly opposed. The production teams must establish sound systems of financial management. All disbursements should observe the stipulated procedures of authorization. The accountants have the authority to forbid any disbursement not in accord with regulations. Moreover, periodic public announcements concerning the state of work-points, food, funds, and other materials should be made. Cadre members at all levels are servants of the people and ordinary workers and should manage the affairs of the people honestly. They cannot have special privileges and must not engage in graft or excess consumption. Personnel charged with assisting and guiding accounting work should strengthen the financial and accounting work of the production team. Individual finance personnel who are incompetent should be shifted.

The effective management of distribution is an important aspect of effective business management. In distribution it is most important to handle conscientiously the relationships between labor and the population and between savings and consumption. Recompense must be based on labor, but considerations must be given to certain households, particularly to those in distress. In the sphere of savings and consumption we must guarantee the income of the commune members and also consider the need for expanded reproduction. This is especially necessary in fishing districts.

(3) Provided that increased food production can be assured, we must diversify our operations to obtain both increased production and increased income. Food is the basis of agricultural production, and precedence should be given to its expansion. At the same time, consideration should also be given to economic crops and the diversification of operations. On the basis of the needs of our county's agricultural and fishery production and the livelihood of the people, we must greatly expand production in forestry, animal husbandry, and subsidiary industries and also in such economic crops as oil-bearing plants, jute, tea, and fruits. Communes in the mountain regions must restore their jute plants and supply the needs of fishery production.

Production teams should expand their activities in agricultural processing shops (flour mills, oil mills, bean-curd shops), handicraft industries (farm tools, kilns, knitting), animal-husbandry industries (the raising of sows and animal breeding, duck raising, chicken raising, bee keeping), transportation, and fertilizer collection in the villages on the basis of the needs and conditions of the given region.

The diversified operations of the production teams may take different formulas and assume different contents. Some can make use of off-season periods to organize labor for short-haul transportation, fishing, and fertilizer collection. Others can make use of skilled commune members to manage various kinds of workshops. Still others may centralize the supplying of raw materials to be worked by scattered commune members.

IV

Production work for this winter and next spring.--The food production planned for the entire county in 1963 is 142 million catties. (Of this, that of the collective is 132 million catties.) We must guarantee the fulfillment of this plan. For this purpose, the entire county must be mobilized and exhorted to diligent labor in a large-scale agricultural-production movement. At the same time that we emphasize food production, we must strive as well for an overall expansion in forestry, fishing, and animal husbandry and in subsidiary and economic crops. Next year's needs are 750,000 tan from the fisheries, 28,000 mou in afforestation, and the raising of 30,000 head of hogs, 14,000 head of cattle, 2,000 head of sheep, and 550,000 domestic fowls. In addition, we must reach the following quotas in economic crops: 3,000 mou of jute, 2,000 mou of peanuts, 1,780 mou of vegetables, 570 mou of taro, 650 tan of tea, 100 mou of ramie, 50 mou of cotton, and 300 mou of sugar cane. The key to the successful completion of next year's production lies in the effective completion of this winter's work, which will have a decisive significance for the entire coming year, in addition to laying the foundation for next year. The People's Daily editorial "Next Spring Depends on This Winter" has discussed this principle very clearly. Our concrete requirements for this winter's work are as follows:

(1) In agricultural production we must reach a collective food production of 132 million catties. This winter we must attend to the following points.

(a) We must work out our 1963 production plans. Next year's plans and the state purchase goal must be studied and set at this meeting, and then rapidly communicated to the production teams. The production team will be taken as the basic unit for the overall awakening of the masses to conscientious discussions of next year's production plans and to the proposals for revisions in the plans. Then, after being put into final form by the higher levels, the plans will serve as the object of struggle for the masses. This work must be completed before the end of the year on the lunar calendar.

(b) A big effort in water-conservation construction: --Based on a policy of "emphasizing small-scale construction completion and repair by the masses," the initial plans for 1963 call for completion and repair of 182 installations. This will require 380,000 man-days, 230,000 cubic meters of earth and stonework, and 700,000 yüan in costs; it will affect an area of 95,000 mou. Of these projects, four--the Pan-tu stream embankment, the flood dike at Ao-chiang, the spillway at Chung-yang, and the spillway at Nan-kung--are to be undertaken by the municipality, 16 by the county, and 162 by the commune.

These 1963 water conservation works must, for the most part, be constructed during the winter, with only a little of the work to be done in the spring. The specific requirements are to complete the embankment and flood dike projects in the spring, to complete 60 per cent of the reservoir and drainage projects before the New Year festival and the rest before spring plowing, and to complete 50 per cent of the river and sea dikes before spring plowing and the rest of them before the summer harvest.

(c) Fertilizer collection. --During 1963 there should be an increase of more than 50 per cent in fertilizer collection in the county. The major sources are: river and pond mud to fertilize 30,000 mou of rice paddies; 35,000 mou of burned-over paddies; 700,000 tan of marine fertilizer; and plant ash, baked earth, turf, and fertilizer purchased from commune families. The method to be used for the fulfillment of this task is the firm implementation of a policy "emphasizing primarily 'barnyard fertilizer' and secondarily commercial fertilizer." We are adopting a three-phase method involving fertilizer collection of both the routine and the commando type, fertilizer collection by mass movement and special corps, and fertilizer collection by the collectives and by commune members. We must rely on the masses to expand the supply of fertilizer, using systems best suited to their respective regions; we must exhort them to raise hogs to provide fertilizer, to actively expand green fertilizer production, and to experiment conscientiously with various new chemical fertilizers such as calcium superphosphates. We must resolutely carry out our fertilizer-collection policies, purchasing fertilizer from farm families and calling upon the fishermen to increase their collection of marine fertilizer in support of agricultural production.

(d) Plowing and pest control. --The county asks that the second plowing be completed before the New Year festival. For this purpose we have requested that all plowers be chosen at once and that the policies of the "two guarantees" (guaranteed area and guaranteed work-points) and the "four fixed" (fixed oxen, fixed plows, fixed time, and fixed quality) be carried out. In caterpillar control we should carry out a policy of "emphasis on early prevention and full control." Labor should be organized, in close cooperation with current production, for digging out and burning rice stalks in order to eliminate pests in paddies that have suffered severe caterpillar infestations during the past several years.

(e) For the effective field management of winter planting, we must sum up the experiences of the past, organize specialized personnel, fix quotas and guarantee their fulfillment, raise quality requirements, and assure good planting and management. These will be the first moves in completing next year's production.

(f) The effective management of year-end distribution. --Each region, after the completion of the state's assignment, should distribute its food in an earnest attempt to stabilize the livelihood of the masses. The results of food distribution should serve to encourage an optimistic outlook among the majority of the masses; this distribution should also assure that hero families, military and worker families, and large families with few workers can reach general standards in food rations. In the distribution of cash, every effort should be made to increase the income of the members. During the course of distribution the enthusiasm of the masses should be aroused, all finances should be made public, and all distribution methods should have the approval of the masses. It is requested that year-end distribution in the agricultural regions of the county be completed before the end of the year on the lunar calendar. Distribution in fishing regions should also be completed on schedule.

In addition, the area of cultivated land should be greatly expanded in all regions. The selection of superior seeds and the purchase and repair of farm tools for next year should be made as early as possible.

(2) Fish production. --In line with a general desire to expand the fishing industry in this county, we should continue to implement the policy of "concurrent catching and rearing" in planning fishery production for 1963. We must restore and develop shellfish and offshore hatcheries, strengthen seaweed production, equip fishing boats with motors, maintain deep-sea fishing grounds, and raise the volume of unit production. We should expand net fishing and restore the hatcheries and shellfish-propagation areas within one or two years. In addition, we must actively expand fresh-water hatcheries, rearing and sowing fish in areas suitable to fish propagation such as reservoirs, ponds, rivers, and the sea.

In order to realize a fishery production of 750, 000 tan in 1963, the following points should be firmly grasped.

(a) The strengthening of leadership in winter deep-sea production. --The winter production units have already begun production at sea. We call upon all fishermen to go out to sea, set out a large number of nets, and work to the utmost to raise unit production. They should make effective use of reports on fishing conditions and pay attention to safety in production at sea. The offshore industries should know when starfish, shrimp, and hair-tail fish are in season and set enough nets to obtain a large catch. On the basis of the successful completion of winter fishing, preparations for spring fishing, and especially the repair of fishing nets, gear, and boats, should be completed.

(b) The management of seaweed production according to the policy of "maintaining high production, economizing on capital, lowering costs, raising production volume, and suitably expanding in the appropriate districts" should guarantee 8, 044 mou for the entire county in 1963. By now the collection of seaweed shoots has been completed, and the essential business at hand is to step up preparations for nurturing the young shoots. In order to bring about the growth of mature shoots and their early separation, each region can study methods for encouraging shoot growth. This year seaweed growth is a week ahead of last year, and it is predicted that separation of sprouts can take place earlier. We

131

request that it be begun in January and completely finished by the end of February. The output quotas for seaweed have been generally set too low. This should be corrected.

(c) In shellfish propagation, the major business is the completion of preparations for next year's work. We must make definite preparations for mussel cultivation, and priority should be given to preparing the hatching grounds. Young clams should be protected for overwintering, and the parent stock should be controlled. Control of the "spring propagation" of oysters should be strengthened. At the same time, the collecting and selling of oysters should be firmly organized.

(d) In fresh-water rearing, the work is to prepare the young stock.

(3) Animal-husbandry production.--In 1963 we wish to obtain a rich harvest in both food and livestock. There are at present three important points that must be grasped. First, we must continue to carry out the County Committee's management ideas and policies concerning pigs and plowing oxen. As to the problem of pigs, it is most important to retain enough feed and maintain a suitable ratio of young pigs for growth to maturity. As for plow oxen, methods should be established for the awarding of work-points to the personnel in charge of the cattle and for encouraging the production of calves. Second, plow oxen should be protected during the winter, fodder management strengthened, sufficient fodder prepared, and proper temperature levels maintained in cattle pens. Third, there should be a good grasp of disease prevention. Special care should be taken in the prevention of epidemics among pigs, oxen, and domestic fowls.

(4) Forestry production

(a) We must continue to work out a forest-ownership policy. The County Committee has an opinion on the solution of the forest ownership problem that can be studied and put into effect. Every effort should be made to complete this work before the New Year festival.

(b) Cases of excessive tree-cutting should be dealt with conscientiously and severely, especially in cases involving cadre members, in order to establish a proper attitude. At the same time, general education should be initiated, and a system should be determined by the masses, to prevent excessive tree-cutting.

(c) During winter, strict measures should be taken to prevent forest fires in the mountains. This should be done primarily by encouraging the masses to set up agreements for forest protection and fire prevention and by initiating a mass movement for these purposes.

(d) Preparations for spring afforestation should be completed. Precedence should be given to the preparation of seeds and young trees and to plans for forest zones. In the afforestation of coastal regions this year, special attention should be given to planting trees to serve as windbreaks and as sources for firewood.

(5) Subsidiary industrial production

Subsidiary production is an activity being developed by the production teams; it is also an important measure for protecting the collectives and increasing income. Leadership in subsidiary production should be strengthened in all regions and plans should be made for annual production. Moreover, there should be further study of, and decisions on, such concrete problems as the disposition of labor, business management, and the disbursement of earnings.

Two principles should be maintained in the effective management of subsidiary production. First, arrangements for subsidiary production must not be allowed to affect agricultural production. "Subsidiary production should be decreased during active farming periods, and increased during inactive periods." Second, with the exception of small-scale enterprises, subsidiary enterprises should be put under the unified operation of the production team.

Before the New Year festival, and after assuring the availability of labor required for plowing preparations, each production team may allot some of its members to engage in subsidiary production so that some cash income can be distributed to the masses.

We shall next discuss trade, coastal defense, and public security. We must now properly carry out the purchase of subsidiary agricultural products in order to guarantee the fulfillment of the state's purchase assignments for the year. Some food is still owed to the state under the state levy and purchase program and an investigation of the execution of this policy should be made in order to fulfill the assignment. The New Year is approaching, and precedence should be given to getting an adequate supply of all kinds of subsidiary food products and to the positive management of the market. We must strengthen the channels for the exchange of goods through state cooperatives and free markets. We must improve the state stores by strengthening management, and improve the attitude and quality of their service. We must strengthen the cooperatives. At the same time, under the leadership of state stores and with the participation of cooperatives, we must develop the positive aspects and limit the negative aspects of the free market. Through a combination of political education, economic measures, and administrative control we shall strengthen our leadership of the free markets. Supplying and marketing cooperatives must participate in and direct market trading and gain greater control over the sources of goods so as to stabilize the market and prices. In addition, sound organs for market control should be established, and strict registration of industrial and commercial enterprises should be enforced in order to prevent speculation and peddling as well as to expand the fight against capitalist business tendencies.

Coastal defense and public security.--As the New Year approaches, past experiences indicate that it is especially on festival days that coastal defenses against enemy attack must be strengthened. Therefore, the coastal regions should be put on the alert, and military sentry posts should be strengthened in order to ensure our safety during the holidays.

We should at the same time get a firm grasp on the work of maintaining social order. A firm attack should be made on the attempts of the Four Class elements to counterattack the old order and destroy the new. Gambling, theft, and forest vandalism should be punished immediately.

V

All sectors of the economy, businesses, and industries should give positive support to agricultural and fishery production and to the collective economy.

All sectors of the national economy must take agriculture as their foundation and put the support of agriculture and the collective economy in first place. We must clarify the direction of our support of agriculture and fishing and, on the basis of their needs, work out plans for the support of agriculture. When formulating plans, investigation and research should be conducted, and in seeking effective measures, the masses should be consulted.

The industrial sector should continue to carry out the Seventy Articles, reform the organization of labor, strengthen management, develop the foundation of industrial strength which has been established since the Great Leap Forward, and, on the basis of the principles of "concurrent repair and construction, giving precedence to quality, adopting optimal methods for a given region, and non-interference with farm seasons," actively produce and supply the means of production for fishing and agriculture. Emphasis should be given to the production of small iron, bamboo, and wooden implements for farming and fishing. There should be further experimental construction of semimechanized and improved farm tools and of machinery for the processing of subsidiary agricultural products.

The handicraft industry should resolve, through Socialist Education, to follow the course of collectivization. On this basis the handicraft industry should strive not only to produce the high-quality medium and small tools needed in agricultural production and in fisheries, according to the specifications and needs of a given region, but also should systematically organize the transfer of its workers to villages and production teams for maintenance and repair work.

The commercial sector should implement a policy that "expands production and safeguards supply," and it should establish a concept of production in which support of agriculture and of the collective economy is seen as the major task of commercial work. It should actively organize the sources of goods and maintain the supply of raw materials and consumers' goods needed daily in the villages. It should implement price policies, policies for the exchange of agricultural and industrial products, and policies to encourage sales. It should effectively carry out the purchase of farm products in order to strengthen further the alliance between industry and agriculture and to stimulate the expansion of agricultural production.

In addition, the fiscal, financial, food, tax, cultural, communication, and transportation sectors should treat agriculture as the foundation of their work and carry out their own work constructively. The credit departments of the banks should support agricultural production with capital. The agricultural science sector should greatly increase its encouragement and training of farm technicians, gradually establish a technical reform corps, and summarize effective production experiences best suited to the needs of given regions.

In order to complete the work discussed above, the ideological attitudes of party and cadre members must undergo reforms. This requires, on the one hand, the establishment of an attitude of service to the people among party and cadre members and the correction of such incorrect attitudes, now prevalent, as are exemplified in the saying "Being a cadre brings misfortune," in the idea of "being a good fellow" (fear of offending people and thus letting mistakes accumulate), and in the expression "leave a way out." We must establish correct attitudes and encourage cadre members to go about their work with courage and self-awareness. On the other hand, within the party and among the cadre members we must clearly differentiate the boundary between right and wrong, maintain principles, and preserve party regulations and national laws. We must wage a struggle against all kinds of incorrect ideology, speech, and conduct, such as illegal house-construction, superstition, extravagance, decadence and corruption, speculative activities, and gambling. In our work, we must learn how to follow mass and class lines, leading the commune members and the masses to the fulfillment of their tasks.

Comrades, the facts of the past few years fully demonstrate that the majority of party and cadre members are good. The tasks and policies of our party depend upon us for their implementation and realization. We must raise high the Three Red Banners of the General Line, the Great Leap Forward, and the People's

Communes, and join together in carrying out the spirit and resolutions of the Eighth Session of the Tenth Plenum, working diligently toward the further strengthening of the collective economy in order to achieve a rich agricultural and fishing harvest next year, and in order to struggle for a new high in our people's economy!

December 21, 1962

Group II
Socialist Education Movements–General

VIII

[THE SOCIALIST EDUCATION EXPERIMENT IN THE HUA-WU BRIGADE OF THE AO-CHIANG COMMUNE]

THE LIEN-CHIANG COUNTY COMMITTEE OF THE CHINESE COMMUNIST PARTY

FUKIEN PROVINCE

(Approved <u>for</u> transmission)

NUMBER:	086	SECRET
TO:	Each commune Party Committee, 3 copies; each brigade Branch Committee, 1 copy; Municipal Committee, 11 copies	
COPIES TO:	County Committee members, county Branch Committees, party schools, People's Committee Office, Public Security Bureau, courts, Procurator's Office, and Youth's, Women's, and People's Military Corps, one copy each; file, 2 copies (total printing: 340 copies)	
THIS ITEM:	Issued by the Office of the Secretary, Lien-chiang County Committee, Chinese Communist Party, December 29, 1962.	

The Lien-chiang County Committee approves for circulation to each commune Party Committee and brigade Branch Committee the report by the County Committee Working Group concerning the Socialist Education experiment in the Hua-wu brigade.

We hereby transmit to you for your examination the summary report concerning the Socialist Education experiment in the Hua-wu brigade.

It should be pointed out here that in the treatment of policy great weight must be attached to maintaining a "firm" spirit. Under ordinary circumstances, changes should not be made at will. If changes must be made, they should be made according to the stipulations of the Sixty Draft Regulations, and they should be carried out after thorough and repeated discussions by the masses and cadre members on a foundation of mature ideology. On the other hand, when changes are made, their scope should not be excessive. This is especially necessary in the problem of the opening of uncultivated land by individual commune members. This problem must be carefully studied and treated. Changes should not be made simply or lightly.

Is this agreeable? We request the Municipal Committee to indicate its views.

LIEN-CHIANG COUNTY COMMITTEE,
CHINESE COMMUNIST PARTY

December 29, 1962

SUMMARY REPORT ON POINTS IN THE SOCIALIST EDUCATION EXPERIMENT IN THE HUA-WU BRIGADE OF THE AO-CHIANG COMMUNE

The Hua-wu experimental Commune Rectification movement began on November 20, and has been under way for more than a month. It is now basically concluded. We summarize below our concrete methods.

I

Excellent conditions have arisen this year in the Hua-wu brigade, as in other places, as a result of the conscientious implementation of all phases of party policy. The total volume of food production has increased over last year, and over the same period animal husbandry has increased by 2.9 times. The average basic ration for commune members has been 23 catties. The masses respond by calling this year the one of "the four many's and the one few" (that is, much food, much visiting of relatives, many marriages, many births, and fewer thieves). This is the mainstream of conditions. However, in strengthening the collective economy and expanding agricultural production many problems continue to exist. These are principally manifested in two aspects. One of them is confusion in ideology. A considerable number of persons do not have a clear understanding of the direction of socialism, and after the summer harvest, a Spirit of Individual Enterprise consisting of Household Contract Production prevailed on a part of the land. All the dry land and part of the distant paddies (altogether 290 mou, comprising 24 per cent of the total cultivated land) were divided among the households for individual management. The upper-middle peasants took the lead in this high tide, and some commune members who were critical of business management also felt that individual enterprise was a "way out." Those cadre members who have partly lost their revolutionary purpose and who intend to resign their membership in the cadre have drifted with the current. Some poor and lower-middle peasants, positive elements, party members, and Youth Corps members clearly understand that this is an evil tendency, but are lacking in prestige and are unable to persuade the others. This, combined with the threats of the upper-middle peasants that "If you do not agree, we will be asking you for food to eat when production decreases," has caused the Spirit of Individual Enterprise to grow even greater. At the time, 18 per cent of the households were actively advocating individual enterprise, 57 per cent were vacillating and undecided, and 25 per cent were resolutely opposed to it. Many people are planning to "divide the paddies according to family size" after autumn. There are problems in actual work. The Sixty Draft Regulations have not been thoroughly carried out, and food distribution within the production team is not equitable. Business-management plans are deficient. Production-team costs are high; there are many expenditures, and the value of the work-points is low. Individual cadre members have been guilty of graft, excess consumption, and engaging in peddling. The central collective leadership of the branch committees and the activities of various organizations have been insufficient. These problems stand in the way of the expansion of the collective economy and also affect the attitude of the commune members toward the collective economy.

Based on the conditions related above, the work policy of this Socialist Education movement was to carry out broad and thorough education concerning class and conditions, to strengthen the collective economy, to turn back the Spirit of Individual Enterprise, to implement further the Sixty Draft Regulations and to stimulate production. Throughout the entire movement, we carried out the following four phases of work. We conducted education concerning conditions and direction in order to raise self-awareness and clarify confused ideology. We implemented policy in depth and solved concrete problems. We reorganized our entire organization, strengthening party leadership, reforming business management, and improving the production teams. We made the plans for next year's production and created a high tide of winter production. After the movement, the political atmosphere of society, team production, and the spirit of the commune members all took on a new aspect.

The attitude responsible for lowered production no longer existed, and the levy and purchase obligations were completely fulfilled. The winter wheat plan was exceeded, and the first plowing was basically completed. There was a high tide in purchasing and collecting fertilizer as well as digging out river and pond mud.

The commune members saw even more clearly the bright future of the collective economy. No one requested individual enterprise. Public opinion on the streets, in the homes, and in the paddies is no longer attuned to the idea of Household Contract Production and "dividing the fields after autumn," but rather to that of study and discussion about how to increase income and how to plan for next year's collective production. Persons who formerly were actively advocating individual enterprise and persons who acted shamefully toward the collective economy now pass on the street with bowed heads. Cadre members are working with great courage, and elementary school students have even begun to wear red scarves. When we look at the change of thought among the twenty-eight commune members in the Huang Ts'eng-hsia production team, we find that originally five persons, or 18 per cent, requested individual enterprise; sixteen, or 57 per cent, were vacillating; and seven, or 25 per cent, were opposed. Now no one requests individual enterprise, and one person, or 3.6 per cent of the total, thoroughly understands that individual enterprise is impracticable. Eleven persons, or 36.4 per cent, clearly understand that the collective is good and that individual enterprise is bad, and sixteen persons, or 60 per cent, have full faith in the collective economy and make up its backbone. When we first looked at changes in ideology among thirty-two party members, we found eight persons, or 25 per cent, whose understanding was not clear, who had lost their direction, and whose ideology was vacillating; seventeen persons, or 53 per cent, whose understanding was clear but who feared difficulty; and seven persons, or 22 per cent, whose understanding was correct and who firmly opposed household contract production. Now twenty-four, or 75 per cent, have correct understanding and actively take the lead in the correction of individual enterprise and in striving for collective production. There are seven, or 22 per cent, whose understanding is quite clear, who can carry out Branch Committee resolutions, and whose work and production is more diligent than before. Only one person, or 3 per cent of the total, remains muddled in his ideology.

The production-team chiefs generally report that their "companies" are easy to lead, that the commune members go out to work on their own initiative, and that they maintain strict mutual surveillance over each other. Hu Sheng-t'ing, a commune member in the Hu Sheng-yü production team, had formerly gone out to work only ten days each month, and was always grumbling and making up strange tales. He now rises early on his own initiative in order to get his farm tools ready and set out to the paddies to work. As the masses say, "If we work with resolve, we certainly shall have plenty to eat next year."

II

We have divided this period of Socialist Education, which lasted more than a month, into three phases.

In the first phase, based on the Tenth Plenum of the Eighth Central Committee, we conducted a propaganda campaign on conditions, the superiority of collectivization, class education, and the Two Road struggle, proceeding from inside the party to the outside and from the cadre to the masses. This step took about twelve days.

We began with the methods of recollection, contrast, and reckoning of accounts. We used as examples the Chou Ch'iu-wang and Huang T'u-kuan production teams in which the collective economy has been quite effective. We used the changes that have taken place during the last few years in the Niu village production team and the improvement in the living conditions of the poor peasants Ch'en I-p'ing and three other households as examples of the tragic conditions that existed before the liberation and of the class polarity that appeared after land reform and before the cooperatives were organized, and contrasted these with the daily improvement in the life of the masses since cooperativization. It was especially pointed out that after the Sixty Draft Regulations have been carried out a bright future will come to the villages, affirming the correctness of the Three Red Banners and affirming that the improvement in village conditions will lead us forever out of poverty along a basic path toward common prosperity. Citing the risks to which the Spirit of Individual Enterprise has led--disorder in production, inability to fulfill the levy and purchase assignments, the appearance of rich and poor class polarization, the failure of party policy implementation-- we have exposed and conquered the kind of incorrect ideology that is expressed in such sayings as "Individual enterprise is good," "With individual enterprise we eat to the full," "Individual enterprise can increase production," and "Individual enterprise is not a class struggle, but simply a way to eat well." We have discredited capitalist ideology promoting individual enterprise and the abandonment of farming for business, and we have affirmed the confidence and resolution of the commune members in following the road of socialism.

Next, we emphasized education among cadre and party members on the long-term nature and complexity of the class struggle. We explained that the overthrown classes will not die out of their own will, that they are continually plotting for their restoration, and that when the opportunity comes they will use any and all methods to attack the socialist system and the Three Red Banners and to strike at the foundations of the collective economy. In addition, we explained that some among the affluent middle-peasants tend toward capitalism spontaneously and that they attempt to follow the road of capitalism. We pointed out that we must analyze the causes of the Spirit of Individual Enterprise in the light of the class struggle and aid them in increasing their understanding, in making distinctions between boundaries so that they may understand that Household Contract Production is individual enterprise, that individual enterprise is the capitalist road, and these are problems of the Two-Roads struggle and a reflection of class struggle.

In addition to ordinary propaganda meetings, we emphasized the following methods of education.

(1) The relating of living events by living persons, explanation through personal example, and statements concerning the "three hardships":

(a) Statement of hardships under the old society. --At the statement meeting, poor peasants Ch'en I-p'ing, Ch'en Ch'üan-ti, and Hu Yüeh-chen said:

> Our ancestors engaged in individual enterprise for several thousands of years. Before the liberation there were 228 households in Hua-wu village, but only twenty-one households owned land. The rich and affluent middle peasants led a very good life, but the other 90 per cent of the people did not get enough to eat and could not dress warmly. After the flood of 1946, two-thirds of the people in the village left, going to Foochow and other places where they worked as baby nurses, ricksha pullers, cooks, and load carriers. The Wu village production team was originally made up of only thirteen households, and during the thirty-eight years of Kuomintang rule only three tile houses were built. In the few years since the cooperatives were organized, seven new buildings (seventy-four rooms) have been built. Before the liberation, the poor peasant Ch'en Ch'üan-ti was out hauling rickshaws at the age of thirteen; he was beaten and he was cold. At seventeen, he had grown only to four and one half feet in height. Now his wife and children have a house to live in, and he is a member of the cadre at the team level. He said: "Some people say that life now is not as good as in the old society. This is really ungrateful." The poor peasant Lin I-chih commented: "Ch'en Ch'üan-ti has disturbed my peace of mind, and I went without sleep for two nights, recalling my father's tragic death and later feeling shame because earlier I had listened to the minority advocating 'individual enterprise.'"

(b) Statement of the hardships caused by class polarization after the land reform and before the cooperatives were organized. --The land reform cadre members Hu Jen-kuan and Hsia Lao-ch'u stated: "After the land reform (before cooperativization), even though the land had been divided up, the poor people lacked plows and had few oxen. What with natural disasters and epidemics, within two or three years more than seventy households had sold their sons, daughters, and homes and borrowed at high interest in order to plant." When they recall the events of the past, their hearts become cold and their jaws harden. After education, Hu I-chieh (a Youth Corps member), who had originally become ideologically disoriented, resolved on the spot to correct his Spirit or Individual Enterprise and work for collective production.

(c) Statement of the hardships of the Spirit of Individual Enterprise. --When the commune member representative Cheng Ta-hua reckoned accounts, he found that after just a half year of individual-enterprise contracting there were forty-six households in which production had decreased and in which living conditions

143

had become difficult. This had a big effect on the commune members. As the woman cadre member Cheng Ta-mei (Branch Committee) said, "If you don't reckon accounts, you are not clear about the situation; once you've reckoned them, you're in for a shock--then you know that no one with any intelligence can agree to individual-enterprise contracting." Commune member Chao Chin-ch'eng said, "If the Spirit of Individual Enterprise is not corrected, socialism will be blown away." A woman commune member said: "We've had a bad time of it this year. In the future, no matter what happens, the important thing is to listen to what Chairman Mao and the Communist Party say."

In the statement of the hardships brought about by the Spirit of Individual Enterprise, we gave special attention to contrasting it with the effectiveness of collective production and the increased income for the commune members, which indicates that individual enterprise is not as good as the collective.

After exposing the evil conduct of the counterrevolutionary element Chao Yüan-yüan, who spread destructive rumors, incited interest in individual enterprise, and induced commune members into abandoning farming for peddling, we taught the commune members to understand that the class struggle will be protracted, that individual-enterprise contracting is what is desired by landlords and rich farmers, and that it is instigated by class enemies.

(2) Varied mountain songs and tunes. --Based on printed materials and taking into consideration the level of village cadres and the capacities of the masses for comprehension, we wrote up a number of materials and brief outlines concerning conditions and policy propaganda for distribution to party and Youth Corps members, cadre members, and propaganda personnel. In the morning and evening we conducted propaganda and question-and-answer broadcasts. We collected material from commune-member discussions and statements of hardships and, in keeping with the tastes of the masses, prepared twelve popular songs, including "The New Appearance of Hua-wu," "Many are the Advantages of the Collective," and "Strengthen the Collective Economy and Expand Agricultural Production." We used opera tunes, verse dialogues, and mountain songs for instructional singing in order to transform these ideas into public opinion.

By means of this instruction, confused ideology was clarified and conditions were clearly understood; it was also discovered that Household Contract Production, the foundation for the promotion of individual enterprise, and the theory that "dividing management among households means better production and more to eat" were bankrupt. There was a great elevation in the class and socialist awareness of the masses of poor and lower-middle peasants. It was understood that the improvement of conditions in the villages was not accomplished by Household Contract Production, and was, rather, the result of the implementation in the villages of the party's major policies; that the capitalist road cannot be taken, that the collective is definitely better than individual enterprise, that only a small minority can grow rich through individual enterprise, and that the prosperity of this small minority cannot long endure.

Now, 29 per cent of the commune members in the Lin Kuo-t'u production team can fundamentally deal with and correct the problem of Household Contract Production.

The second step was the further implementation of the Sixty Draft Regulations, the solution of concrete policy problems, and the strengthening of the collective economy. This step was completed in ten days.

On the basis of the "Resolutions of the Central Committee for the Strengthening of the Collective Economy of the People's Communes and the Expansion of Agricultural Production," the spirit of the Provincial Committee resolutions, and the Revised Draft Regulations and in the context of the problems discovered during the first step of the education program, we carried out a deep and repeated program of policy study and policy dissemination. On the basis of a clear knowledge of conditions, the affirmation of accomplishments, the summarization of experiences, and the clarification of policy, we organized the commune members in discussions on how they might further strengthen the collective economy. We stimulated the commune members to investigate their own production teams (or brigades) to discover those activities not in accord with the Sixty Draft Regulations and to determine how these should be corrected. During the discussions, many concrete problems were brought out and several methods for their solution were proposed. For the sake of caution, the Branch Committee collected these problems and methods and, after further study through a meeting of commune members' representatives, made resolutions for their implementation. The work groups gave special attention to assisting third-class teams in carrying out policy, solving concrete problems, correcting the spirit of individual enterprise, elevating the work capacities of the production-team cadre members, establishing trust and pride in the collective economy, and overcoming the fear of difficulty.

Methods for handling specific problems [were as follows].

(1) After full and repeated discussions, it was decided that all Household Contract Production land (altogether 296 mou, comprising 24 per cent of the total farmland area) would revert to the production teams for farming after autumn. After the levy and purchase requirements are met, the food produced will be applied to offset the basic ration.

(2) As to the excess allotments of private land, which were not determined according to policy, conditions differ in each team. Some deliberately gave extra shares; for example, the Chao Huo-kuan production team gave each person an extra 0.05 mou. Others have given small extra allotments to individual commune members having bad land or for the convenience of farming; for example, the Hu Sheng-yü production team gave an extra 0.6 mou. The Chao Huo-kuan team, after commune-member discussions had raised their level of understanding, returned the extra portion to the production team. The Hu Sheng-yü team must be made to see that their understanding is incorrect. However, no change will be made for the time being. In the future neither production teams nor individuals may exchange or add to their private plots.

(3) At spring planting, the brigade took over 19 mou of team paddies as "mobile land" and assigned the cultivation of this land to the brigade's industrial workers. The income, with the exception of rations for the workers, went to the brigade·for the construction of a hall. This problem should be seen as an error in the diversion of funds. At the same time, because the building of a hall was not consistent with the principle of frugal commune management, discussions were held and its construction halted. The paddy lands and the income in food were all returned to the individual teams. The problem was investigated and corrected by the cadre members at the brigade level.

(4) Concerning the problems of the loss of 2.6 mou of land taken over by the commune members when the team was redivided and the loss of 11.9 mou when collective land was opened up and usurped by commune members, it was decided that all the land should be returned unconditionally to collective farming or redistributed to the production teams.

(5) Concerning the problem of commune members who, in opening up un-cultivated land, have destroyed land and water maintenance, mountain forests, grass plains, and water conservation works and have impeded communications—for the entire brigade, a total of 13 strips of 31.9 mou—it was decided by discussion in a meeting of the production team and the commune-members' representatives to have a showdown with these persons and to prohibit them from continuing to farm.

(6) How should we handle the problem of commune members who have opened up uncultivated land in excess of policy regulations as to private-plot portions? There are, in all, thirty-one households (comprising 11 per cent of the total households) who have done so. The commune members studied the matter from three aspects: the amount in excess, the general attitude toward collective labor, and the degree of completion of the fertilizer assignment. It was decided to confiscate the reclaimed land of seven households, but not to confiscate that of the rest for the time being. It was also determined that future opening of uncultivated land must first be discussed by the commune members and reported to the brigade for approval and that no one may open up uncultivated land at will.

(7) Concerning the problem of those commune members whose raising of flocks of ducks and geese has affected collective production, the following measures were adopted: mature ducks were bought up, and ducklings, small geese, and mother ducks reverted to production-team management with compensation. Through discussion it was decided that in the future no individual may affect collective production by raising domestic fowls.

(8) Labor quotas were newly determined and adjusted. We eliminated the firm differentiation between the labor force and nonlabor force according to age, and determined the basic labor quotas for all those capable of taking part in labor (including auxiliary labor). As for handicraft-industry workers (principally earth-workers and stonemasons), after a discussion, the teams adopted the general method that their incomes be surrendered to the teams in return for work-points. Provisions were also made for uniform distribution and for rewards for exceeding quotas. It was decided not to supply food at low prices for those engaged in peddling and those who had run off [to the cities].

(9) A study was also made of the purchase ratio for young pigs. The brigade had originally determined to purchase 20 per cent of each litter. This has been adjusted to 50 per cent.

(10) Concerning the problem of food distribution within the production teams, it was determined after study to guarantee basic rations, increase the share distribution according to labor, raise the basic rations, and convert the differentiated rations into a uniform ration.

In addition to these, other problems relating to management, the disposition of cadre members, and the line of demarcation between collective and home subsidiary industries were handled according to policy.

After these problems had been handled, the commune members were generally satisfied. Those engaged in peddling stopped, and more than fifty persons who had run off returned. Persons for whom no labor quotas had been originally set asked to participate in collective production, and the labor force of the production teams increased 15 to 17 per cent.

The third phase was organizational reform: establishment of sound systems, strengthening of party leadership, strengthening of production-team construction, further implementation of the policies of democratic and frugal commune management, elevation of the leadership level and work capacities of members of the production-team cadre, improvement of the business-management system, planning for next year's production, and stimulation of a high tide of winter production.

First, through summarizing the leadership experiences of the Branch Committee and the work of Socialist Education, party members were organized and stimulated to examine themselves and to conduct criticism and self-criticism according to the Eight Points to Observe for Communist Party members, according to the nature and mission of the party. The results of the education were affirmed and the required systems established. Three new party members (not yet approved) emerged.

Second, we reorganized and improved the organization of the Communist Youth Corps and the Women's Representatives Committee, selected new leadership personnel, passed on six new corps members, and persuaded five overage members to withdraw from the corps.

Third, we reorganized and reelected the team committees, reinforced the poor and lower-middle farmer leadership framework within the production teams, and determined the production-team supervisory personnel.

Fourth, we further implemented the policy of democratic and frugal commune management. Year-end accounts were balanced, the next year's preliminary production plans were set for each team, and the commune members pledged to love the nation and the commune.

At the same time, we conducted among the cadre and commune members another educational campaign on conditions and missions; on the correct handling of the relationships between the state, the collective, and the individual; and on the policies of frugal and democratic commune management. The masses were called upon to effect production economy and frugal commune management, unite in strengthening the collective economy, and complete winter production effectively in a struggle for attaining a rich harvest next year, meet the new high tide of the nation's economy, and achieve a new victory of socialist construction.

For party members, we also conducted an educational campaign emphasizing basic party knowledge, class struggle, devoted service to the people, and being a good Communist Party member. We called upon them to develop the fine traditions of the party, raise the level of their political ideology, improve their work attitudes further, serve the people even better, bear their responsibilities conscientiously, and be courageous in their struggle against persons and acts harmful to the collective interest. We explained that the Branch Committee is the bastion of the villages and that it functions as the model and the vanguard in the class struggle and in the Two Road struggle.

For the women masses, we conducted an educational campaign to promote production, economy, and frugal household management, to eradicate superstition, and to oppose marriage-by-sale. We called upon them to participate actively in collective labor, make precise calculations, consolidate their household duties and manage them harmoniously, and, with the prerequisite of not affecting the collective interest, strive to expand household subsidiary enterprises and increase their income.

For the militia, we conducted an educational campaign on the Three Great Disciplines, the Eight Points to Observe, and the Ten Rules to Obey. We called upon them to participate actively in collective labor, increase their watchfulness, strengthen their struggle against the enemy, maintain public order, and strengthen the rear echelon.

III

Strengthening the collective economy and correcting the tendency toward individual enterprise make up a serious political and ideological struggle and also require a broad range of difficult and detailed organizational work. There are problems of class struggle (including the Two-Road struggle), problems of ideology and understanding, and problems of concrete policy. When ideology and understanding are not uniform, then the phenomena of obstinacy and obstruction will occur. Once understanding is uniform and direction is clear, concrete problems are easy to handle. We have at this stage come to appreciate the following points.

(1) The concepts embodied in the questions "Can individual enterprise increase production?" and "Is individual enterprise a reflection of class struggle, or is it merely for the purpose of getting enough to eat?" need to be clarified through the reckoning of accounts and by debate before we can attain our objectives of heightened awareness, clear understanding of direction, and unified ideology. If rectification of the Spirit of Individual Enterprise and the handling of concrete policy problems are discussed in this way, the feeling that "the government has not asked us to work" will not arise and a determination to eliminate poverty permanently and protect the collective interest will be established.

(2) The facts prove that by means of recollection, contrast, and the summarizing of experiences a great many events may be used to conduct education about class and direction, that many living examples can be used to assist the commune members in clearly understanding the glorious future of collectivization, that clear banners can be set up to stimulate the commune members into an enthusiasm for effective collective production, and that reason can be used to convince people and solve ideological problems.

(3) We must implement the class line. Whether in conducting education on conditions and classes or in handling concrete policy problems, we must rely closely on the poor peasants (including the lower-middle peasants) and unite with the middle peasants. Many events have proved that the lower and middle peasants are not only numerous, but also that their awareness is high, that they are the most obedient to the party, and that they are the most active in supporting collectivization. They constitute the backbone of the party's power in all work in the villages, and . . .[1]

---

[1] The remaining three to four hundred characters are illegible.

IX

[COMMUNE RECTIFICATION PLAN OF THE LIEN-CHIANG COUNTY COMMITTEE]

THE LIEN-CHIANG COUNTY COMMITTEE OF THE CHINESE COMMUNIST PARTY, FUKIEN PROVINCE:

COMMUNE RECTIFICATION PLAN OF THE LIEN-CHIANG PARTY COMMITTEE FOR THIS WINTER AND NEXT SPRING

NUMBER: 004

TO: Each Commune Party Committee, 3 copies; Brigade Party Branches, 1 copy each, Work Group Chiefs, 1 copy each; Municipal Committee, 11 copies

COPIES TO: County committeemen; Party Committee of the 6579th, 6720th, 6581st and 6662d Corps; each branch of the County Committee; Youth, Womens' Workers, and Military Corps; People's Committee; and the Public Security Bureau--one copy each; file, 2 copies (total printing: 375 copies)

ITEM: 6 pages, issued by the Office of the Secretary, Lien-chiang County Committee, Chinese Communist Party, January 5, 1963

The agricultural communes in our county, having undergone several years of readjustment and improvement, are basically sound. The majority of communes, brigades, and teams are very well managed. However, a series of problems have occurred this year after the rise of the Spirit of Individual Enterprise. The major problem is that some cadre and commune members have lost their direction. They have become confused in their ideology. Tendencies toward low production, emphasizing the individual, and neglecting the collective have become widespread and severe. Furthermore, a number of problems in operation and management remain to be solved. A major problem has arisen because we have not maintained work records and work-point evaluations, and because we were lax about the labor-and fertilizer-management system. For these reasons, we have not been distributing rewards and punishments. At the same time, there are some areas in which problems in work attitudes exist among cadre members and are displayed in undemocratic attitudes, in not maintaining open financial transactions, and in greed, corruption, and excess consumption. On this basis the County Committee's proposal to hold a commune rectification movement this winter and next spring is completely necessary and timely. We must by means of this commune rectification movement strengthen socialist education, strengthen the stand of socialism in the villages, and maintain faith in collectivization. On this foundation and on the basis of the Sixty Draft Regulations we shall solve our policy problems, establish sound systems of operation and management, reform work attitudes among cadre members, and strengthen the solidarity between the cadres and the masses, bringing about an even stronger expansion of the people's communes.

I. THE REQUIREMENTS AND CONTENT OF COMMUNE RECTIFICATION

The essence of the commune rectification movement is Socialist Education and the implementation of the Revised Draft Regulations Governing Rural People's Communes. On this foundation, we shall correct the Spirit of Individual Enterprise, improve operation and management, and improve the production teams.

(1) There are four aspects to Socialist Education: education about conditions (the present good conditions in the villages), class education (the struggle between the two classes and the Two Roads), education in patriotism (subordination to national interests, support of cities and industry), and policy education (on the basis of the Sixty Draft Regulations in combination with other policies). In addition, we must also conduct education on internationalism. Through education, we shall bring the cadres and the masses to a clear understanding of the following points.

(a) Present conditions are excellent, and the future is bright. The principal causes of these excellent conditions are the leadership of the party, the correctness of the Three Red Banners, the elimination of confusion in understanding, and the maintenance of faith in victory.

(b) Classes exist, and the class struggle will be lengthy, complex, repeated, alternately resurgent and recessive, and sometimes acute.

(c) The Spirit of Individual Enterprise is a reflection of the two-class, Two Road struggle. The party's basic line in the agricultural problem is, first, to bring about the collectivization of agriculture, and, second, to bring about mechanization and electrification. This is the basis of the maintenance of socialism and the defeat of capitalism.

(d) To bring about an understanding of the superiority of the collective and of the harmfulness of individual enterprise, the emphasis will be on comparing their differences in the overcoming of natural and personal calamities, in the achievement of socialist industrialization, and in the mechanization of agriculture. It will then be understood that we cannot pursue individual enterprise and that it is only through socialism that the peasants can divest themselves of poverty.

(e) A clear understanding of the relationships between the state, the collective, and the individual. --We must subordinate ourselves to the interests of the state, and at the same time clarify the relationship and strengthen the alliance between industry and agriculture.

(2) The implementation of the Draft Regulations Governing Rural People's Communes and the systematic solution of related policy problems. --After education, the eradication of the Spirit of Individual Enterprise should become the urgent demand of the masses. This will naturally lead to the handling of policy problems. We know that we must give careful consideration to the handling of policy, and that under ordinary conditions we should not act indiscriminately. In principle, our point of departure should be the strengthening of the collective economy and the beneficial expansion of production. At the same time, we should differentiate between the Spirit of Individual Enterprise and correct management on the one hand, and between

it and domestic subsidiary industries on the other, so that we will not go to the opposite extreme.

(3) Systems for the effective management of production teams and the establishment of sound management institutions. The "five goods" represent the standard for effective production-team management. These five goods are: first, a firm stand, democratic work attitudes, and fairness in handling affairs; second, good operation and management, with increased production and income; third, good distribution and open finances; fourth, good performance in fulfilling obligations to the state; and, fifth, good solidarity and education. After the policy problems have been dealt with, the masses should be mobilized to investigate, study, and summarize past business-management systems and methods (especially in the fields of labor and fertilizer distribution), preserving those that are good and revising, supplementing, and systematizing those that are unsuitable in order to make them good. Finally, these should be put into effect through either a representative or a commune-membership meeting.

(4) The reform of the work attitudes of cadre members.--In the course of the commune rectification movement, we must organize cadre and party members to study the basic party doctrines for the self-education of Communist Party members, to study the Three Great Disciplines and the Eight Points to Observe, and also to study the seventh chapter of the Draft Regulations Governing Rural People's Communes, concerning the cadre problem. This is in order to raise the class awareness of cadre members and to make them feel that it is an honor to be of service to the people, and also to establish a firm stand, a clear understanding of our direction, the courage to struggle against bad tendencies, and the reform of such incorrect attitudes as "fear of failure" and the "doctrine of being a good fellow." In addition, we wish to educate the cadre members to maintain principles, and to take the lead in observing national and party laws, and to discourage them from engaging in corruption or excess consumption, breaking regulations, and falling into depravity. They should be taught to work honestly and to perform their work effectively. After commune rectification, there should be a democratic election of cadres, [which will be] a summons to the cadres to reform their deficiencies and to complete their work well. We should encourage the cadres to seek reelection. More than two-thirds of those elected should be from the poor and lower-middle peasant groups.

II. METHODS, STEPS, AND TIME REQUIREMENTS IN THE COMMUNE RECTIFICATION MOVEMENT

(1) The commune rectification movement is an ideological education movement, the essence of which is Socialist Education. If Socialist Education can be made profound and far-reaching, other policy and business-management problems can be effectively handled. We must therefore resolve to carry out Socialist Education effectively. Of its methods, the most important are recollection (recollection of conditions before the liberation), the airing of complaints (complaints about past political, economic, and private enterprise hardships), contrast (the contrasts between the old and the new societies and between collective and private enterprise), and the reckoning of accounts (taking stock of the changed economic and political accounts, party support of peasants, and the class polarity and production losses accompanying private enterprise). In certain regions small-scale exhibitions may be held, and education by contrast and living example may be conducted. The point of emphasis in Socialist Education should be the struggle between socialism and capitalism and between the two classes. So far as the Spirit of Individual Enterprise is concerned, the most representative points of confusion in a region should be

151

brought out and thoroughly clarified through discussions, comparisons, and the presentation of facts and arguments. Socialist Education must be broad and deep. For this purpose, the methods of education must be flexible, detailed, and varied. Education may be conducted through large meetings, in small discussion groups, or by visits to inquire about hardships and accumulate lists of hardship cases. In addition, all types of propaganda devices should be put to thorough use--for example, rustic songs, street plays, blackboard reports, slogans, and express reports--so that the message will reach into the homes and become fixed in the people's minds.

(2) The rectification movement in brigades may, in general, be carried out in three steps.

The first step is the calling of meetings at all levels to arouse the masses and to initiate Socialist Education. In this step, the method is to hold meetings and conduct education from the inside to the outside, and from above to below. Ideology and direction should be clarified. The time required for this step should be long enough to permit a thorough solution of problems.

The second step is to solve problems related to policy. The revised Sixty Draft Regulations should first be made known and seriously discussed among the masses. After this, through meetings of representatives of the cadre members, the masses, and commune members there should be repeated study and solution of problems related to policies that are not consistent with the Sixty Draft Regulations. The Sixty Draft Regulations should be well carried out.

The third step is to organize and arouse enthusiasm for production and, through the movement, to clarify internal conditions and problems in the party, the Youth Corps, the militia, and the women's organizations. After this, criticism and self-criticism should be initiated through general meetings of party members and meetings within all organizations in order to correct tendencies toward error and to raise the level of understanding. During the movement, emphasis should be placed on making examples of good cadre members, good party personnel, and good commune members. At the same time, positive elements should be cultivated and those qualified should be absorbed into the Youth Corps and the party. Finally, a mass meeting should be held to announce the conclusion of the commune rectification and to inspire the masses to attain a high tide of production. In this way, the Socialist Education of a brigade can be accomplished in about one month.

(3) The Socialist Education movement in this county has been planned in two groups. The first group will comprise about 100 brigades and will be managed by county and commune cadres. However, after the conclusion of the commune meetings, the Socialist Education will be fully carried out in both the first and second groups. The second group of brigades will rely principally on the party Branch Committee for management, rather than on cadres. After the period of education, problems related to present production as well as clear and easily resolvable policy problems may be handled by the party Branch Committee. Only the harder-to-handle policies and concrete problems of the third step need await the attention of cadres after the completion of the work in the first group. In this way, the county can complete the first step of Socialist Education by about the end of January, complete the work of the first group by the middle of February, and complete the entire movement during the first third of March. Because of the early onset of spring in 1963, each region must make a strict allotment of time and, in a spirit of "moving ahead rather than falling behind," strive to complete their work.

III. SOME PROBLEMS NEEDING ATTENTION DURING THE COMMUNE RECTIFICATION MOVEMENT

(1) The heart of the commune rectification movement must be production. The purpose of commune rectification is the expansion of production, and the two must not impede each other. This will require the party Branch Committee to assign personnel to manage production and to investigate its program section by section. When initiating Socialist Education and handling specific policy problems, we must start with and proceed around production, to prevent its disassociation from production. It is especially in the handling of policy that we must give our attention to solving policy problems related to present production, in order to inculcate a positive spirit of collective production among the masses and effectively to complete production.

(2) The commune rectification movement must have education as its center of gravity, pointing out good persons, good deeds, good cadre members, and good commune members as examples. Struggle meetings and key-point criticism should not take place during the movement, but the counterattack, restoration, and destructive conduct of Four Class elements should be attacked according to law.

(3) The emphasis in Socialist Education will be on party and cadre members. If the ideology of these persons can be resolved, then all work will proceed well. Therefore, education should first be conducted within the party and among the cadres. This should consist of linking it to ideology by appropriate criticism and self-criticism. The ideology of party and cadre members must be made deep and clear.

(4) In the course of the commune rectification movement, attention must be given to the poor-peasant line and to the mass line. Rely on the poor and lower-middle peasants, and unite the middle peasants. In the handling of concrete problems, democracy should be fully practised and the masses should be relied upon to complete the work.

(5) In order to carry out the commune rectification movement effectively, each commune should concentrate its efforts on one brigade, drawing experiences and discovering problems therefrom and thereby furthering the expansion of the movement.

LIEN-CHIANG COUNTY COMMITTEE,
CHINESE COMMUNIST PARTY

January 5, 1963

X

HOW THE LIEN-T'ENG BRIGADE UNITED THE SOCIALIST EDUCATION MOVEMENT WITH SOLVING THE PROBLEM OF THE LABOR FORCE THAT HAD EMIGRATED

The Lien-teng brigade was one of the brigades in the Ao-chiang commune with a poor work foundation. The Spirit of Individual Enterprise was quite intense, and many members of the labor force had run off [to the cities]. Since last year, the number of brigade members who left at various times to engage in earthwork, carpentry, odd jobs, and dealings in oxen and pigs totaled 106 persons and comprised 50 per cent of the total labor force. In the Li T'ai-an production team, in which this was most severe, nineteen persons of a labor force of twenty-three, or more than 80 per cent of the total force, successively emigrated and there was essentially no one to handle collective production. Of the 106 persons who emigrated, there were sixty-two, or 58 per cent of the total number, who went to work (among these, thirty-one were earth workers and stonemasons, three worked as carpenters, and twenty-seven did odd jobs). Forty-four, or 42 per cent of the total number, entered into speculative business and reaped large profits, amounting to 8,200 yüan (among these, there were four persons who each made more than 1,000 yüan). These persons, with the exception of a minority who had received approval to engage in technical work, for the most part emigrated on their own accord and did not hand over their income to the collective. Even more serious were the instances of six technical workers who took up work as foremen outside [the collective] and engaged in exploitation. For example, since spring of last year, Li Chao-fang has undertaken seven construction projects, from which he earned 7,500 yüan. In addition to lending out 4,200 yüan, he bought silks, cotton, foreign cloth, a watch, gold bars, oxen, farm tools, and furniture. He said to his wife: "You don't have to take part in collective labor. Even if there were a three-year drought, we could not starve to death." After the masses had seen this, their eyes brightened, and everyone thought about going out and doing the same. As a result, there was no one left to handle collective production . . .[1]

I

They felt out the situation, made use of contrast, concentrated their forces, and took a firm grasp on ideological education. At first, many persons were thinking of going outside to work rather than staying at home to work in agriculture. They said: "If you go outside to work, you will have a big income and will get rich quickly. Besides, it is relaxed and free, compared with staying home and working in agriculture."

---

[1] A section is missing here.

In order to solve this problem, model teams and model households from the brigade were selected for instructing the masses through reckoning of accounts and contrast, by means of real persons and events. The T'ang Hsiang-ti production team was one of those selected. Last year, very few in the labor force of this team emigrated, there being in fact only one (and he only for a little while) from the team's labor force of nineteen persons. Because they had concentrated their forces and because everyone's ideology was stable, collective production was managed very well and food production and ration standards were very high, each person being able to eat, on the average, 27 catties a month (including the work rations). Another was the Li T'ai-an production team, in which conditions were fundamentally similar to those in the T'ang Hsiang-ti team but an excessive number had emigrated, nineteen out of a total labor force of twenty-three persons, and consequently production was managed very badly and food production and income decreased. Each person had a monthly average ration of only 17 catties, and the value of the work-points was only about half that of the T'ang Hsiang-ti team. After a detailed reckoning of accounts and a concrete contrast in this manner, right and wrong became clearly distinguished, the understanding of the commune members was raised, and everyone realized that although some could earn some money by running off to work, it was impossible to make up the losses from decreased food production. All expressed a desire to return to farming. For example, commune member Li Chao-chien undertook self-examination in everyone's presence; he examined his past faults of running off as he pleased, not taking part in collective labor, and not concerning himself with collective production. He even instructed the masses by telling the facts of his own misfortunes. He said: "We cannot just reckon small accounts and neglect the big accounts, giving up watermelon to grow sesame. If you do not understand this principle, you will run into misfortune eventually."

II

As the movement matured, party and cadre members took the lead in action, especially in bringing about the return of persons among their own families, relatives, and friends. This led to good results. For example, Branch Committeeman Chou Te-shih, on the day following the completion of instruction, went off to P'an-tu to influence his younger brother Chou Ts'ai-tzu toward returning. By means of his patient persuasion and instruction, not only did he get Chou Ts'ai-tzu to return, but four other persons, including T'ang I-chin and T'ang Chin-t'ai, who had accompanied him, returned with him of their own accord and stated that they would not again act in such a manner, guaranteeing that they would remain contentedly at home and take part in collective production.

III

Grasp the essential points, attack the vital parts, and initiate a back-to-back struggle. --On the basis of completed ideological education, they stimulated the masses, using the methods of enumeration of facts and discussion of principles, and relentlessly exposed and criticized the deceitful means and exploitative conduct of foreman Li Chao-fang, revealing his true nature and, moreover, causing him to be viewed by the masses as disreputable. Their principal method was to gather a number of good commune members who had been severely exploited to serve as the injured persons, and to conduct disclosures and complaints of hardships at all meetings. For example, commune member Li Chao-chien said: "Li Chao-fang wanted us to take the road of capitalism and exploitation of others. Last year, after the summer disaster, he came to my house to get us aroused, saying that there was no profit to be had from farming and that by going outside to work for a month we could get several hundred yüan in income and that after a year of this, we would still have plenty to eat even if we went for two or three years without doing any labor. And what were the results of this? Seven persons in the team ran off and there was a decrease in the autumn food production. Even though I earned more than 300 yüan, my expenses on the outside were high, and when I returned I had to buy rations and make up my quota, so that I ended up having to borrow more than 170 yüan. This is what I call a loss for both the individual and the collective."

Commune Members Chou Chin-shui, T'ang I-mao, and Li T'ai-ch'üan made a disclosure, saying: "Last year Li Chao-fang asked us to go to Huang-ch'i to undertake a construction project. More than 800 yüan was realized from the project. He himself did not do any work, but he took more than 500 yüan." Commune member Li Kuang-ti said: "Li Chao-fang's methods of exploiting others are very cruel. For example, anyone he chooses to go out to work with him must first give him three to four days of voluntary labor (handling his private plot for him)." These methods of exploitation are even worse than those of the capitalists and landlords under the old society. After these disclosures and criticisms not only was Li Chao-fang viewed as disreputable, but the awareness of the broad masses of commune members was raised and their direction clarified. In addition, there was active coordination with the tax authorities, who investigated Li's taxes. He was fined 4,300 yüan, of which he has up to now paid 1,100 yüan. This kind of action has led to a good response from the masses. They say: "This is really the way to manage things. Otherwise, it is like a bolt of thunder without any rain and cannot solve problems."

IV

After the education program, they stimulated the masses to study related policy problems, set off clear boundaries, and determine their objectives. What are workers? What does being both a worker and a farmer mean? After a discussion of these problems, everyone came to realize that those who went out to work before 1958 were considered to be workers (thirty-one persons out of the entire brigade), and that those who studied masonry and carpentry after 1958 were considered to be both workers and farmers. (1) Workers are permitted to go out to work on a permanent basis. Those who are both workers and farmers work principally at farming, and during off-seasons they are uniformly organized by the production teams in working outside. Their incomes should be surrendered to the collective, and they cannot move about as they please. (2) Those workers who go out for long periods are divided into classes and pay the team at fixed intervals. Individuals are separated into three classes according to their technical level and their physical strength. Each person in the first class must pay the production team 40 yüan a month, each person in the second class must pay 35 yüan a month, and each person in the third class must pay 30 yüan a month. Payment is made monthly and accounts are balanced annually. After they pay the money to the production team, they will be credited with work-points. Six work-points are given for each yüan of cash, and these work-points are distributed like agricultural work-points, including treatment as excess-output rations and subsidiary agricultural goods. (3) They put the reward-and-punishment system into strict effect on the basis of complete reward or complete indemnity. A reward of six work-points was given per yüan of excess, and similarly six work-points were subtracted per yüan of deficiency. (4) In the future, when technical workers go out to work, they may not ask production-team farm labor to accompany them. If they really need the assistance of odd-job workers, they should obtain in advance the approval of the production team, which will organize the required work force. They may not organize it privately, or they will be required to make good the production losses. By means of the measures related above, labor has, by and large, been stopped from leaving the collective. Within the brigade, forty-four peddlers have given up their activities, and sixty-two persons (excluding thirty-one who work outside on a permanent basis) have returned to participate in collective production, thereby hastening the progress of preparations for planting and production.

February 14, 1963

XI

THE "FOUR CONTRASTS" MATERIAL
OF THE SHANG-SHAN BRIGADE

During the Socialist Education movement we utilized persons and events from our own teams and organized the "four contrasts" material for the purpose of conducting education among the masses. In this way, right and wrong were clearly distinguished and made easy for the masses to comprehend. The four contrasts were as follows.

(1) The contrast between the Liu Yu-sai production team, which through maintenance of collective production increased its production and income, and the Yang Li-en production team, which through the Spirit of Individual Enterprise seriously decreased its production and income, follows.

Cadre members of the Liu Yu-sai production team were united and the commune members liked the collective. Last year, rice production was 914 catties per mou, and work-points were valued at 1.07 yüan for each ten points. Each commune member had an annual basic ration of 350 catties, to which was added 22 catties per person from the spring harvest, 12 catties in excess-quota food production, and about 15 catties from the Small Freedoms sector. Thus, the entire annual ration reached 404 catties, an average of 47.5 catties per person per month.[1] After autumn, the spirit of the commune members was even higher. Resolving to complete production and strengthen the collective, they actively invested their capital in production. Now 80 per cent of the estimated 25 tan of fertilizer per mou for the spring planting has been collected, and preparations are being made to buy an additional 150 tan of marine fertilizer in order to assure that this year's rice production will reach 1,000 catties per mou. The entire team is striving to attain a goal of 1,001 catties.

The principal reasons why this team was able to operate effectively are as follows.

(a) Cadre members were united, direction was clear, resolve was great, production measures were forceful, and methods were correct. The commune members responded by saying: "The team chief is the helmsman, and the Four Personnel are the pilots who both direct and take the lead in production."

(b) The commune members were diligent, their faith was strong, and they put the collective interest ahead of private interests. When contradictions arose between private and collective production, they were able, with self-awareness, to

---

[1] The separate elements of the annual ration add up to 399 catties, not 404, and the average monthly ration figures out to 33.25 or 33.75 catties (at 399 or 404 per year), not 47.5.

give precedence to the collective and only after that to pursue their private interests. The work-attendance rate was regularly above 90 per cent. For example, in the War Preparation period, other teams engaged in the farming of private land to a great extent. This team, however, still maintained the collective course, actively gathering more than 4,000 tan of fertilizer and thereby solving the problem of the shortage of fertilizer on 50 mou of land during spring planting and assuring a rich summer harvest.

(c) Finance was open, and the details of the accounts were clear, the accounts being balanced annually and monthly. Accounts were made public every ten days. The commune members were satisfied, and their positive spirit in production was thereby stimulated.

[In contrast,] the chief of the Yang Li-en production team took the lead in emigrating to do odd jobs, and eleven full-time workers, or 26 per cent of the total labor force, followed his example. The collective-production work-attendance rate was only 45 to 50 per cent. Production was not completed effectively, the production of rice reaching only 706 catties per mou (land conditions were similar to those of the Liu Yu-sai team), and work points being valued at only 0.96 yüan for each ten points. The annual basic ration for the commune members was 144 catties, to which were added 11 catties per person from the spring crop, and about 10 catties from private farming, bringing the total annual ration to 165 catties, or only 15.5 catties per person per month.[2] The commune members have become critical, and the cadre cast blame on the commune members. At present the team has collected only 50 per cent of the 25 tan of fertilizer per mou required for spring planting.

This team is backward for the following reason.

(a) The cadre members of the production team have problems. They are severely afflicted with the ideology of individual enterprise and do not like serving as cadres; they feel that serving as a cadre is a misfortune. Since they themselves cannot participate in the farming of free land, they took the lead in going out to do "rat work" and thereby exerted great influence on the commune members.

(2) The contrast between commune-member Lin Tsu-jui, who loved the collective and was intent on collective production, and commune-member Liu I-chung, who was not intent on collective production and who left to work outside, follows.

There are four members (and a labor force of two) in the family of commune-member Lin Tsu-jui. Last year they made 2,200 work-points which were exchanged for 325 yüan in cash. Adding to this the income from family subsidiary enterprises, there was a surplus after the costs of food and sundry expenses for the entire family had been deducted.

Liu I-chung (a family of four, with a labor force of two) thought only about getting rich and was not intent on collective production. During the first half of last year he ran off to Chien-ning to work for three months. After paying for his food and other expenses, he did not have enough money for his return fare. Finally, he sold his wool and cotton clothing and, after his return, borrowed 120 catties of rations from the production team. He came to grief, and had a good lesson. During the last half of the year, he actively participated in collective production, and when the year-end accounts were balanced, he was given a cash share of 70 yüan.

---

[2] The monthly figure should be 13.75, not 15.5.

159

(3) The contrast between the free marriage of Hsieh Chih-chien and the marriage-by-sale of his cousin Hsieh Chih-hsiang follows.

Hsieh Chih-chien is the cousin of Hsieh Chih-hsiang. Last year he and his sweetheart, Yang An-mei, fell in love and were married. Before the marriage, Yang An-mei's mother objected to the low wages of 33 yüan which Chih-chien received as a cadre member. An-mei, however, was resolute. She said, "Even if I have to live under the eaves, I shall marry Chih-chien." Since their marriage, the two have lived together happily, have a good livelihood, and have not had any quarrels. Now she is pregnant.

Hsieh Chih-hsiang's marriage had been arranged by his father before the liberation, and the couple did not know each other before the marriage. Since their marriage, in 1956, their relationship has not been good. They are at odds with each other two days out of three and quarrel on the third, and each feels resentment toward the other. In the eight years up till now they have had no children, to the displeasure of their parents.

(4) The contrast between commune member Cheng Shui-mei, who is diligent in household management, and commune member Yang Ts'ung-t'ai, who is extravagant, follows.

Commune member Cheng Shui-mei has a family of six. Her eldest daughter is thirteen years old and her youngest son is five. Her husband works outside, and his wages are about 30 yüan. Of the family, only she participates in labor for collective production, and their circumstances are very difficult. However, she is careful in her household calculations, and has their livelihood well ordered. As a result, everyone lives happily.

Commune member Yang Ts'ung-T'ai has a family of four, of whom two are workers. Although their circumstances are quite good, she is not skillful at organizing their livelihood. Last year, they had a cash surplus of more than 50 yüan and a food surplus of more than a hundred catties. This year she gave a thirty-nine-table birthday party for her father, on which she spent more than 500 yüan. After allowing for the receipts for birthday presents, she was still short more than a hundred yüan. Their food supply was exhausted, and she also had to sell cloth-ration coupons worth ten feet of material.

February 28, 1963

XII

MATERIAL FOR PROPAGANDA PERSONNEL

(For oral dissemination only)

A large-scale Socialist Education movement has already begun in our country. Why must we conduct a Socialist Education movement? Our principal reasons for initiating a Socialist Education movement are to heighten the awareness of socialist ideology on patriotism, collectivism, and internationalism among the people of the county and to establish good social tendencies. We also wish to stimulate diligence, to strive for production and economy, and to give powerful support to agriculture in order to obtain a rich harvest this year, completely fulfill state plans, and win a new victory for socialism.

As everyone knows, there has already been an extensive growth of socialism in our nation and a great change in the form of the nation's economy as a result of construction under the two five-year plans. This year, we entered on the first year of the third five-year plan for the development of socialism. We must continue the hard struggle and exert heroic labor to establish a strong socialist nation with modern industry, agriculture, science, culture, and defense. There are now many tasks that face us and many kinds of work to be done. On what do we rely? On the people. We rely on the awareness and diligence of the people, because all work must depend on the people for its execution. If the people have a high awareness and are industrious, the work will be done well. The People's Liberation Army, with its inferior weapons and equipment, could defeat powerfully armed enemies because of the high awareness and great bravery of its soldiers. Our victory over three years of successive and severe natural disasters was due to the awareness and persistence of the nation's people in overcoming difficulties. Therefore, the expansion of Socialist Education is the key to the effective completion of all our work.

In regard to the problem of raising socialist awareness, we shall discuss the following eight problems. [1]

(1) First the collective, then the individual. Our nation is a socialist state in which public ownership is basic. There are two kinds of public ownership, one being ownership by all the people and the other being collective ownership, both of which are forms of socialist ownership. Individual ownership is merely an aid and

---

[1] The phrases describing the eight problems occur also in Documents XVIII and XIX.

161

a supplement, and it occupies only a subordinate and secondary position. Our nation's production and the livelihood of the people rely primarily on the economic systems of collective ownership and ownership by all the people. For this reason we must firmly support and strengthen these latter systems of ownership.

(2) <u>First the nation, then the individual.</u> Only when we have a nation can we then have families. The nation is now under the leadership of the Communist Party, and we are a nation of workers and peasants--of all people who work. Only if our nation grows strong and prosperous can we divest ourselves of poverty and backwardness. The policies, plans, and tasks set by the party and the state are for the general good, reflecting the needs and representing the best interests of the majority of the people. We must therefore consider the needs of the nation first and those of the collectives and the individual later.

(3) <u>First ask of oneself, then of others.</u> This is the necessity for a spirit of self-sufficiency,[2] in which one relies primarily on one's own strengths, and only afterward on outside assistance and support from the state. We must have faith in and rely on the masses if our work is to be accomplished quickly and well. We must not seek assistance from above in all our affairs, nor ask others for things. We must develop the Communist characteristic of "keeping our difficulties to ourselves, and extending our conveniences to others."

(4) <u>First reprimand oneself, then reprimand others</u>. That is to say, in our relationships with others we should be strict with ourselves and lenient with others. When contradictions occur with others, we must first examine ourselves. We must conduct self-criticism and self-examination, first reprimanding ourselves and later assisting and criticizing others. If everyone asks of himself in this way and sincerely helps others, then we can bring to fruition a new spirit of mutual concern, mutual accommodation, mutual assistance, and common progress.

(5) <u>First give one's concern to the public interest, then to private interests.</u> We must take a comprehensive viewpoint. If overall conditions are not going well, it is not enough that individual conditions are much improved. If overall conditions are good, then we need have no fear of local difficulties, no matter how great, for they will be easy to resolve. One should not practice parochialism and fragmentationism.

(6) <u>First work for the public interest, then for the private interest</u>. Communist Party members and revolutionary cadre members are the servants of the people, and the worker class is the master of the nation. In whatever we do and in whatever problems we consider, we must place the interests of the nation and the collective in first place and the interests of the individual in second place. We must put hardship first and pleasure after.

(7) <u>I work for all the people; all the people work for me.</u> All the people, as referred to here, indicates the entire body of laboring people who, under the direction of the worker class, are following the road of socialism. When we plan for the welfare of all the people, we ourselves, our families, and our sons and grandsons will benefit from the general affluence of all the people. For this reason we must consider the people and the nation in all things. Our nation is great. Our people are great. Our armies are great. Our party is great, and our Chairman Mao is great. We must be obedient to the party and to Chairman Mao.

---

[2]Or "spirit of revival through one's own effort" (<u>tan-li keng-sheng</u>).

(8) <u>I work for the world; the world works for me.</u> This is the requirement of having an internationalist spirit. Now that our revolution has been victorious, we must help others. Assisting the people of other nations in their revolutionary movements is our international duty. Actually, assistance to others is in our own interest. Because imperialism has not yet been destroyed in the world, and because the American imperialists are still pursuing their war policy, our safety is still threatened. They are still supporting the remnants of the Chiang K'ai-shek group in their plots for restoration. For these reasons we must be ever watchful, complete our work, and actively support the revolutionary struggles of the people of the world. If revolution is carried on everywhere in the world, and if everyone opposes the policies of war and aggression by American imperialism, then we will be able to tie its hands, unceasingly strengthen revolutionary forces, and finally annihilate imperialism. This kind of revolutionary struggle is of great assistance to us. We must therefore strive to perfect our production and our work in support of the revolutionary movement of the people of the world.

The general spirit of the above eight points gives precedence to the public interest and subordinates private interests.

Comrades, commune members, let us quickly move into action, vigorously expanding the Socialist Education movement and the production and economy movement, and, under the leadership of the party, let us continue to raise high the Three Red Banners of the General Line, the Great Leap Forward, and the People's Communes. Let us unite in further raising socialist awareness of patriotism, collectivism, and internationalism. Let us with great diligence struggle for a massive strengthening of agriculture and the perfection of all phases of production and work so that we may reap a rich harvest this year, completely fulfill the nation's plans, and struggle heroically for a new victory for socialism.

March 1, 1963

XIII

[EXPERIENCES OF THE HU-PING BRIGADE IN UNITING THE SOCIALIST EDUCATION MOVEMENT WITH CURRENT PRODUCTION]

THE LIEN-CHIANG COUNTY COMMITTEE OF THE CHINESE COMMUNIST PARTY, FUKIEN PROVINCE

(Approved for transmittal)

NUMBER:	029	SECRET
TO:	Each Commune Party Committee, 3 copies; State Farm and Brigade Party Branches, 1 copy each; Municipal Party Committee, 11 copies; Provincial Committee Socialist Education Office, 3 copies	
COPIES TO:	County Standing Committee, County Committee members in rural areas, other County Committee members, People's Committee Office, Youth Office, Women's Office, Farm Office, and Agricultural Bureau, one copy each; files, 2 copies (total printing: 340 copies)	
THIS ITEM:	Issued by Office of the Secretary, the Lien-chiang County Committee, Chinese Communist Party, March 25, 1963	

The Lien-chiang County Committee has approved for circulation the report of the Hu-p'ing brigade on uniting the Socialist Education movement with current production.

With this document we are circulating the experiences of the Hu-p'ing brigade in uniting the Socialist Education movement with current production. We believe that the experiences of the Hu-p'ing brigade are very good and are worthy of widespread study. Especially prominent is their effective treatment of fertilizer and capital. Their methods were concrete. Each region should imitate the methods of the Hu-p'ing brigade and master the two key problems of fertilizer and capital in their preparations for plowing, and achieve a new high level in plowing preparations.

Some teams are still backward in their plowing preparations, and capable cadre members should be sent to strengthen their leadership and reform their character as soon as possible.

COMMUNIST PARTY COMMITTEE OF LIEN-CHIANG COUNTY

March 25, 1963

THE EXPERIENCES OF THE HU-P'ING BRIGADE IN
UNITING THE SOCIALIST EDUCATION MOVEMENT
WITH CURRENT PRODUCTION

During the Socialist Education movement, the Hu-p'ing brigade took effective measures to unite the movement closely with current production. Not only did this assure the smooth progress of the movement, but it also greatly stimulated current production, causing the Socialist Education movement to become a great force in strengthening the collective economy and in expanding agricultural production as well as in reaping a rich harvest this year. In all the teams, new conditions of production have emerged. The percentage of workers reporting for work is high, they start work early, and their work efficiency is high. In short, farm work is of good quality, and progress in production is rapid. Now, more than 300 of the total brigade labor force of 330 persons daily participate in collective labor, an increase of more than 30 per cent over that before the movement. In addition, there are also twenty old people and children who assist in the labor and who take the initiative in requesting tasks from the production teams, participating actively in all the work of which they are capable. For these reasons, preparations for production have proceeded quickly. According to statistics, the brigade's total area of burned-over paddies has now reached 351 mou, 51 mou in excess of the original plan and more than a threefold increase over last year for the same period. River mud amounting to 189 mou has been dug out--more than double the amount for last year for the same period. In addition to this, 11,300 tan of fertilizer (meaning concentrated fertilizer) have been collected from households, an increase of more than 40 per cent over last year for the same period. This has provided 96 per cent of the fertilizer required for this year's spring plowing. In addition, 652 mou of paddies have been plowed the second time. This is 94 per cent of the total area and basically completes our original plan. Our twelve water-conservation projects have been completed ahead of schedule. In completing the conservation work, ground was leveled which expanded the farming area by five mou. In order to increase the incomes of commune members and solve the problem of capital for production, 125 brigade laborers were assigned to engage in subsidiary production. Within half a month, a total income of more than 1,850 yüan was obtained. This basically solved the problem of insufficient capital for production.

The rapid and effective completion of current preparations for production has raised the spirit of the commune members. This is reflected in the statement, "In this way, we have solved both ideological and practical problems and have assured a rich harvest this year."

The principal methods used by the Hu-p'ing brigade for uniting the movement with production were as follows.

First, we conducted a resolute and timely study, solving the key problems most closely related to current production and most urgently requiring solution by the masses. These were problems such as production plans, methods of food distribution,

165

and the determination of labor quotas and fertilizer assignments. Although we had already studied these problems before the New Year festival, we had not made definite decisions by that time. For this reason, during the movement, we took three or four evenings for the continued discussion and solution of these problems, discussing and resolving each item one-by-one. This had a highly stimulating effect on production by the commune members. For example, after labor quotas had been set for the Hu-lien production team, there was an increase of five to six persons in the average number of commune members daily participating in collective labor. After the fertilizer quota had been set, the Hu-kuang production team fulfilled its assignment for March in only five days.

Second, we set up a model team and used examples of good persons and good actions. We launched competition in production and stepped up the Study, Compare, Emulate, and Assist movement. The brigade set up the superior Hu-lien production team as a model and organized the other teams to study its experiences and to exchange their experiences with it. First-class production teams within the brigade have increased from the original three to eight, and the state of two third-class teams has changed completely. The production teams, through the movement, had singled out for commendation seventeen good cadre members, four good Youth Corps members, and twelve good commune members. They were set up as examples to other cadre and commune members. This was an encouragement to the people concerned, and served to instruct others. As a result, seven team leaders who had stated that they did not wish to serve are now intent on their work. Furthermore, they led the way in participating in collective labor and led the commune members in carrying out production.

Third, we conscientiously expanded production and earnestly assisted the production teams in the solution of specific problems. During the movement, we devoted two days to intensive investigation (in which thirty brigade- and team-cadre members and old farmers participated) and discussed and solved, individually, the problems brought to light during the investigation. During the investigation, we discovered that in eleven out of twelve production teams the early rice seed could not be used. The brigade immediately dispatched cadre members to the Ma-pi, P'u-k'ou, and Sha-chiang communes to obtain 60 tan of good seeds. This rapidly solved the seed problem. As another example, when six production teams, including the Hu-chin, Hu-feng, and Hu-hsin teams, made a poor beginning in their fertilizer collection work, the brigade assisted them, on the one hand, in enlarging their fertilizer sources, in bringing their labor force up to sufficiency, and in greatly increasing their household fertilizer, and, on the other, it mobilized them to utilize their income from subsidiary enterprises to go to Ch'eng-kuan, Foochow, and P'u-k'ou in order to purchase 500 tan of such kinds of concentrated fertilizer as rotten fish, dried shrimp, and human excrement. This resulted in their quickly reaching the level of advanced teams in fertilizer collection.

Fourth, we strengthened the concrete leadership of the cadres. A suitable division of labor was made between the seven principal cadre members and the three work groups of the brigade. It was decided that five persons, including the branch secretary and members of the work groups, would lead the movement, and that five persons, including the brigade chief, would lead production. We thus achieved uniform leadership and division of responsibilities, involving mutual cooperation and coordination. The production-team cadres took charge of both the movement and production, participating in production during the day and leading discussions in the evening, thereby advancing the movement.

March 25, 1963

XIV

[COMMUNICATION CONCERNING A STRICT
PETITION AND REPORT SYSTEM]

THE LIEN-CHIANG COUNTY COMMITTEE OF THE CHINESE COMMUNIST PARTY,
FUKIEN PROVINCE, COMMUNICATION

NUMBER: 035   SECRET

PRINCIPAL RECIPIENTS: Each Commune Party Committee, 3 copies;
                           each Brigade Party Branch Office, 1 copy;
                           Municipal Party Committee, 10 copies

COPIES SENT: County Standing Committee; Organization,
                           Propaganda, Agriculture and Industry,
                           Coastal Work, and Supervisory divisions of
                           County Party Committee; Party Committees,
                           in organizations under the direct jurisdiction
                           of the County Public Security Bureaus,
                           Courts; and Procurator's Office, one copy
                           each; file, 2 copies (total printing: 330
                           copies)

THIS ITEM: 2 pages, issued by the Office of the Secretary,
                           Lien-chiang County Committee, Chinese Com-
                           munist Party, April 12, 1963

Communication from the Lien-chiang County Committee concerning a Strict
Petition and Report System

All Commune Party Committees, Brigade Branches, and the Municipal Committee:

Recently in the course of the Socialist Education movement it has been discovered that a minority of areas have independently advocated and adopted unlawful beating, struggle, search, and disciplinary methods in dealing with problems and that, as a consequence, deaths have repeatedly occurred. Even more serious is the fact that there are some places in which persons do not petition before taking action when problems develop and do not report after taking action. This has created work losses. These practices must be firmly corrected.

In order that the petition and report system be strictly carried into effect, we again issue the following communication:

(1) In any doubtful problems occurring during the Socialist Education movement, and particularly in those problems concerned with policy, a petition must be filed before action is taken. In order to avoid deviations, hasty decisions as to treatment should not be taken before a reply is received.

(2) In all situations requiring arrest, court action, or struggle through argument, county approval must be received before such action may be carried out. Before approval has been granted, neither struggle nor arrest will in any case be permitted. In addition, using struggle under altered names such as "key-point criticism" or "key-point assistance" is not permitted.

(3) Conducting unlawful searches, or search under any other name, among the masses is not allowed. If search is required, approval must be obtained from the county. Neither the commune Party Committee nor the Brigade Branch has the authority to grant approval.

(4) Such illegal actions as beatings and collective discipline are strictly prohibited. Even the Four Class elements and other bad elements guilty of destructive conduct must also be punished according to lawful procedures. Approval may be given to the production teams to carry out struggle and instruction, but beatings by the cadres are strictly enjoined.

(5) All abnormal deaths during the movement must be reported to higher authorities on the day of their occurrence. In addition, those regions in which unlawful beatings, struggle, search, and collective discipline have taken place must reform their ideological attitudes and work methods through the examination and summarization of their experiences. Suitable discipline should be dispensed to individual elements guilty of serious illegal conduct.

It is requested that the above communication be immediately put into effect. The Municipal Committee is requested to indicate any unsatisfactory points contained herein.

CHINESE COMMUNIST PARTY COMMITTEE OF
LIEN-CHIANG COUNTY

April 12, 1963

XV

[STATISTICAL TABLES RELATING TO THE SOCIALIST EDUCATION MOVEMENT IN THE CH'ANG-SHA BRIGADE OF THE P'U-K'OU COMMUNE]

[Note: Some tables are apparently missing from the captured documents. Those presented here (and in Document XVI) are arranged as far as possible in their presumed original order. It has, however, not always been possible to do this, as some have no page numbers and are not clearly dated. The data contained in the tables are not always consistent with one another. Component parts, for example, sometimes do not add up to the totals.]

TABLE XV-1

PERIODIC PROGRESS REPORTS ON SOCIALIST EDUCATION, NO. 1

Report date: 27

Has the brigade set up a Poor and Lower-Middle Peasants' Representatives' Committee? 15

Number of persons participating: 95

    Poor peasants: 59
    New upper peasants: 11
    New lower peasants: 17
    Old lower peasants: 8
    Party members: 12
    Youth Corps members: 20
    Brigade cadre members: 8
    Team cadre members: 42

Number of poor and lower-middle peasant groups established: 7

    Of these, number of groups established in factories and plants: ...

Total number of poor and lower-middle peasant households in the brigade: 127

    Number of households participating in poor and lower-middle peasant groups: 72

Total number of poor and lower-middle peasants: 286

    Number participating in poor and lower-middle peasant groups: 95

Poor peasants

    Total households: 70
    Number of households participating: 46
    Total number of persons: 61
    Number of persons participating: 59

New lower-middle peasants

    Total households: 18
    Number of households participating: 18
    Total number of persons: 64
    Number of persons participating: 17

New upper-middle peasants

    Total households: 16
      Number of households participating: 10

    Total number of persons: 40
      Number of persons participating: 11

Old lower-middle peasants

    Total households: 13
      Number of households participating: 5
    Total number of persons: 21
      Number of persons participating: 8

Number of cadre, party, and Youth Corps members participating in poor and lower-middle peasant groups:

Party members: 12
Youth Corps members: 20
Brigade cadres: 8
Team cadres: 42

PERIODIC PROGRESS REPORTS ON SOCIALIST EDUCATION, NO. 2

Report date: 27

Number of production teams: 7

Number of teams in which election has been held: 6

Number of persons elected: 42

    Number reelected and reappointed: 37
    Number of team chiefs reelected and reappointed: 6

Number of team chiefs not reelected: ...

    Number transferred to be deputy chiefs: ...
    Number transferred to be committee members: ...
    Number not acting as cadre members after losing election: ...

Progress in mass discussions on reform and the opening of uncultivated land:

    Number of teams in which production plans have been decided upon: 7
    Number of teams in which food distribution has been decided upon: 7
    Number of persons for whom labor control has been decided upon: 7
    Number of teams in which fertilizer control has been decided upon: 7

Land that should be confiscated
    Excess shares of free land:
        Number of households: ...
        Number of mou: ...

    Land illegally occupied by commune members
        Number of households: ...
        Number of mou: ...

    Uncultivated land involving the "five destructions" [i.e., land
        previously cultivated, but now in disuse]
        Number of households: ...
        Number of mou: 18

Land already confiscated
    Excess shares of free land:
        Number of households: ...
        Number of mou: ...

    Land illegally occupied by commune members
        Number of households: ...
        Number of mou: ...

    Uncultivated land involving the "five destructions"
        Number of households: 135
        Number of mou: 18

Land not confiscated which has been planted by commune members:

Number of households: ...
    Excess shares of free land: ...
    Land illegally occupied by commune members: ...
        Uncultivated land:
    Bad land involving the "five destructions": ...
    Uncultivated land newly opened this year: ...

PERIODIC PROGRESS REPORTS ON SOCIALIST EDUCATION, NO. 3

The problem of excess tree-cutting:

Commune members from whom retrieval should be made
    Number of teams: ...
    Number of households: ...
    Number of trees: ...

Commune members from whom retrieval has been made
    Number of teams: ...
    Number of households: ...

Statistics of retrievals
    Number of households: ...
    Materials:
        Pine trees (number of trees): ...
        Pine trees (number of trees): ...

Abandonment of farming for peddling:

> Number of persons who should return to the teams: 16
> Number of persons who have returned to the teams: 16

Individual handicraft industries:

> Number of persons who did not hand over the Three Funds in the past: 13
> Number of persons who have reformed: 11

Working outside on odd jobs:

> Number of persons who should return to the teams: 4
> Number of persons who have returned to the teams: 4

Religious swindlers:

> Total number of persons: ...
>> Number of persons who have ceased their activity: ...

Witchcraft practitioners:

> Total number of persons: ...
>> Number of persons who have ceased their activity: ...

Taoist priests:

> Total number of persons: ...
>> Number of persons who have ceased their activity: ...

Marriage go-betweens:

> Total number of persons: ...
>> Number of persons who have ceased their activity: ...

Geomancers and fortunetellers:

> Total number of persons: ...
>> Number of persons who have ceased their activity: ...

Private brewing of wine:

> Total number of households: ...
>> Number of cadre-member households: ...
>> Number of catties: ...

Private slaughter of pigs:

> Number of households: ...
> Number of head: ...
> Number of head on which tax was evaded: ...
> Number of head for which tax indemnity made: ...

PERIODIC PROGRESS REPORTS ON SOCIALIST EDUCATION, NO. 4

Number of cadre members requiring reform:

> Brigade cadre members: 8
> Team cadre members: 22
> Party members without duties: 1
>> Total: 31

Stolen goods and materials that should be retrieved from cadre members:

    Money (yüan): ...
        Graft: ...
        Misappropriations and excess expenditures (yüan): 300

    Food (catties): ...
    Land (mou): 4
    Lumber (number of pieces): 5
    Cloth or cloth-ration coupons (feet): ...
    Farm tools (pieces): ...
    Fishing tools (pieces): ...

Number of persons whose faults have been corrected:

    Brigade cadre members: 8
    Team cadre members: 22
    Party members without duties: 1
        Total: 30
            Number completely reformed: 24
            Number partly reformed: 6

    Nature of faults
        Economic problems: 1
        Problems of ideology and work-attitude: 18
        Other: 11

Stolen Goods and Materials Retrieved:

    Money (yüan): ...
        Graft: ...
        Misappropriations and excess expenditures: ...
        Other: ...

PERIODIC PROGRESS REPORTS ON SOCIALIST EDUCATION, NO. 5

Report date: ...

Has there been a need to hold brigade struggle and criticism meetings? ...

Number of production-team struggle and criticism meetings required: ...

Total number of persons requiring struggle and criticism: ...

    Number of persons for whom data have been reported and approved: ...
    Number of persons for whom data have been reported, but for whom
        approval has not been granted: ...
    Number of persons for whom data have not been reported: ...

Total number of Four Class elements requiring struggle and criticism: ...

    Number of persons for whom data have been reported and approved: ...
    Number of persons for whom data have been reported, but for whom
        approval has not been granted: ...
    Number of persons for whom data have not been reported: ...

Current progress in struggle and criticism:

    Number of persons already subjected to struggle and criticism in
        brigade mass meetings: ...
    Number of Four Class elements among them: ...

Number of persons about whom struggle and criticism have been conducted in interbrigade mass meetings: ...

Number of Four Class elements among them: ...

Number of persons about whom struggle and criticism have been conducted in team meetings: ...

Number of Four Class elements among them: ...

The state of treatment of those about whom struggle and criticism have been conducted

Number of persons arrested and tried by law: ...

Number of Four Class elements among them: ...

Number of persons put under surveillance: ...

Number of Four Class elements among them: ...

Number of persons placed under supervised labor in production team: ...

Number of Four Class elements among them: ...

EXPLANATION: The above five tables should be reported on between the third and eighth [day of the month].

The previous report forms are no longer used.

TABLE XV-2

PERIODIC REPORTS ON SOCIALIST EDUCATION, NO. 1

Report date: 15

Progress of meetings:

Branch Committee Meetings
Frequency: 6
Number of persons in attendance at each meeting: 12

Expanded Cadre-member Meetings
Frequency: 1
Number of persons in attendance at each meeting: 88

Youth Corps-member meetings
Frequency: 1
Number of persons in attendance at each meeting: 26

Womens' Association Meetings
Frequency: 1
Number of persons in attendance at each meeting: 66

Militia meetings
Frequency: 2
Number of persons in attendance at each meeting: 80

Meetings of positive elements
Frequency: 7
Number of persons in attendance at each meeting: 15

Meetings of propaganda personnel
  Frequency: ...
  Number of persons in attendance at each meeting: 7

All types of discussion meetings
  Frequency: ...
  Number of persons in attendance at each meeting: ...

Mass meetings
  Number of persons who should attend: 232

  Group I. Number of days of discussion: ...
     Number of teams: 1
     Number of persons participating: 38

  Group II. Number of days of discussion: ...
     Number of teams: ...
     Number of persons participating: ...

  Group III. Number of days of discussion: ...
     Number of teams: ...
     Number of persons participating: ...

State of the organization and training of Class Corps:

Number of persons in class groups: ...

  Number of poor and lower-middle peasants: ...
  Number of party members: 7
  Number of Youth Corps members: 18
  Number of brigade cadre-members: 3
  Number of team cadre-members: ...

Number of training sessions held: 2

PERIODIC REPORTS ON SOCIALIST EDUCATION, NO. 2

(Due on the third and seventh of each month -- to be reported by
telegraph by P'u-K'ou Party Committee personnel)

Report date: 17

Exemplary persons and acts:

  Number of good production teams: 1
  Number of good cadre-members: 17
   Among these, number of brigade cadre-members: 1
  Number of good party members: 2
  Number of good Youth Corps members: 4
  Number of good commune members: 22
  Number of good women: 16
  Number of good militia members: 7

Present state of cadre-members exhibiting the Three Evil Tendencies:

  Number of brigade cadre-members having the Three Evil Tendencies: 8

   Number of persons with minor problems who have repented
    and reformed: 5

Number of persons with rather severe problems who take criticism with open minds and have repented and reformed: ...

Number of persons with rather severe problems who do not take criticism with open minds and who have not resolved to reform their errors: ...

Number of team cadre having the Three Evil Tendencies: 34

Number of persons with minor problems who have repented and reformed: 20

Number of persons with rather severe problems who take criticism with open minds and have repented and reformed: 14

Number of persons with rather severe problems who do not take criticism with open minds and who have not resolved to reform their errors: ...

Number of cadre-members in factories having the Three Evil Tendencies:

Number of persons with minor problems who have repented and reformed: ...

Number of persons with rather severe problems who take criticism with open minds and have repented and reformed: ...

Number of persons with rather severe problems who do not take criticism with open minds and who have not resolved to reform their errors: ...

PERIODIC REPORTS ON SOCIALIST EDUCATION, NO. 3

(Due between the third and seventh day of each month by telegraph. Issued by the P'u-k'ou Party Committee.)

State of Reform

Report date: ...

Number of cadre-members already reformed: ...

Brigade cadre members: 5
Team cadre members: 20
Other cadre members: ...

Materials retrieved (including materials retrieved from cadre members and masses)

Cash (yüan): ...
Lumber (number of pieces): 5
Land (mou): ...
    Including open uncultivated land (mou): 2.8
Food (catties): ...
Cloth-ration coupons (feet of cloth): ...

Planned retrieval by installments:

Cash (yüan): ...
Lumber (meters): ...
Land (mou): ...

Including open uncultivated land (mou): ...
Food (catties): ...
Cloth-ration coupons (feet of cloth): ...

TABLE XV-3

STATISTICAL REPORT ON THE ATTENDANCE AT EXPANDED BRIGADE CADRE
MEETING OF CH'ANG-SHA BRIGADE

Members of brigade cadres:

    Planned participation: 9
    Actual number participating: 9

Members of brigade factory cadres:

    Planned participation: 27
    Actual number participating: ...

Production-team chiefs:

    Planned participation: 21
    Actual number participating: 20

Other production-team cadre members:

    Planned participation: 24
    Actual number participating: 24

Members of militia cadre:

    Planned participation: 4
    Actual number participating: 4

Members of women's associations:

    Planned participation: 15
    Actual number participating: 15

Other Cadre members:

    Planned participation: ...
    Actual number participating: ...

    Planned participation: ...
    Actual number participating: ...

    Planned participation: ...
    Actual number participating: ...

    Planned participation: ...
    Actual number participating: ...

    Planned participation: ...
    Actual number participating: ...

Active elements:

    Planned participation: 18
    Actual number participating: 18

Total:

Planned participation: 90
Actual number participating: 88

Party members: 12
Youth Corps members: 27
Women: 18

TABLE XV-4

STATISTICAL TABLE ON CONDITIONS AMONG CADRE MEMBERS INVESTIGATED BY THE BRIGADE CADRE EXPANDED MEETINGS

	Group classification			
	Brigade Cadre	Production-Team Cadre	Other Cadres	Active Elements
Number of persons participating.....................	9	39	22	--
Investigated:				
Number of persons investigated and passed by the conferees.........................	7	25	10	--
Number investigated and adjudged as not too satisfactory	2	9	5	--
Number investigated and adjudged as poor......	--	5	2	--
Number of persons not yet investigated	--	--	5	--
Number of cadre members with Three Evil Tendencies faults participating in expanded cadre meetings	8	34	15	--
Number thoroughly investigated	6	25	9	--
Number not too thoroughly investigated.........	2	9	6	--
Number not thoroughly investigated............	--	1	--	--
Number not investigated	--	--	--	--
Total number investigated	84	45	18	--
Capitalism:				
Number of individual-enterprise households	--	1	--	--
Number of persons advocating household-contract production	--	9	--	--
Number of persons abandoning farming for peddling	--	--	--	--
Number of persons lending money at high interest ....,.................	11	--	--	--
Number of persons practicing labor contracting	--	--	--	--
Number of persons hiring labor	--	--	--	--
Number of persons doing rat work.........	--	--	--	--

	Group classification			
	Brigade Cadre	Production Team Cadre	Other Cadres	Active Elements
Number of persons not handing over fertilizer to the collective	--	--	--	--
Number of laborers emigrating	--	--	2	--
Number of persons actively opening uncultivated land	--	5	6	--
Subtotal	--	--	--	--
Feudalism:				
Number of marriages-by-sale	--	--	--	--
Number of gamblers	--	--	--	--
Number of girls brought up in home of fiancé	--	--	--	--
Number of bridegrooms married into the home of the bride	--	--	--	--
Number of persons engaging in superstitious practices	--	--	--	--
Number of persons participating in religious exercises and worshiping idols	--	--	--	--
Number of persons making and repairing tombs	--	--	--	--
Subtotal	--	--	--	--
Extravagance:				
Number of persons holding feasts	--	--	--	--
Number of persons giving parties and sending presents	--	--	--	--
Number of persons engaging in other extravagance	--	--	--	--
Subtotal	--	--	--	--
Breaking laws and regulations:				
Number of persons engaging in graft	--	--	--	--
Number of persons engaging in misappropriation	4	2	--	--
Number of persons engaging in theft	--	--	--	--
Number of persons engaging in speculation	1	5	--	--
Number of persons engaging in decadent behavior	--	--	--	--
Number of persons engaged in excess cutting of trees	--	--	--	--
Number of persons privately slaughtering hogs	--	--	--	--
Number of persons extorting money	--	--	--	--
Subtotal	--	--	--	--

	Group classification			
	Brigade Cadre	Production Team Cadre	Other Cadres	Active Elements

Other:

Number not acting as cadre members.......	3	6	3	--
Number with bad work attitudes............	--	--	4	--
Number engaging in excess consumption	1	6	4	--
Number serving private ends but pretending to serve public ends	--	--	--	--
Number of production teams in which work is not well recorded and work-points not well evaluated	--	1	--	--
Number of production teams not having clear accounts	--	3	--	--
Subtotal	--	--	--	--

Cadre-member classification:

Number of persons without the Three Evil Tendencies.........................	1	5	7	--
Number of persons with some Three Evil Tendencies	8	34	15	--
Number of persons with serious Three Evil Tendencies....................	--	--	--	--

TABLE XV-5

STATISTICAL TABLE ON CADRE INVESTIGATION: PROBLEMS AND OTHER DETAILS, CH'ANG-SHA BRIGADE

State of cadre investigations:

Leading brigade cadre members

Number of persons attending meetings: 5
Number of persons investigated: 5

Production-team chiefs

Number of persons attending meetings: 7
Number of persons investigated: 7

Other

Number of persons attending meetings: 7
Number of persons investigated: 2

Cadre members investigated:

Courageous investigations: 10
Those with some reservations: 4
Those with serious ideological conflicts: ...

Investigation of actions:

Number of persons engaging in peddling: 5
Number of persons advocating household-contract production: 2
Number of persons lending money at high interest: ...
Number of persons contracting labor: ...
Number of persons participating in gambling: ...
Number of persons taking the lead in superstitious activities: ...
Number of persons acting as marriage go-betweens and flesh peddlers: ...
Number of daughters sold into marriage: ...
Number of persons engaging in excess parties and waste: ...
    Number among these holding parties to make money: ...
Number of persons engaging in graft, theft, and misappropriation: ...
Number of persons engaging in excessive consumption and taking
    special privileges: 7
Number of persons engaging in decadent conduct: ...
Number of persons privately slaughtering hogs: ...
Number of persons not serving as cadre members: ...
Number of persons participating in excess felling of trees: ...
Number of persons serving self-interest, but pretending that their acts
    are in the public interest: ...
Number of persons frequently engaging in individual subsidiary
    production: ...
Number of production teams in which work is recorded but points not
    evaluated: ...
Number of production teams in which finances have not been made public
    for long periods: 3

Explanation:

The leading brigade cadre members are the chief and assistant branch
secretaries, the chief and assistant brigade chiefs, the Youth Corps
secretary, the Women's Corps chairman, and the Militia Corps chief.

"Investigation of Actions" indicates incorrect acts committed by the
cadre members present. Names of persons may be repeated. For
example, if Chang San engages in peddling, does not serve as cadre
member, and is decadent, then his name should be recorded in each
appropriate blank.

TABLE XV-6

STATISTICAL TABLE ON CONDITIONS OF BRIGADE CADRE MEMBERS AS DISCLOSED IN EXPANDED CADRE MEETINGS

Number of persons attending meeting: 88

Nature of opinions presented to brigade cadre members:

Number of persons courageously presenting opinions: 40
Number of persons presenting ideas, but not courageously: 22

Number of persons not presenting opinions to the brigade: 26

Total number of brigade cadre members: 9

Number of persons criticized: 6

Number of opinions presented to the brigade cadre: 35

Suspicions

Suspicions of graft: 1
Suspicions of engaging in peddling: ...

Correct criticisms

Criticisms of engaging in peddling: 2
Criticisms of graft: ...
Criticisms of superstition: ...
Criticisms of slipshod work: 9
Criticisms of excess consumption: 15

Constructive criticism

[Illegible]: 4
[Illegible]: 3

Explanation:

1. Tables should be reported immediately upon conclusion of meetings.
2. Figures should be checked to avoid rough guesses.
3. Add whatever is necessary in blank spaces.

Supplementary materials: Issued by P'u-k'ou Party Committee,
February 27, 1963

The period for brigade cadre expanded meeting investigations is one day and one night, of which brigade-cadre investigations are half a day and night.

The brigade cadre members make public inquiries of three persons during the meetings.

TABLE XV-7

STATISTICAL TABLE ON THE THREE EVIL TENDENCIES DURING 1962

Capitalist activities:

Number fully engaged in individual enterprise: 9
Number abandoning farming for peddling: 9
Number abandoning fishing for peddling: ...
Total number of craftsmen of all kinds: 16

Number handing over their earnings: 9
Number doing rat work and not handing over their earnings: 7

Number of persons hiring labor: ...

High-interest loans

Number of persons: ...
Amounts of money: ...

Number of persons having labor quotas: 19

    Number of these not fulfilling labor quotas: 19

Number of households with fertilizer quotas: 153

    Number of these not fulfilling fertilizer quotas: 153

Activities based on superstition:

Temple repair:

    Number repaired: ...
    Repair in preparation: ...

Temple construction

    Number constructed: ...
    Construction in preparation: ...

Newly made Bodhishattva idols: ...
Number of witchcraft practitioners: ...
Number of Taoist priests: ...
Number of religious swindlers: ...
Number of geomancers: 10
Number of fortunetellers: ...
Number of persons taking part in lantern parades: ...

Feudal marriages:

Number of persons married or engaged in 1962 (indicates women):   12

    Of these, number of persons having free marriages: ...
    Of these, number of persons entering marriage by sale: 11

Number of go-betweens: 2
Number of girls brought up in home of fiancé: 2
Number of bridegrooms married into the families of brides: 1

Extravagances:

Marriage feasts

    Number of households having marriages: 1
    Number of households holding feasts: ...
    Number of tables: ...

Feasts to celebrate new buildings

    Number of households having new buildings: 40
    Number of households holding feasts: 1
    Number of tables: 2

Birth feasts

    Number of households having births: 24
    Number of households holding feasts: ...
    Number of tables: 2

Birthday feasts

    Number of households having birthdays: ...
    Number of households holding feasts: ...
    Number of tables: ...

Other feasts

Number of households: ...
Number of tables: ...

Number of teams holding one feast in 1962: 7
Number of teams holding two feasts in 1962: 2
Number of teams holding three feasts in 1962: ...
Number of teams holding more than three feasts in 1962: ...

TABLE XV-8

STATISTICAL TABLE ON THE THREE [EVIL] TENDENCIES AND OTHER
ACTIVITIES REVEALED AMONG THE MASSES, CH'ANG-SHA BRIGADE

Total number of households: 153 (including 5 affluent middle peasants)

Households without problems: 80 (including 3 affluent middle peasants)
Households with minor problems: 73 (including 3 affluent middle peasants)
Households with major problems: . . .

Attitude toward the movement:

Number of households taking initiative in having nothing more to do with the
Three Evil Tendencies: 50
Number of households taking initiative in returning stolen goods and
materials: 13
Number of households with bad manifestations: ...

Number of households having the Three Evil Tendencies problem: 100

As percentage of the total adult population: 24 per cent

Number of cases disclosed through investigation: 85

Promoting individual enterprise (persons): 8
Abandoning farming for peddling (persons): 2
Hiring labor and exploitation (persons): ...
Acting as labor contractors (persons): 2
Running out to do rat work (persons): 1
High-interest loans: ...

Number of households: ...
Amounts of money: ...

Speculation

Number of persons: 11
Amount of profit (yüan): 8,009
Number of persons among these making more than 1,000 yüan: 11

Usurpation of collective land

Number of households: 15
Number of mou: 4

Theft

Grain and fodder
Number of persons: 3
Number of mou: 3.50

184

Other materials (persons): 32

Swindlers (persons): ...
Pickpockets (persons): ...

Private slaughter of hogs:

Number of households: ...
Number of head: ...

Excess cutting of trees:

Number of households: ...
Number of cedars: ...
Number of Manila pines: ...

Extortion of money:

Number of persons: ...
Amount of money: ...

Number of households privately brewing wine: ...
Religious processions (frequency): ...
Construction of shrines and repair of temples:

Number newly constructed: ...
Number repaired: ...

Number of households having images of the bodhisattva: ...
Taoist priests (persons): ...
Geomancy: 1 (affluent middle peasant)
Fortunetelling: ...
Witchcraft practitioners: ...
Religious swindlers: ...
Flesh peddlers: ...
Marriage go-betweens: 1
Girls brought up in the home of fiancé: 1
Gamblers: ...
Beatings of cadre members: 5

In business together with cadre members:

Number of persons: ...
Amount of money: ...

Not returning advance payments on time:

Number of households: ...
Amount of money: ...

Explanation: It is not necessary to include statistics on cadre members which have previously reported, or on the Four Class elements, which are reported elsewhere.

TABLE XV-9

PROGRESS TABLE OF CRITICISM AND STRUGGLE

Report date: ...

Need for criticism and struggle: ...

> Does the brigade need to hold big criticism and struggle meetings? ...
> Production teams requiring big criticism and struggle meetings: 2
> Number of persons in brigades and teams requiring criticism and
> struggle: ...
>
>> Number of persons with internal problems: 2
>> Number of persons with hostility toward us: ...

Four Class elements:

> Number of persons requiring struggle: ...
>
>> Number of those engaging in speculation, graft, theft, and
>> breaking laws: ...
>> Number of most serious offenders among these: ...

Criticism and struggle already held:

> Number of persons undergoing criticism and struggle at brigade mass
> meetings: ...
>
>> Number of persons with internal problems: ...
>> Number of persons harboring hostility toward us: ...
>
> Number of persons undergoing criticism and struggle at team meetings: ...
>
>> Number of persons with internal problems: 2
>> Number of persons harboring hostility toward us: ...
>
> Number of persons undergoing criticism and struggle at interteam mass
> meetings: ...
>
>> Number of persons with internal problems: ...
>> Number of persons harboring hostility toward us: ...

Treatment of hostile elements who have undergone criticism and struggle:

> Number of persons remanded to production team for education: ...
> Number of persons placed under restraint: ...
> Number of persons arrested and tried by law: ...

Notes:

TABLE XV-10

REPORT ON THE DESTRUCTIVE ACTIVITIES OF THE FOUR CLASS ELEMENTS AND THEIR TREATMENT

Team:

Total number of Four Class elements: 3

Total number engaging in destructive activity: ...

As percentage of Four Class elements: ...

    Promotion of individual enterprise: ...
    Emigration: ...
    Speculation: ...
    Insulting and cursing of cadre members: ...
    Beating of cadre members: ...
    Counterrevolutionary activities: ...
    Incitement of destruction: ...
    Class revenge: ...
    Gambling: ...
    Superstition: ...
    Theft: ...

Requiring attack:

    Arrest and trial: ...
    Restraint: ...
    Struggle: ...

TABLE XV-11

STATISTICAL TABLE OF SOCIALIST EDUCATION DATA, I

Cadre Investigation

Leading brigade cadre members: ...

    Total number of persons: 7
    Number of cadre members with problems: 6

        Personal problems already solved: 6
        Major personal problems already solved: ...
        Major personal problems not yet solved: ...

General brigade cadre members:

    Total number of persons: 3
    Number of cadre members with problems: 3

        Personal problems already solved: 3
        Major personal problems already solved: ...
        Major personal problems not yet solved: ...

Production-team chiefs:

    Total number of persons: ...
    Number of cadre members with problems: 12

Personal problems already solved: 11
Major personal problems already solved: ...
Major personal problems not yet solved: 1

Other cadre members (includes the Seven Personnel of production teams and factory cadres):

Total number of persons: 44
Number of cadre members with problems: 26

Personal problems already solved: 21
Major personal problems already solved: 3
Major personal problems not yet solved: ...

STATE OF REFORM OF CADRE PERSONNEL WITH PROBLEMS

Leading brigade cadre members:

Number of persons who have actually returned stolen goods and who have resolved to correct their errors to the satisfaction of the masses: 3

Number of persons who have acknowledged their errors, who have corrected some minor problems, and who are preparing to correct their major problems: 2

Number of persons who refuse to investigate their errors and who have an ideological conflict over returning stolen goods: 1

General brigade cadre members:

Number of persons who have actually returned stolen goods and who have resolved to correct their errors to the satisfaction of the masses: 1

Number of persons who have acknowledged their errors, who have corrected some minor problems, and who are preparing to correct their major problems: 2

Number of persons who refuse to investigate their errors and who have an ideological conflict over returning stolen goods: ...

Production-team chiefs:

Number of persons who have actually returned stolen goods and who have resolved to correct their errors to the satisfaction of the masses: 10

Number of persons who have acknowledged their errors, who have corrected some minor problems, and who are preparing to correct their major problems: 1

Number of persons who refuse to investigate their errors and who have an ideological conflict over return of stolen goods: 1

Other cadre members (includes the Seven Personnel of production teams and factory cadres):

Number of persons who have actually returned stolen goods and who have resolved to correct their errors to the satisfaction of the masses: ...

Number of persons who have acknowledged their errors, who have corrected some minor problems, and who are preparing to correct their major problems: 4

Number of persons who refuse to investigate their errors and who have an ideological conflict over returning stolen goods: ...

Explanation:

1. Leading brigade cadre personnel includes the chief and assistant branch secretaries, the chief and assistant brigade chiefs, the Youth Corps secretary, the Women's Corps chairman, the Militia Corps chief, and the chief accountant.

2. The number of cadre members with problems and the number of cadre members with problems who have been classified must agree.

STATISTICAL TABLE OF SOCIALIST EDUCATION DATA, II

Classification of commune members:

Total number of adult commune members: 224
   Number of persons having the Three Evil Tendencies: 131

   Number of persons thoroughly corrected: 95
   Number of persons not thoroughly corrected: 21
   Number of persons with ideological conflicts still not corrected: 15

Four Class elements:

Landlords

Total number of persons: ...
   Number engaging in destructive conduct: ...

   Number of persons now converted: ...
   Number of persons not well converted: ...
   Number of persons not converted and continuing in destructive acts: 1

Rich peasants

Total number of persons: ...
   Number engaging in destructive conduct: ...

   Number of persons now converted: ...
   Number of persons not well converted: ...
   Number of persons not converted and continuing in destructive acts: ...

Counterrevolutionaries

Total number of persons: ...
   Number engaging in destructive conduct: ...

   Number of persons now converted: ...
   Number of persons not well converted: ...
   Number of persons not converted and continuing in destructive acts: ...

Bad elements

Total number of persons: 1
   Number engaging in destructive conduct: ...

Number of persons now converted: ...
Number of persons not well converted: ...
Number of persons not converted and continuing in destructive
    acts: ...

STATISTICAL TABLE OF SOCIALIST EDUCATION DATA, III

Number of teams in which production-team leadership authority has been taken
    over by the Four Class elements: ...

Number of teams in which this has been corrected: ...

Number of Four Class elements or their children who have infiltrated the ranks
    of the cadre: ...

Number who are production-team chiefs: ...
Number who are deputy team chiefs: ...
Number who are included in the Seven Personnel: ...
Number who are brigade cadre members: ...
Number who are serving as other kinds of cadre members: ...

Number of persons who have been removed from office in reelection: ...

Number who have been removed from office as team chiefs: ...

Amount of land discovered during the movement to have been pre-empted
    secretly in the past: ...

Number of teams: ...
Nonpayment of rent: ...

        Paddy land: ...
        Dry land: ...

Public property confiscated during the movement which had been taken home by
    cadre and commune members:

Farm tools (pieces): ...
Fishing gear (pieces): ...
Privies (individual): ...
Tables and chairs (pieces): ...

Number of production teams in which accounts were not made public and commune
    members were critical: 3

Production teams which have been assisted in clearing up their accounts: 3

Number of production teams in which cadre members were found engaging
    in graft and misappropriation involving large sums: ...

Number of production teams in which members were found engaging in
    graft and misappropriation not involving large sums: ...

Number of teams in which cadre members engage in graft and mis-
    appropriation: 2

Please report the preceding two tables together with those entitled
"Statistical Tables on the Three Tendencies and Other Activities Revealed
among the Masses" and "Report on the Treatment of Destructive Activity
of Four Class Elements" to the Party Committee before the fifteenth of the
month.

XVI

[STATISTICAL TABLES RELATING TO THE SOCIALIST EDUCATION MOVEMENT IN THE CH'ANG-SHA BRIGADE OF THE P'U-K'OU COMMUNE]

TABLE XVI-1

STATISTICS ON PROBLEMS OF BRIGADE MEMBERS AS REVEALED IN THE
SOCIALIST EDUCATION MOVEMENT, 1963

Number of persons: 224

Capitalism problems:

> Promotion of individual enterprise: 1
> Abandonment of farming for peddling: 16
> Labor contractor: 2
> Emigration of labor force: 13
> Excessive opening of uncultivated land: 24
> Failure to fulfill fertilizer quotas: 2
> Speculative activities: 5

Feudalism problems:

> Marriage-by-sale: 9
> Marriage go-betweens: 1

Extravagance problems:

> Large-scale parties: ...
> Giving parties and sending presents: ...
> Holding theatrical performances: ...
> Building assembly halls: ...
>
> Subtotal: ...

Other problems:

> Theft: 6
> Cutting down trees: 4
> Beating cadre members: 1
> Slandering the government: 8

TABLE XVI-2

STATISTICS ON PROBLEMS OF PARTY MEMBERS, BRIGADE CADRE MEMBERS, TEAM CHIEFS, AND THE SEVEN PERSONNEL AS REVEALED IN THE SOCIALIST EDUCATION MOVEMENT, 1963

	Party Members	Brigade Cadre Members	Team Chiefs	Seven Personnel
Number of persons...................	13	9	7	26
Capitalism:				
Promotion of individual enterprise..	--	--	2	3
Abandonment of farming for peddling	--	--	--	1
Benefitting oneself at expense of public	--	1	1	2
Emigration of labor force.........	--	--	--	1
Excess opening of uncultivated land........................	--	--	--	2
Extravagance:				
Excessive consumption	5	4	1	1
Other abuses:				
Misappropriation	--	--	--	1
Theft...........................	--	1	1	2
Speculation......................	3	1	2	3
Decadent behavior................	1	--	--	--
Refusal to act as cadre...........	2	1	--	9
Bad work attitude................	--	--	--	1

Group III
Socialist Education Movements–
Expanded Cadre Meetings

XVII

[REPORT ON WASTE, EXTRAVAGANCE, AND INFRACTIONS OF LAWS AND REGULATIONS BY MEMBERS OF THE COMMUNE AND BRIGADE LEADERSHIP CADRE IN THE P'AN-TU COMMUNE]

THE LIEN-CHIANG COUNTY COMMITTEE OF THE CHINESE COMMUNIST PARTY, FUKIEN PROVINCE

(Approved for transmission)

NUMBER:	084	SECRET

TO: Each Commune Party Committee, 3 copies; each Brigade Branch Committee, 1 copy; Municipal Committee, 5 copies

COPIES TO: County Committee Standing Committee, County Committee Groups, Propaganda Sections, Farm Work Sections, Coastal Work Sections, Supervisory Committees, People's Committee Offices, Public Security Bureau, Courts, and Procurator's Office, one copy each; file, 2 copies

THIS ITEM: 5 pages, issued by the Office of the Secretary, Lien-chiang County Committee, Chinese Communist Party, December 18, 1962

The Lien-chiang County Committee of the Chinese Communist Party hereby transmits the report of the P'an-tu Commune Party Committee on waste, extravagance, and infraction of laws and regulations by members of the commune and brigade leadership cadres.

ALL COMMUNE PARTY COMMITTEES AND BRIGADE BRANCH COMMITTEES:

We hereby transmit to you the report of the P'an-tu Commune Party Committee on waste, extravagance, and infraction of laws and regulations by members of the commune and brigade leadership cadre. It is hoped that each area will organize party-member discussions with the Branch Committee as the basic unit.

We feel that the waste, extravagance, and infraction of laws and regulations by members of the commune and brigade leadership cadre of the P'an-tu commune are extremely severe. This situation is not an isolated one, but exists in varying degrees of severity in other places in the county. Not only does this serious phenomenon destroy the relationships between the party and the masses and between cadre members and the masses, but even more seriously, it also directly destroys the strength of the collective economy. For this reason, we must call this to the attention of all leadership levels. We request that you, like the Party Committee of the P'an-tu commune, conscientiously conduct investigations and discussions and propose effective measures to stem the tide of this evil tendency as quickly as possible.

In regard to such conduct among cadre members as engaging in graft, misappropriation of public funds, private cutting of trees, extravagances for parties, speculation, and superstitious practices, after examining the circumstances and considering the severity of the acts and the individual's attitude toward his errors, severe punishment should be given in order to put a stop to the continued development of this improper situation.

LIEN-CHIANG COUNTY COMMITTEE,
CHINESE COMMUNIST PARTY

December 28, 1962

REPORT OF THE P'AN-TU COMMUNE COMMITTEE, CHINESE COMMUNIST PARTY, ON WASTE, EXTRAVAGANCE, AND INFRACTION OF LAWS AND REGULATIONS BY COMMUNE AND BRIGADE LEADERSHIP CADRES

COUNTY COMMITTEE:

According to our most recent investigation, extravagance, waste, and infraction of laws and regulations by some members of our commune and brigade leadership cadres are severe. They take advantage of such occasions as house buildings, marriages, and births to hold large-scale parties, invite guests, give presents, eat and drink heartily, and engage in waste and extravagance. According to our statistics, of nine committee members (not including members of Commune units under the Commune and Brigade committees) of the commune Party Committee, four, or 45.5 per cent, gave parties when their sons or daughters were married and when they had babies. Of the twenty-four commune and brigade branch secretaries and brigade chiefs, seven of them, or 29.1 per cent, gave parties under similar circumstances. Some among them, because of house building and party giving, unscrupulously appropriated public funds, used collective food, and cut down cedar trees by their own authority, thereby destroying the strength of the collective economy. Some extorted money by holding big parties. These kinds of incorrect conduct are extremely harmful. First, let us enumerate a few examples below:

In the Ch'ih-shih brigade, Brigade Chief Chang Tseng-kuan, Accountant Chang T'ien-hsiang, and Cashier Chou Ch'un-ti (all three of whom are party members), together with Party Branch Secretary Chou Huo-chiao as the leader, have engaged collectively in graft of public funds. From September 1961 to September 1962 they did not record income on the accounts. They falsified blank receipts, destroyed stubs, and appropriated cash under false names. They committed graft amounting to 1,394.93 yüan, involving misappropriation for sale of brigade cedar and bamboo and the misappropriation of funds. In addition they borrowed 422.72 yüan of public funds. Of the 1,394.93 yüan appropriated, Chou Huo-chiao took 339.70; Chang Tseng-kuan, 311.70; Chang T'ien-hsiang, 493.70; Chou Ch'un-ti, 249.83. After Chou Huo-chiao, Chang Tseng-kuan, and Chang T'ien-hsiang received these funds, Chou Huo-chiao suggested that they pool the money to build a house. After a discussion with Chang Tseng-kuan and Chang T'ien-hsiang, the three decided to build a house together. (Later two more commune-member households were drawn into participation.) Chou Huo-chiao invested 450 yüan, Chang Tseng-kuan 360 yüan, and Chang T'ien-hsiang 450 yüan, making a total of 1,200 yüan. After obtaining the capital, in successive periods and amounts, they cut 500 cedars belonging to the collective. (This is the figure that they admit. The masses say it came to about 1,000 trees.) At present they have basically completed the construction of a nine-room, two-storied building. While the three were building the house, they unscrupulously took 1,800 catties of feed belonging to the brigade and 250 catties of seeds as supplementary rations for the masons and carpenters and planned to hold a sixty-seven-table party from which they intended to extort another huge sum. This was stopped after the commune discovered it.

Ch'en Chen-jui (party member), brigade chief of the P'o-hsi brigade, held parties and invited guests in order to extort other people's money. In January of this year, under the pretext of the marriage of his daughter Ch'en Yu-ti to Chang Sheng-yen, he held an eight-table party at which 733 yüan was received as gifts. After expenses of 203 yüan, there remained 470 yüan. He bought a 105 yüan watch and used the remaining 305 yüan as the basic capital for the building of a house. In order to construct a three-room building, in September 1962 he ordered three times in succession, on his own authority, the cutting of 45 cedars belonging to the collective (paying only 40 yüan). He also took 20 cedars that were left over from bridge building by the 9144 Corps, five poles and beams from the P'o-hsi commune hydro-electric station, 40 feet of board from the P'o-hsi ranch, and 41 rafter boards. The value of the wood that he appropriated was about 188 yüan, but Ch'en paid only 120 yüan. While he was building his house, he reckoned his accounts and, estimating that he would be in financial difficulty, gave a twenty-table party for the entertainment of friends and relatives. By this means he was able to extort even more money through gifts and thus solve his financial difficulties. During the party he used the method of pledging presents. He suggested to his brother-in-law Lin Huo-ti (credit accountant of the Kao-yüeh brigade, who was discovered to have taken 92 yüan in graft) that he pledge a present of 100 yüan. Lin Wan-tien (Ch'en's maternal uncle), because of his financial circumstances, was only prepared to pledge 30 yüan. After Ch'en found this out, he secretly lent him forty yüan through his wife so that altogether 70 yüan were recorded on the gift register, putting him in the second place of honor. As a result, Lin was constrained to offer 70 yüan. In this way, the number of gifts that were offered grew. According to the gift register, 120 persons together offered 1,000 yüan. After paying out 270 yüan in expenses, he made a profit of 730 yüan. For his party, he privately slaughtered a hog of 78 catties net weight, (for which he was fined 17.8 yüan). He sold eight catties of this at the high price of 24 yüan, and used the remaining 70 catties for his party. He wasted 942 catties of food. Apart from 150 catties of his own, 300 catties that he bought at a high price from Kao-yüeh, and 250 catties that he borrowed from three commune-member households, he also used 242 catties of work rations belonging to the brigade and to the Hsia-lai production team. The assistant branch party secretary of the Tung-an brigade, Lan I-shui, cut down 55 cedars belonging to the collective (of this total, the brigade had approved 20) in order to build a private house. During the busy periods of this year's autumn harvest and winter planting, he was busy constructing his own house. On October 25, when the County Committee reviewed the work of the Forest Rights Working Group, it was discovered that 900 cedars had been cut by both cadre and commune members in that brigade. Records were made immediately, and, at a brigade cadre meeting, a resolution about the cedars already cut was passed, to the effect "not to use them and to await orders before making any disposition of them." Thereupon, the Commune Party Committee issued a decision that they should be bought up by the state. The commune members, in general, respected the decisions of the commune and

197

the brigade, and did not make use of even one piece of timber. However, Lan I-shui, himself the party branch secretary, paid no attention, and continued construction, using cedars that were already registered. In preparation for a beam-raising party, he sent out invitations to the Tung-an, Kuei-an, Hsi-li, Jen-shan, Kao-yüeh, P'o-hsi, and T'an-p'o brigades, and dispatched people to Foochow and other places to shop for the party. On November 19 of this year, he gave a nineteen-table beam-raising party. In addition to his friends and relatives, the commune Youth Corps committee secretary, the P'o-hsi brigade chief and supply and marketing chief, the Tung-an brigade branch secretary, and the T'ung-an brigade chief attended the feast. He received a total of 1,079 yüan in gifts, with a profit of more than 200 yüan. He wasted 800 catties of food and a 100-catty pig. He also privately brewed 70 catties of yellow wine (on which no taxes were paid). Because of Lan's activity in house building and party giving during the busy autumn harvest and winter planting periods, not only was he an ineffective leader, but he also made use of the labor days of the commune members to assist him in his work. This had a serious effect on production. For example, the Shang Pai-an production team in Lan's region had a winter-planting assignment of 20 mou, but up to November 23 had planted only one mou, and of the levy-purchase obligation of 257 tan had completed only 63 tan. (This was with the assistance of troop labor in transporting grain.)

Wang Sung-ch'un (party member), the brigade chief of the Tung-an brigade, in September of this year, together with Lin I-yü, the brigade Credit Section accountant, commune member Wang Hsiu-ken, Wang I-chien (freed after labor reform), and Chiang Ching (a thief) cut down 21 camphor trees and, after sawing them into seven-meter strips, sold them at high prices to the Kuan-t'ou shipyard and the T'a-t'ou shipyard through the confederation of Wang I-chien with the two peddlers Huang Chao-jui and Wang Ch'ang-ch'un. From this they obtained 830 yüan. After expenses of 387 yüan for transportation and sawing, their net income was 443 yüan. Each of the five took equal shares of 88 yüan.

After the disclosure of their actions and after education, these seven persons and Chou Huo-chiao resolved to correct their faults and do good work. In order to handle this problem strictly, we are now further verifying the facts. Later, we shall carry out individual punishment on the basis of the nature, seriousness, and attitude as seen in the different problems.

If there are unsatisfactory points in the above report, we request the County Committee to indicate them.

> P'AN-TU COMMUNE COMMITTEE,
> CHINESE COMMUNIST PARTY

December 18, 1962

XVIII

FURTHER DEVELOPMENT OF A LARGE-SCALE
SOCIALIST EDUCATION MOVEMENT FOR THE
PROMOTION OF PRODUCTION AND
ECONOMY, BY CH'EN FU-LUNG

February 9, 1963

(A copy of the report made in the three-level County
Expanded Conference for cadre members)

Today we convene this Expanded Conference for cadre members above the branch-secretary level. Participating in the conference are the first secretaries of the commune Party Committees, party branch-secretaries, some commune and brigade chiefs, and all work groups. The major purpose of the conference is to study how to launch a large-scale Socialist Education movement for increased production and economy.

Most recently we conducted a Socialist Education movement. However, because it was not adequate, we are holding this meeting in order to study how we may conduct another one more thoroughly and effectively.

Today, I shall discuss principally three problems.

I. THE STATE OF THE PREVIOUS SOCIALIST EDUCATION MOVEMENT

Like our brother counties, we have already conducted a Socialist Education movement. Although it has gone on for almost a month since the last expanded meeting and up to the present, there was an interruption, owing to the New Year festival, during the period. Consequently, Socialist Education has actually been conducted among the masses for only about ten days. During this stage, preliminary education has been conducted from the cadre members to the masses and from the inside to the outside. In general, this has been quite effective, and in some cases, extremely effective. According to county statistics, training was received by 12,247 cadre members above the production-team level, accounting for 93 per cent of all cadre members, and 5,093 party members, accounting for 94.2 per cent of total party members. Seventy to 80 per cent of the adult public also received instruction. During this stage we also held meetings in which examples of good persons and good acts were presented. Examples of 3,621 good cadre members, 1,053 good party members, 742 good Youth Corps members, and 5,644 good commune members were presented. As a result, a good atmosphere began to prevail and the bad atmosphere declined. Therefore, our work up to this point seems good, and the development of the movement has been regular and healthy. We have made the following major accomplishments:

First, through this phase of education, the majority of cadre members have reached a higher socialist awareness. They have come to understand that cadre members are to serve the people, and they have reaffirmed their faith in the revolution. Many cadre members have gotten rid of their previous lack of interest in acting as cadres and are now frequently found saying, "If we don't take charge, who will?" Consequently, they are very courageous in their work. According to statistics, before the movement there were 172 cadre members at the brigade level and 1,016 at the production-team level who had stated that they did not wish to serve as cadres and who had requested discharge. After the movement, the majority have changed their feelings, and now there are very few who do not wish to serve as cadres. According to the report of the meeting, there are only four persons at the brigade level and only 163 remaining at the production-team level who do not wish to serve as cadres. Statistics from the Ao-chiang commune indicate that while 105 cadre members requested dismissal originally, only eleven now do so. This is a great accomplishment.

Second, the level of understanding of the masses of commune members (including cadre members) has begun to rise, and they are beginning to be clear about direction. Their understanding has reached a point where they recognize that Household Contract Production, individual enterprise, and the distribution of land, farm tools, and fishing gear is wrong, and further, that these are problems of the struggle between socialism and capitalism and reflect the class struggle. In consequence, the majority of cadre members have voluntarily returned the Household Contract Production land and farm tools originally distributed to individuals. These have reverted to the collective ownership of the production teams. According to statistics, 755 production teams, or 96.3 per cent of the total number of teams, have already taken back land under Household Contract Production. This represents a total land area of 4,218 mou, or 97.5 per cent of the total Household Contract Production land. In addition, 5,722 farm tools, or 70 per cent of the total, which had been distributed to households, have been taken back. Also 121 boats and 43 fishing nets have been taken back. This is a phenomenal development.

Third, the bad attitude is on the wane, and a correct one is arising. The enthusiasm of many commune members toward collective production has begun to rise, and the number of persons abandoning farming for peddling has greatly decreased. The majority of those who left [for the cities] have returned, and those who at first would not participate in collective production now participate in it. Few, if any, commune members now engage in indiscriminate reclamation of uncultivated land and excess cutting of trees. Fewer persons now engage in feudalistic superstitious practices. Some cadre members and members of the masses have even voluntarily removed and destroyed the images of the Bodhisattvas. This phenomenon is very marked in the coastal regions. In the past, construction of temples to Bodhisattvas and the practice of superstition continued. Little temple construction is going on now, and in some places images have been removed and the temples transformed into storage houses. Extravagance and gambling (particularly the latter) decreased sharply during this year's New Year festival in comparison to last year's, and as a consequence social order has been enhanced.

Fourth, as a result of this movement, transformations have begun in some backward brigades and teams and in brigades and teams in distress. There are 86 brigades in the county whose present production is excellent. Among these, 21 brigades that were formerly backward in production are now operating well. Some have already overtaken originally advanced brigades. The Ao-chiang commune originally had 98 backward production teams. Sixty-one of these, or 62 per cent, have already been transformed. In the past, the Wang-ya brigade of Tan-yang was consistently backward in production. However, as a result of this work, its production has already begun to improve, and is now very effective. It is now considered to be one of the better brigades in the entire commune. Similar conditions exist in other places. In the past there were twelve production teams in the Kuei-an and Chu-pu brigades of P'an-tu that were rather backward, and some of them were in extreme distress. As a result of this work, the majority have improved, and some have already exceeded the production of the advanced teams several times and have surpassed them in paddy plowing, field burning, digging out river mud, and collecting fertilizer.

In short, there has been an elevation in the ideological consciousness of the broad body of cadre members and masses. An enthusiastic tide of production has formed, the bad attitude is on the wane, and a correct attitude is on the rise.

These are general accomplishments. Yet, we should also be aware of our problems. Our work has not been adequate. This is particularly true in . . . [1] Judging by the spirit of this conference, our work is still insufficient, and many problems still exist. What are our problems? They are principally as follows.

(1) The scale of the movement that we have been conducting has not been sufficiently large, and, in particular, a large-scale mass movement has not been formed. Using up time in going through the formal motions still occurs. Ideological problems have not been solved in depth, and great discrepancies have been found to exist in some places. Some persons have not even attained the county requirements.

(2) From the overall county standpoint, the situation is good, and great accomplishments have been made. However, these are not uniform. The good are very good, and the bad, very bad. Some brigades and teams have not even held meetings, and this includes cadre and Youth Corps members. In some, only a score of people out of a hundred came, and in others, only 40 or 50 per cent of the members received instruction.

(3) The content of this Socialist Education movement was not sufficiently comprehensive and was somewhat monotonous. Consequently, problems were not solved in depth. As everyone knows, the content of the education was principally concerned with "conditions," "class," and "policy." But, as we can now see, this was insufficient. We did not touch upon feudalism and extravagance, and as a result, bad attitudes have not yet been suppressed. We have not dealt effectively with the problems of speculative activities, superstition, worship of idols, and marriage-by-sale (not ordinary sale, but sale of human beings).

Why do these problems exist and what are their causes? During the two days of the expanded conference of the County Standing Committee, we have come to understand that the basic causes of these problems are insufficient comprehension of the great significance of the Socialist Education movement and failure to realize in what area that significance lies. As a result, our determination was not sufficiently great, our forces were not sufficiently organized, and our study of problems was insufficient. This is to say that the principal and most basic cause was our inadequate comprehension of the significance of the Socialist Education movement. This is our major problem at present, and this is the point that should be examined by the County Committee. We cannot blame the brigades, the teams, or the work groups.

---

[1] Four characters are illegible.

II. FURTHER COMPREHENSION OF THE SIGNIFICANCE OF
THE SOCIALIST EDUCATION MOVEMENT

Why must we initiate a large-scale Socialist Education movement to increase production and encourage economy? As everyone knows, overall conditions in Lien-chiang County, like those in the province and the nation at large, are good and are improving from year to year. However, we wish to achieve even better conditions in 1963 and in the future. What is our most important task at present? Speaking basically, and from the standpoint of work, it is the problem of working out methods for the attainment not only of a bumper crop in food, but of an over-all bumper crop, and an overall increase in production. Chairman Mao said in a speech at the most recent Party Representatives Conference, "Let us unite, struggle vigorously, overcome difficulty, and attain victory." This states the objective of our work. Conditions are improving from year to year, but this is still not enough. Difficulties still exist. Even when the food problem is solved, problems of clothing and commodities used in everyday life remain. It is for this reason that Chairman Mao spoke of uniting, struggling vigorously, overcoming difficulty, and attaining victory. If we wish to bring about an over-all production increase and bumper harvest in 1963, we must, on the basis of this directive from Chairman Mao, encourage all party members, Youth Corps members, cadres, and positive elements to join in the leadership of the masses and in the effective completion of all phases of production. However, if we are to complete production effectively, we must rely on the people and on their positiveness, their consciousness of purpose, and their initiative. Without this, production will not be satisfactory. Production must be accomplished by the people and by the masses, and it must be led by the party and the cadre members. However, if our cadres have not been mobilized and if their sense of purpose is low, production cannot be effectively managed. In order to attain our objectives, we must initiate a large-scale Socialist Education movement to promote production and economy, based on the recommendations of the Provincial Committee. This work is our most important, most urgent, and most critical task of the moment. As we all know, we are only one-and-a-half to two months from spring planting. Chairman Mao has said: "We cannot miss our opportunity. The time will not come again." Now is an excellent time. All organizational levels above the branch level and the entire body of cadre members must take advantage of it, concentrating their energies and resolving to carry out this movement effectively. This is to say, we request that on the basis of the previous movement the Socialist Education movement be carried out on a more effectual and greater scale and that the work be conducted in greater depth. Why do we say that this movement is our most important, urgent, and critical task at the moment? The reasons are as follows.

(1) Everyone knows that in the management of production and in the carrying out of all phases of work, if the most basic ideological problems are not solved, production and work cannot be effective. Chairman Mao has said that consideration of things rather than persons is what causes work to be ineffective. The "consideration of things rather than persons" is, in other words, the consideration of concrete things rather than consideration of ideology. Our present work is of many kinds, and a great deal of work has to be done in production, farming, forestry, animal husbandry, the subsidiary industries, and fishing. However, most basic and most important is the mastering of ideological work. The Socialist Education movement cannot be effectively carried out if this is not done. As everyone can clearly see, even after only one month (in reality, only about ten days among the masses), there has been a great change in conditions in the villages as well as great changes in the state of society, production,

and the spirit of the people. If we carry out the movement in even greater depth, even greater changes can be made. Production is a struggle with the natural world with which we are fighting just as the Liberation Army fought. Why is it that the Liberation Army could attain victory, overcome American imperialism, annihilate eight million Kuomintang troops, and, most recently, gain a great victory at the China-India border, annihilating and capturing several thousands of men? It is because of ideological and political work. Our troops fought at temperatures of thirty degrees below zero, in the thin air of high mountains where breath comes hard, where the land is frozen and covered with snow, and where noses and ears freeze. The Indian troops were not equal to this, and they surrendered after the first blow. It is therefore extremely clear that we cannot consider things while neglecting persons and that we cannot grasp concrete situations while neglecting ideological work. As everyone also knows, in the ten years since the liberation we have had a great educational campaign devoted to the spread of the General Line in 1953 and another educational campaign in 1958. In addition, we have had a program of education concerning the organization of cooperatives. General improvement took place after these were carried out. In the past few years we have encountered difficulties, and there have been a number of defects in our work. We have relaxed the Socialist Education of the cadres and the masses, so that capitalist and feudal ideology has arisen in some persons' minds. If we grasp only concrete work and production and neglect ideological work, then our handling of the situation will be ineffective.

(2) This Socialist Education movement is not only for the benefit of present production, but for that of the future as well. This point must be clearly understood. To view its purpose as that of bringing about great production and a great harvest for this year only is an oversimplification. If it is to be satisfactory, it must lay the ideological foundation for the next few years, decades, and even centuries. If it is not done in this way, our work will be only a spot treatment in which we deal with symptoms but do not treat fundamentals.

What do you say? Is it right not to oppose a bad attitude? Is it right not to put it down? No, it is not right. You want to manage production, but they want to engage in speculation, worship Bodhisattvas, and stage idolatrous processions. At present, marriage-by-sale, flesh peddlers, religious swindlers, and gambling have returned. In the Hua-wu brigade at Ao-chiang, eighteen girls of an average age of fourteen years were sold at an average of 750 yüan each. In Pai-sha there is a girl who has been married thirteen times. In some places girls are sold like hogs at so much a catty. Even worse is that some people make a business of buying and selling girls. They get fifty yüan merely for making an introduction. Some do not work but opportunistically go into business. In some places where extreme extravagance and waste exist, public savings have been spent to the point that even the shares for distribution to the commune members have been used up, depriving commune members of capital for production and making it necessary for them to borrow from the state. Since this atmosphere exists, we must deal with it on a large scale.

As everyone knows, we oppose revisionism, and we oppose it internationally. Our nation is a socialist state of which the people and the masses are the head. Would it be possible for us to become a capitalist nation if our work were not done well? This has already occurred elsewhere. As everyone knows, Yugoslavia was once a socialist state: now capitalism has been restored; land can be freely bought and sold; there are many rich farmers; and more than 90 per cent of the land is privately managed. We must give thought to our nation and devise methods to prevent it from following that example. Everyone knows that if these bad tendencies, such as capitalism and feudal ideology and behavior, are not put down and suppressed, but are allowed to expand gradually, capitalism will be restored. The problem will become serious. Therefore we are conducting this movement, not only to improve production and other work, but also to assure that our nation will always remain a socialist state. Thinking in this way, is it right not to conduct the movement in depth? The world situation is one in which the east wind is prevailing over the west wind. However, in some cases the east wind is not prevailing over the west wind; rather, the west wind is prevailing over the east wind. Therefore, we must resolve to carry out this movement effectively.

We must have a movement, but must we have a big movement? Yes, we must. We must let our banners fly and sound our battle drums and conduct the movement with great vigor. This cannot be an ordinary movement. We must arouse the masses. We must understand clearly that if we do not conduct it on a large scale, we can neither suppress the evil tendencies of capitalism and feudalism, nor elevate the awareness of the masses and the cadres. Accomplishments were registered in the previous phase of the movement. Have they, however, been firm accomplishments? Some who have engaged in individual enterprise and speculation are watching and waiting for the movement to pass, and afterward they will take up these practices once again. Other bad persons start rumors and take the lead in inciting those whose level of ideological awareness is not high into following them into Household Contract Production, promotion of individual enterprise, and speculation. Therefore, we must conduct a large-scale movement in the manner of the 1953 General Line and the 1958 Great Leap Forward movements.

Must we struggle? This is a great problem. Struggle still is necessary. If you do not use struggle, other people will compel you to. Struggle is necessary for those whose characters have been severely transformed by capitalism and feudalism. By "struggle," however, we are referring principally to ideological struggle. Struggle must be conducted in various forms and by various methods. To be sure, there are some persons who must be dealt with by law and some who will require punishment. There are those within the ranks of the party, the Youth Corps, and the cadres who should be so handled. Individual bad elements must be dealt with by law. This, however, holds only for a small number of individual cases. In general, it is ideological struggle that should be conducted. Ideological struggle should be conducted even among those who require legal handling. At present a minority of comrades are considering whether this great movement might not lead to errors and troubles. If it should, then our branch secretary, brigade chiefs, commune chiefs, secretaries, and work groups would find it difficult to go on with their work effectively. Afterward, we would be subject to criticisms, investigations, and punishment to the extent that we would have to make apologies, express regrets, and reverse decisions. We must not let this disturb us. The movement must still be carried out, and struggle must still be extended. Everyone knows that during the last two years we have promoted conscientiousness in work. However, in spite of this, the movement is still necessary. We need worry only if it is not carried out correctly. We can now see that it will not be satisfactory if it is not on a large scale. A minority of persons still engage in speculation, buy and sell people, work as flesh peddlers, and rely on superstition for their livelihood.

Why must we struggle? Struggle still exists fundamentally. Classes still exist, and as a result, class struggle exists. This is an objective existence. If you do not struggle, people will engage in Household Contract Production, speculation, and peddling. Do you say that we should deal with it or not, and do you say that we should struggle or not? We must understand a very important principle, that of recognizing the existence of classes and class struggle. If we fear class struggle and do not keep it up, but live together in peaceful coexistence without struggle, we shall be guilty of revisionism. Therefore, it is not necessary for anyone to be afraid of creating problems, committing errors, and being investigated. Our present treatment of struggle is different from what it was in the past. We now have gained in experience and can manage it more effectively. To avoid the occurrence of problems we need only to study earnestly, conduct our affairs according to regulations rather than personal whim, and give our attention to work methods based on party policy and regulations. Everyone knows that the level of our cadre members, including those above the county level, is still not very high. Our experience with this aspect of struggle is still insufficient. For example, we still fail to differentiate between the two kinds of contradictions. We do not have sufficient understanding of the complexity of the class struggle. It has political, military, economic, and cultural aspects, and it exists both with and without form, both openly and secretly, and both within and without the party. It is thus extremely complex. In addition, we lack sufficient understanding of the difference between class struggle in the period of socialism and in the period of democratic revolution. Class struggle differs before and after the attainment of political power. We do not yet sufficiently understand the struggle techniques of the socialist construction period. However, we need not be concerned. If we study what we do not understand, conscientiously manage our affairs according to party regulations, and resolve to study in the course of our work, then we can succeed in the successful completion of our tasks.

III. THE CONTENT OF SOCIALIST EDUCATION

It can now be seen that our original arrangements for Socialist Education were not comprehensive and that we must study them again on the basis of the requests of the Provincial Committee. As for the content of Socialist Education, at the East China Advanced Agricultural Collectives Representatives Conference, held in Shanghai, Premier Chou spoke on eight problems which the East China Bureau had already decided to adopt as its general program for conducting the Socialist Education movement in villages and cities throughout the entire East China region. The themes of the eight problems are as follows.

(1) First, the collective, then the individual. This refers to systems of ownership and problems in agricultural production.

(2) First the nation, then the individual. This refers to problems in production work.

(3) First ask of oneself, then of others. This also refers to problems in work and production.

(4) First reprimand oneself, then reprimand others. This refers to the problem of the interrelationships between people that exist in work and labor.

(5) First give one's concern to the public interest, then to private interests. This refers to the problem of distribution.

(6) First work for the public interest, then for the private interest. These are problems in the political and ideological sphere.

(7) I work for all the people; all the people work for me. "All the people" means the whole body of laboring people who are establishing the socialist road under the leadership of the working class.

(8) <u>I work for the world; the world works for me</u>. This refers principally to internationalism.

The Provincial Committee has, at this meeting, advocated the "three three's" as the content of Socialist Education for the entire province.[2]

The first "three" is the propagation of the three doctrines of collectivism, patriotism, and socialism.

The second "three" is opposition to the Three Evil Tendencies of capitalism, feudalism, and extravagance.

The third "three" is the firm support of the three demands: the demand for following the socialist road, the demand for being concerned with the protection of the collective, and the demand for democratic and frugal commune management (which includes the education of commune members in frugal household management).

We must now make it clear why we must act in this way, why we have advocated the "three three's," and especially why we must oppose the three evil tendencies. Everyone should realize that the advantage in proceeding this way is that our banners are clear! What we want and what we want to support become very clear. In this way, the masses are also clear about what we oppose, what we support, what we want, and what we do not want. Otherwise the banners of our movement will be unclear, without force, and lacking in full content. In this way our objectives will be easy to understand and remember, our banners will be clear, and the movement easy to manage. Once our banners have been made clear, right and wrong and bad and good become easily distinguishable and confusion cannot occur. Similarly, once the banners have been made clear, the movement gains in force and takes on a rich content. This is a correct procedure. Is it right not to oppose the spirit of feudalism and extravagance? It is not. In the previous phases of our work, our points of emphasis were education about "conditions" and "class." This was not bad, and accomplishments were great. The struggle between socialism and capitalism was also brought out very clearly. However, we did not deal effectively with the spirit of feudalism and with extravagance. Fundamentally, we did not make any inroads against marriage-by-sale, flesh peddling, and trading in women. Although ideological education about conditions, the struggle between capitalism and socialism, and about classes has been handled effectively, it is not right that these problems have not yet been solved. If we do not oppose the spirit of feudalism, it will be difficult to maintain the strength and growth of the collective economy. We did not understand this point clearly in the past, but it has now been clarified. In the past, we simply opposed Household Contract Production. But, as you now know, when a girl is sold into marriage, the price may be more than 800 yüan and may even be as high as 1,000 or 2,000 yüan. Now people are saying that some engage in speculation for no other reason than [. . .][3] to marry. In this way, the labor force is dispersed, and there is no one to work on the collective.

Is it right not to attack speculation? It is not. Lenin has said:

The proletariat in its victory over the capitalist class must, from beginning to end, act upon the following basic

---

[2] Reference to the "three three's" also occurs in Document XIX.

[3] Three characters are missing from the text here.

policy line toward farmers, which is the differentiation by
the proletariat between laboring peasants and those having
private property, between farmers who work and those who
[. . .]^4 and between those who farm and those who are speculators. This differentiation is the essence of socialism.
Providing for hungry workers in the cities according to the
state's fixed price and transferring 40,000,000 poods^5 of
food to state agencies although there still are shortcomings
in these agencies (shortcomings which are clearly understood by the workers and the state, but which are unavoidable in the initial transitional stage to socialism), these
farmers are laboring peasants, unashamed of being the
comrades of socialist workmen. They are the partners
upon whom the socialist workers can most rely and are
the close brothers of the socialist workers in their struggle
of opposition to capitalist oppression. There are, however,
other kinds of farmers who deceive the state and everywhere
exert their effort to carry on [. . .]^6 plundering, and
speculation, and who have made use of the hunger and hardship of the city workers to sell 40,000,000 poods of food
at prices ten times those set by the state--these farmers
are villainous merchants, the allies of capitalism, the
class enemies of the working people, and exploiters.^{7}

Therefore, our targets in this campaign against the spirit of feudalism and
the spirit of capitalism are speculation, flesh peddling, religious swindling, and
gambling. These must be smashed.

We must also oppose extravagance, which is antagonistic to frugal commune
management. At present, neither production nor living conditions are too good;
they are, in fact, very difficult. Nevertheless, some people and even some
cadre members, desiring to construct an attractive assembly hall or to build
an attractive house, have spent several thousands or tens of thousands of yüan
from the year's income, which should be used for distribution to members, or
from reserve funds. Some have called upon the masses for volunteer work in
the cutting of trees, and some have used bricks belonging to the collective. On
these scores the masses are critical of us. If such practices are not opposed,
it will become difficult to strengthen and to develop the collective economy of the
people's communes. It is for this reason that the Provincial Committee has
advocated the "three three's" as the content of this movement.

During this stage, cadre members at all levels who commit bad acts should
be investigated, and criticism and self-criticism should be carried out. Individuals who seriously violate laws and regulations should be punished. It is at
this stage that the masses have been critical of us. For example, if a minority
of cadre members do not behave properly, or if they build houses illegitimately,
the masses become very critical. It is commonly said, "How can one of our
cadre members who has a monthly wage of only twenty or thirty yüan build such
a fine, big house!" This represents a common suspicion among the masses.
However, as we agreed at the last meeting when we discussed the problem of

^{4}Two characters are missing.

^{5}A Russian unit of weight equal to about 36.11 pounds.

^{6}Two characters are missing.

^{7}The quotation is retranslated from the Chinese translation.

house building by cadre members, if done properly, it is all right, and when required, assistance may be given wherever possible. However, some people do not proceed properly or with complete correctness. Some take public savings and funds intended for distribution to the commune members, others cut trees belonging to the collective, and still others make use of brigade capital and bricks, and even of labor and land. These are all exceedingly evil practices. There are even some who, in order to build houses for themselves, make assessments on commune members on false pretexts. This is even more incorrect. All these tendencies can be classed as evil, and they must be resolved during this movement. If they are not, the masses will remain critical and unwilling to submit. At this point, many among the masses say: "Socialist Education is only for the masses, not for the cadres. What does this mean?" Because we have not solved the severe and predominant problems concerning the cadres, the masses are critical.

XIX

REPORT ON THE EXPANDED CADRE MEETING
OF THE CH'ANG-SHA BRIGADE

The purpose of this meeting is to initiate a large-scale Socialist Education movement to promote production and economy. The previous Socialist Education movement that we conducted was not sufficiently thorough, and as a result the higher-level party committee has once again issued a directive. On the basis of this directive we have called this second expanded conference of cadre members of the Ch'ang-sha brigade. Although, as everyone knows, we spent more than a month on the previous stage of the movement, several problems remain which we wish to discuss.

Accomplishments and existing problems in the previous stage were (1) the further development of a Socialist Education movement to promote production and economy, (2) the development of the content of the education, and (3) how the movement should be developed.

Although the previous stage of the movement lasted one month, education was actually conducted for just a little more than ten days because of the New Year festival. No great number of persons received instruction, and the movement did not develop evenly. For example, although it should have been well carried out among the masses, there was no true organization of discussions, and only a minority received instruction. Many old people and women received no instruction. In addition, the methods of instruction were monotonous.

After the movement was carried out, a correct attitude began to arise within the Ch'ang-sha brigade, while the bad attitude began to decline. Several accomplishments were registered. We observed the following.

(1) The majority of cadre members, after education, recollection, and contrast, raised their socialist understanding, established firm convictions, learned about conditions, and reached a clear understanding that being in the cadre and in the service of the people was an honor and a responsibility. Frequently cadre members were heard to say, "If we don't serve as cadre, who will?" Moreover, in their work they changed from being timid to being courageous, positive, and active. At the same time, in their leadership of labor and production they established labor quotas and fertilizer collection quotas for each individual.

(2) There was a great improvement in the ideology and knowledge of the masses and commune members and also clearer understanding that we must follow the road of the socialist collectives. We rectified the incorrect methods of household-contract production, the Spirit of Individual Enterprise, and the Small Freedoms. At the same time, it came to be understood that these practices are, in essence, a

concrete reflection of the Two Road struggle and the class struggle. When we set the quotas for the collection of organic fertilizer, all the commune members actively participated, and many exceeded their quotas.

(3) The attitude of the commune members and the masses toward collective labor and production improved greatly. This year our basic requests were met, as, for example, in hauling sand and in collecting fertilizer. This indicates accomplishment through education. Nevertheless, several problems still exist.

(4) A minority of persons believe that the cadre members were responsible for the decrease in income in 1962, and for that reason bear a grudge against them. The cadre members, on the other hand, believe it was a result of the recalcitrance of the commune members and the masses. This has led to a feeling of mutual grievance between the cadres and the masses. After studying the Sixty Draft Regulations and after mass discussion of agricultural income and expenditures in 1962, the causes of the decrease in income were ascertained. Of these, the most important were the effects of the Spirit of Individual Enterprise, speculation, and abandonment of farming for peddling. During the previous stage a minority of commune members who were temporarily confused in their ideology succumbed to the influence of bad persons. They spread rumors, saying: "There is no future here in Ch'ang-sha. Income will continue to decrease from now on." After a program of propaganda, everyone clearly understood that the land belonging to the Ch'ang-sha brigade has a great future. There are the mountains, the sea, and the plains, which is to say, "We have the mountains, the sea, and the fields and gardens all nearby." Consequently, the masses have all resolved to overcome difficulties and to strive, during 1963, for a rich harvest in agriculture, fishing, animal husbandry, subsidiary industries, and forestry. However, we must understand that we shall of necessity encounter difficulties on the road ahead, but that these difficulties will be only temporary and need not be feared. For example, after the disaster last year our brigade's food supply was tight. However, under the correct leadership of the party, with the strong support of the state, and through reliance on the power of collective production and the efforts of the commune members and masses, the most difficult juncture was passed within a few short months. For example, because of the decrease in income last year, the brigade did not have enough capital to cultivate oysters this year. The state then made loans, and the commune members actively invested. We have now basically passed the difficult juncture occasioned by the lack of capital for cultivating oysters. As Chairman Mao has said, "Unite to overcome difficulties and strive vigorously for victory." Although there were accomplishments in the previous stage of Socialist Education, we did not make sufficient progress in implanting the thought of protecting the collective, firmly following the socialist road, and carrying out production systematically and with economy.

Many problems still exist, such as time wasting and "going through the motions," inability to solve everyone's ideological problems, incomplete suppression of evil tendencies, and poor solution of policy problems. The principal problems that still exist, which we ask everyone to discuss and resolve, are as follows.

(1) Individual commune members keep good fertilizer for themselves and hand over to the brigade fertilizer containing water. When the manure appraisers give them only a percentage of the total price, they make trouble, argue, and even curse the appraisers.

(2) Some do not go out to work after their quotas have been set, but surreptitiously attend to their own Small Freedoms and open up uncultivated land. Some have said to the team chiefs, "You cannot set a quota for me, as I do not have any

labor force," and yet they have opened up several mou of uncultivated land, thereby contravening the policy of giving precedence to the collective over the individual.

(3) Some work because discipline requires them to do so, and the efficiency of their work is not high. They go to work late and finish early; they skimp on their work and waste time. They have not attained self-awareness and initiative.

(4) Some rely on state support and do not strive to stand on their own feet. They have delayed in repaying state-assistance loans, have even gone so far as not to repay them, and have distributed state funds among the commune members. To be sure, state assistance to us is correct. But we should repay the funds when they are due.

(5) The Spirit of Individual Enterprise continues, even though we oppose it. Individual production teams have understood the conditions; they have discovered that even a small area of land given over to Household Contract Production has bad effects; but they have persisted in establishing Household Contract Production for 1963.

(6) The felling of trees has continued side-by-side with Socialist Education, harming collective wealth and destroying collective forests.

(7) Some have abandoned farming for peddling and industry. Some persons engage in speculation and peddling. Some who abandon farming for peddling ask to become apprentices. Some workmen accept apprentices and thus exploit others. Some who abandon farming for subsidiary industries let flocks of ducks and geese damage crops. Work of the labor force was reduced by emigration.

(8) Some steal valuables such as farm tools, fertilizer, and materials that belong to the collective. Fishermen also steal fish belonging to the collective.

(9) We still have not suppressed the evil tendencies of capitalism, feudalism, and extravagance and, as a result, cannot manage collective production effectively.

The educational content of this meeting. --The previous stage of education in our brigade, as in all others, was very [...][1] and not comprehensive. We dealt only with the problems of opposing the Spirit of Individual Enterprise and individual-enterprise contracting, the contrasts between the new and the old society, and the Two Road struggle. Responding to the requests of the Provincial Committee, however, we submitted the matter for study again, and here at this general meeting, today, we are again conducting education. What is the content of this stage of Socialist Education? On the basis of the spirit of higher-level directives, the outline for Socialist Education to be conducted in the villages and cities consists of an eight-theme program.

(1) <u>First the collective, then the individual</u>. This refers to the viewpoint of the commune member toward collective production, such as attitudes toward opening uncultivated land, fertilizer, and labor.

(2) <u>First the state, then the individual</u>. This refers to production and work as, for example, the purchase of subsidiary agricultural goods from the commune members, the fulfillment of assigned tasks, and the unified purchase of food.

(3) <u>First ask of oneself, then of others</u>. This refers to whether cadre members should rely on themselves or others in work and production.

(4) <u>First reprimand oneself, then reprimand others</u>. This refers to the need to make more severe demands of one's self and to treat others more leniently. In

---

[1]Illegible character.

this, our cadre members should set the example through their own conduct.

(5) <u>First consider the public interest, then the private interest.</u> This refers to the problem of distribution, as in the handling of the income from the oyster industry by our brigade.

(6) <u>First work for the public interest, then for the private interest.</u> This refers to problems in political ideology. Party members, Youth Corps members, and cadre members should give special attention to this.

(7) <u>I work for all the people; all the people work for me.</u> This refers principally to the laborers who are working collectively to establish socialism under the leadership of the working class.

(8) <u>I work for the world; the world works for me.</u> This refers principally to the internationalist movement. At the same time, the Provincial Committee has drawn up the "Three Three's" as the content of the Socialist Education movement for the entire province.

The first "three" is the propagation of the three doctrines of collectivism, patriotism, and socialism.

The second "three" is opposition to the Three Evil Tendencies of capitalism, feudalism, and extravagance.

The third "three" is The firm support of the three demands: the demand for following the socialist road, the demand for being concerned with the protection of the collective and the demand for democratic and frugal commune management (which includes the education of commune members in frugal household management).

We now wish to make clear why we must proceed in this manner, why we have drawn up the "three three's," and especially why we must oppose the Three Evil Tendencies. Everyone should realize that the greatest advantage in this is that the banners of our socialism will become clear. At the same time, it will make us understand what we want. We want collectivism, patriotism, and socialism. What must we support? We must support the socialist road, care for and protect the collective, and support democratic and frugal commune management (as well as frugal household management on the part of the commune members).

What do we oppose? Capitalism, feudalism, and extravagance.

What do we want? What do we not want? We want the collective, but we do not want individual enterprise. We want socialism, not capitalism. We want frugal commune management, not extravagance.

In this way, matters will be very clear, and everyone will understand what we oppose, what we support, and what we do not want. Otherwise, the banners of the socialist movement will not be manifest and the movement will be weak and incomplete in content. In this way, however, it will be extremely easy for the cadre members and the masses to understand and remember, and because its banners are manifest, it will be easy to manage. Once the banners have been made manifest, right and wrong and good and bad will be clearly differentiated and we will not go astray. Once our purposes have been made manifest, the movement will have strength and, therefore, a rich content.

Furthermore, it will be wrong not to proceed in this manner. Indeed, it is improper not to oppose the spirit of feudalism and extravagance.

In the first stage of our work we emphasized education concerning conditions and class. This was not bad. Our accomplishments were great, and we made the Two Road struggle very clear. However, we were not effective in our treatment of the spirit of feudalism and of extravagance. For example, in the previous stage of the movement we did not conduct education against such basic problems as marriage-by-sale, trading in human beings, and the use of women as articles of trade. Although education on conditions, the Two Road struggle, and class have, as one can see, been handled very well, it is not satisfactory that these Three Evil Tendencies remain unresolved. If we do not oppose the spirit of feudalism, it will be difficult to strengthen the collective economy. This is a point we did not thoroughly understand in the past, but we now understand it more clearly. In the past we simply promoted opposition to household-contract production. Now, however, everyone is aware that marriage-by-sale is a restoration of the remnants of feudalism. For example, a girl being married off can be bought for 400, 500, 800, 900, or even 1,000 or 2,000 yüan. Some men say, "With wives so expensive, I cannot get one even if I work myself half to death at my farming."

Is it right if we do not attack speculation and profiteering? Of course, it is not. As everyone knows, speculation and profiteering and engaging in peddling destroy collective production and strike at the foundations of socialism. Some people are, therefore, not intent on agricultural production and depart from the collective, so that there is no one to handle collective production. Naturally, there are some persons whose eyes light up and whose palms begin to itch when they see this, and they say, "If you are going to do it, I will do it too." In this way speculation and profiteering can destroy state plans and affect the solidarity between agriculture and industry and the relationship between city and country. It is just as Lenin said: "The broad masses of peasants are willing to take the course of socialism, but it is very easy for them to be influenced by capitalistic thought. Whenever a nation has temporary difficulties, it causes their minds to waver."[2] Recently, for example, a small number of persons have engaged in speculation and profiteering, peddling, and contracting of labor and have thereby exploited others. If they continue in this way, they will become enemies of the people and of the masses, and friends of the bourgeoisie. Since they are not close brothers of the people and of the masses, this indicates the extreme importance of ideological reform for them. At the same time, we should awaken to the true state of affairs, namely, that capitalism is beginning to take form in our socialism. Therefore, if we do not put capitalism under control, the bourgeoisie will push socialism to the rear. This occurred, for example, when some of our comrades did not want to serve as cadres during the previous stage. They held such incorrect views as believing that those serving as cadre members were at a disadvantage, were afraid of trouble, and were cursed by the people. We must, however, realize that at present if we poor peasants are not prepared to serve as cadres, then bad men will be our leaders and we shall once again suffer oppression and exploitation. We believe that no one wishes that to happen. Therefore we have made speculation and profiteering, trading in human beings, religious swindling, witchcraft, and gambling the objects in this campaign of opposition to the spirit of feudalism and capitalism.

We must also oppose extravagance, because it is antithetical to frugal commune management. At present, production and standards of living are not good and difficulties remain, even though some persons are demanding and extravagant with everything. The problem of excessive eating and drinking is also very severe and is also prominent among cadre members. As a result, a number of those among

---

[2] This statement is retranslated from the Chinese translation.

213

the masses have said that if we do not oppose these evil tendencies, it will be difficult to strengthen and expand the collective economy of the people's communes. This is the reason why the Provincial Committee has drawn up the "three three's" as the major content of this Socialist Education movement.

Cadre members at all levels have done some bad things. These should be investigated, and criticism and self-criticism should be conducted. It is essential that each serious infraction of laws and regulations should be dealt with severely. Since we did not thoroughly solve this problem during the previous stage, the masses have been very critical of us. This is especially so in regard to the problems of excessive eating and drinking, taking of special privileges and conveniences, and excessive spending and borrowing by the cadre. These are all evil tendencies which we must resolve this time; if we do not, the masses will be critical and naturally unsubmissive. Many conspicuous problems have not been clearly solved. For these reasons, another influential and vigorous Socialist Education movement is extremely necessary.

What objectives must we attain in this movement? There are five principal points. These may also be used as standards in judging whether the Socialist Education movement is being carried out thoroughly within the teams. We should see:

(1) Whether the awareness of the overall majority of the commune members has been heightened, whether they have truly united in following the road of socialism, and whether socialist ideology has suppressed feudalistic and capitalistic ideology--this is to say, whether the east wind is overcoming the west wind.

(2) Whether evil tendencies have been suppressed and good tendencies are increasing.

(3) Whether there has been increased enthusiasm in the attitude of the overall majority of commune members toward collective production, and whether a high tide of collective production has been built up in the teams.

(4) Whether the party's Sixty Draft Regulations have been put into actual operation, whether the work attitudes of cadre members have changed, and whether Communist Party members, Youth Corps members, and cadre members are behaving in a manner becoming their stations.

(5) Whether the overall atmosphere of the society has changed.

If these five provisions have been adequately met, this indicates that the movement in a given region has been effective and has met the requirements.

February 20, 1963

XX

[REPORT ON THE SOLUTION OF PROBLEMS AMONG CADRE MEMBERS BY THE EXPANDED CADRE MEETING OF THE SHANG-SHAN BRIGADE]

THE LIEN-CHIANG COUNTY COMMITTEE OF THE CHINESE COMMUNIST PARTY, FUKIEN PROVINCE

(Approved for transmission)

NUMBER: . . .   SECRET

TO: Each Commune Party Committee, 3 copies; each Brigade Branch Committee, 1 copy; Municipal Committee, 11 copies; Provincial Committee Socialist Education Office, 3 copies

COPIES TO: County Committee Standing Committee, Regional County Committeemen, each County Committee Section, Youth Corps Office, Women's Corps Office, Militia Office, and People's Committee Office, one copy each; file, 2 copies (total printing: 330 copies)

ITEM: . . . pages, approved for transmission by the Lien-chiang County Committee of the Chinese Communist Party and approved for transmission by the County Committee and issued on February 27, 1963, by the Secretariat of the County Committee

ALL COMMUNE PARTY COMMITTEES AND BRIGADE BRANCH COMMITTEES:

We hereby transmit to you the report of the Shang-shan brigade on the expanded cadre meeting's solution of problems among cadre members.

We believe that it is extremely important to solve the personal problems of cadre members and that this should be a major item in the expanded cadre meetings. The Shang-shan brigade has handled this matter well and, because it has acted in this way, it was able not only to bring the cadre to a positive and courageous leadership of the movement, but also, owing to the personal example set by the cadre members, to influence and teach the masses even more positively. Therefore, we must resolve to assist the cadre members in the solution of personal problems.

It would appear that it should take about two days for expanded brigade meetings to solve cadre problems (in regions where there are big problems, the time may be somewhat longer). Because their problems have directly involved the masses and because the ideological struggle is extremely intense, these problems cannot be solved in too short a period. At the same time, we must repeatedly promote ideological mobilization, analyze harmful conditions, and raise the level of understanding, in order that the examination and treatment of problems will become voluntary [matters] for cadre members.

In addition, during investigation, attention must be given to immediate rectification after a revelation is made, in order to show the masses that we are true to our word. Problems whose solution is obvious and easy should be corrected at once. The Shang-shan brigade has given attention to this problem and has begun work which, we feel, is very good. In this way, we can arouse the masses more easily.

Is the above satisfactory? Please indicate.

LIEN-CHIANG COUNTY COMMITTEE,
CHINESE COMMUNIST PARTY

February 27, 1963

REPORT ON THE SOLUTION OF PROBLEMS AMONG CADRE
MEMBERS BY THE EXPANDED CADRE MEETING
OF THE SHANG-SHAN BRIGADE

In compliance with the County Committee directive and for the purpose of solving personal problems of cadre members and helping them to clarify their ideology and enter actively into the movement so as to assure its favorable development, we devoted a day of the meeting to assisting cadre members in ideological understanding. The meeting followed a procedure whereby first the problems at brigade cadre members and then those of production-team cadre members were solved. Initially an investigation of the brigade was made by Branch Secretary Hsieh T'ien-tseng, Assistant Branch Secretary Yang Hsüeh-chü, Brigade Chief Liu Yu-tzu, and Youth Corps Branch Secretary Wu Ch'ing-jen. The meeting was divided into groups for the discussion and presentation of opinions. Later, with the groups as units, problems of production-team cadre members were solved and self-examination and mutual criticism were conducted. The meeting was very successful, spirits were high, and there were many speeches. The brigades all took an attitude of courageous responsibility and raised many points of criticism of the brigade cadre members. Many problems were revealed, which were reduced to 48 items. Of these, 13 were questionable criticisms, 25 were correct criticisms, and ten were constructive criticisms. The chairman of the Brigade Women's Representatives Committee was also requested to make a self-examination before the brigade, and in group examinations the majority of the cadre members also vigorously examined their own problems and assisted their comrades in good faith. According to our statistics, of the 294 persons examined (those not examined were some of the positive elements among the commune members and some women cadre members), making up 70 per cent of the people and 92 per cent of the cadre members who attended the meeting, there were 198, or 67 per cent among them, who examined themselves thoroughly and manifested sincere attitudes, to the satisfaction of all. There were 77 persons, or 25.8 per cent, who did not examine themselves thoroughly and had problems which were not solved. There were 21 persons, or 7.2 per cent, who did not examine themselves thoroughly, whose attitudes were not good, and of whom everyone was critical. By means of self-examination and mutual assistance, several problems were revealed. Of these, the most common were obstinacy in work attitudes, unwillingness to serve as cadre members, lack of thoroughness in work, extravagance and waste, misappropriation of public funds, inaccuracy in accounts, superstitious practices, and the taking of special privileges. A minority of the cadre members was enthusiastic about opening uncultivated and free land, working outside, and engaging in peddling and gambling. On the basis of incomplete statistics, among the cadre members there were two persons who had engaged in peddling, 40 who had committed graft and misappropriation, ten who had gambled, five who had privately slaughtered hogs, three who had arranged marriages-by-sale, one who had engaged in superstitious practices, three who had given extravagant parties, and 36 who had been unwilling to serve as cadre members. In short, the meeting was quite successful and reaped a large harvest; basically, it reached the stage described in the saying, "Everything that was known was said, and everything that was said was said completely." Enthusiasm was high, as the statement "From now on we should have two meetings like this every year" reflects. Production-team Chief Huang Te-shun said, "This is the most satisfactory movement we have had since 1958." Liu Ch'eng-ts'un, a positive element, said: "Working in this way helped the cadre members and instructed us. Problems could be solved and major criticisms eliminated."

We came to understand four major points.

(1) The repeated explanation of significance and objectives, and the initiation of self-conscious examination among the cadre. --The meeting mobilized the people, explained the major points of significance, clearly indicated why the personal problems of the cadre members must be solved, and also indicated what is beneficial and what is harmful. Points such as the following were emphasized. Is it right for the problems of cadre members not to be solved? What harm is it to the nation, the collective, and the cadre members themselves? What effect can these [problems] have on the masses? After mobilization, everyone expressed the belief that one must conscientiously examine and solve one's own problems. It was recognized that this was very important. Many people said, "Now that reprimanding one's self before reprimanding others is being advocated, if the cadre members do not solve their own problems, how can they teach the masses?" As Team Chief Wu Chin-mu (Branch Committee) said: "Capitalist ideology was widespread in our team and was, for the most part, inspired by my growing of sweet potatoes--I raised more than seven tan. Now I must take the lead in reform so that I can then persuade the masses." In addition, some persons having problems truly understood that the purpose of this movement was to help the cadre. Some persons also came to feel that they had begun to take an incorrect course and that if they did not reform, their characters would be altered. As Brigade Chief Liu Yu-tzu said: "My problems were very serious. I had already begun to take the road of capitalism, and if it had not been for this meeting I would have fallen into the pit of capitalism." He vowed to examine his own problems thoroughly and solve them. Assistant Secretary Yang Hsüeh-chü said, "If we do not examine our errors and they continue to grow, we will degenerate into Kuomintang pao-chia chiefs." In this way everyone's understanding was increased and examinations conducted were with self-awareness.

(2) The solution of ideological problems, the unification of ideology and knowledge, and the elimination of doubts from above to below and from inside to outside. Before the movement began, and although the majority of people realized that this movement was extremely important, there were, nevertheless, some cadre members among whom there existed thought of the "four kinds" type. The first was

that cadre members with problems had fear of struggle, of punishment, of change, and of returning funds. The second was fear of attack and revenge. The third was fear that criticisms would be useless because they would not lead to reform. The fourth was fear of becoming involved personally. They said, "If it keeps on, we are afraid that we will become involved ourselves." Team Chief Chu Cheng-feng said, "If we make criticisms, we are afraid that we will be sentenced to labor reform like those who made criticisms in 1958." Huang Shao-yun, a work-point recorder in the P'in-yu team, said: "The handle of the sword is always in the hands of the cadre. We are powerless, whether there is a reform or not." Some said: "On the surface cadre members are moral and virtuous, but in their hearts they are devious. Their speech and their conduct are not consistent. They do not do as they say." There are great ideological conflicts among cadre members with problems. Chang Hui-ying, the chairman of the Women's Representative's Committee, has not attended to her work, has participated in very few of the meetings, and has not attended the two expanded meetings of commune cadres. She said: "After working several years, I find things have turned bad, and the masses are very critical of me. I have decided to give up being a cadre member." We took the following four methods in dealing with the above thought.

(a) We began with the leadership. On the basis of criticisms, we conducted supplementary examinations of the branch secretary, the brigade chiefs, the Youth Corp secretary and the chairman of the Women's Association. As a result of the examinations the branch secretary, the assistant branch secretary, and the brigade chiefs were found satisfactory. There was basic satisfaction with the examination of the Women's Association chairman, and dissatisfaction with that of the Youth Corps secretary (who avoided the serious and concerned himself with the trivial, and was transferred to continued brigade examination). When members of the team cadre saw that brigade self-examination had been conscientious, they then conducted their own self-examinations scrupulously.

(b) The repeated communication of policy and the indication of the future of rectification. -- The Women's Association chairman, Chang Hui-ying, at first did not want to be a cadre member and did not submit to self-examination. After the consequences were indicated to her (principally, by explaining that it is only necessary for a person to correct his errors for the masses to trust in him, and that if he does not submit to self-examination, then the masses will not forgive him, and he will never again be respected by them), she examined her own problems fundamentally, and she has now adopted a good attitude.

(c) For cadre members with serious problems, individual discussions should be conducted by the work groups and the branch secretaries. For example, in order to build a house, Brigade Chief Liu Yu-tzu spent 700 yüan of brigade funds, borrowed 500 catties of food belonging to the team, privately slaughtered one hog, and used boats belonging to the collective to transport the materials for construction. (In the construction of the house he processed 80 tan of shell lime, used 1,500 bricks, and dug up 6,000 foundation bricks.) He also used to burn incense and engage in practices arising from superstitious beliefs. After six individual discussions with the work groups and after assistance from the branch secretary, he resolved to submit to a thorough examination at the meeting.

(d) Cadre members with problems should be subjected to education and examination, which should be boldly utilized. For example, a brigade chief should be allowed to participate in the Branch Committee meeting, and the committee members should study and work together with him so that he will not feel greatly oppressed, and so that unnecessary doubts will be dispelled.

(3) Emphasis should be on thoroughgoing methods, which should be like a pleasant breeze and a gentle rain. We believe the question of being like a pleasant breeze and gentle rain is principally a problem of method and consists of positive education. In stimulating self-conscious examination, we must basically investigate and disclose existing problems. This work must be strictly performed, but there can be some leeway in the choice of method. It must be done so that intense struggle does not occur, yet mutual criticism should be encouraged. Problems must be thoroughly handled, and obstinacy and recalcitrance prevented. Some persons hold the incorrect view that a pleasant breeze and a gentle rain means "no breeze and no rain," and this idea should be changed. How does one make a "pleasant breeze and a gentle rain"? We feel that it is done principally by using "four repetitions." That is, the repeated explanation of the importance and significance of the solution of cadre members' problems, repeated examinations (if examination is not thorough, it can be repeated two, three, or four times), repeated demonstration of attitude (demonstration of an open-minded desire to accept others' criticisms and to reform thoroughly), and repeated discussions (principally concerning the difference between right and wrong, correct reformation, and resolution of doubts). In addition, the brigade cadre and work groups should participate in the examinations conducted by the teams, give them encouragement and leadership, and get a concrete grasp of the situation. After this, we should attain the "two satisfactions" (satisfaction for the individual and satisfaction for everyone) as a basis. Everyone not only felt that this meeting was like a pleasant breeze and a gentle rain, but that there actually was a breeze and a rain. As the woman assistant brigade chief, Wu T'u-chin, said: "In the past, movements ran like storms and consisted of struggles. As a result, there was not enough rain. This time it was like a pleasant breeze and a gentle rain falling drop by drop, and it was both deep and thorough."

(4) Simultaneous rectification and reform must be emphasized. In this problem, there is ideological struggle. Brigade Chief Liu Yu-tzu was hesitant at first about returning materials and funds. After this work, he demonstrated a resolve to return them and satisfied the cadre members present. The principal method of reform is treatment on the basis of individual conditions. That which can be reformed should be reformed quickly. (For example, the problems of cadre members' using production-team land and excess private plots were solved on the second day by the return of the land to the production team. Cotton bedding that belonged to the militia and had been taken home by cadre members was immediately returned.) We should resolve to reform as soon as possible that which for the time being cannot be reformed. Our forces should be organized to clarify and later correct that which is for the time being not clear. (For example, specialized personnel should be organized for the reckoning of all brigade accounts and foods.) By thus presenting suggestions for reform in individual and concrete situations, everyone will be satisfied.

> SHANG-SHAN BRANCH,
> CHINESE COMMUNIST PARTY
>
> SHANG-SHAN WORK GROUP

February 27, 1963

XXI

REPORTS ON THE EXPANDED CADRE MEETINGS
OF THE SHANG-SHAN AND CHU-CH'I BRIGADES

THE LIEN-CHIANG COUNTY COMMITTEE OF THE CHINESE COMMUNIST PARTY, FUKIEN PROVINCE

NUMBER: 018   SECRET

TO: Each Commune Committee, and the Tung-hu
                 Farm Party Committee, 3 copies; each Brigade
                 Branch, 1 copy; Municipal Committee, 11 copies

COPIES TO: County Committee Standing Committee, each section
                 of the County Committee, the Youth Corps Office,
                 Office for Women's Corps, Militia Office, and
                 People's Committee Office, one copy each; file
                 2 copies (total printing: 330 copies)

THIS ITEM: ...pages, issued by the Office of the Secretary, Lien-
                 chiang County Committee, Chinese Communist Party,
                 February 23, 1962[1]

The Lien-chiang County Committee approves for transmission the reports on two expanded meetings of brigade cadre members.

TO EACH COMMUNE PARTY COMMITTEE AND BRIGADE BRANCH:

We hereby transmit to you the reports on the expanded cadre meetings held by the Shang-shan brigade of the Ao-chiang commune and the Chu-ch'i brigade of the Kuan-t'ou commune. We believe that each of these meetings has its strong points as well as its limitations. We now present the following opinions on the successful handling of expanded meetings of brigade cadres based on the experience and lessons of these two brigades.

(1) Attendance at meetings.--The major purpose of the expanded cadre meetings is the training of all cadre personnel (including production-team committee cadre), all party and Youth Corps members and positive elements. How many positive elements should be absorbed? We feel that one or two per small team is enough (if there are too many, they are hard to control, and if there are too few, a framework cannot be built up) and that a few more may be added to the

---

[1] The discrepancy between this date and the date February 22, 1963, in the body of the document appears thus in the original.

minority of backward teams. Representative positive elements (such as old revolutionaries, old peasants, fishermen, model workers, retired military persons, youths, militiamen, and women) should be selected. Special attention should be given to poor and lower-middle peasants with relatively high awareness. In this way we can assist the brigades in conducting successful meetings and lay the foundation for the organization of good Class Corps.

(2) What problems should the brigade meetings solve? Taking the methods of these two brigades as a basis, we believe that in the brigade meetings, in addition to making reports (the communiqué of the Tenth Plenum of the Eighth Central Committee, and the revised sections of the Sixty Draft Regulations, and the resolutions of the Provincial Committee should be disseminated and read), emphasis should be given to the discussion and solution of the following five problems: (a) discussion of the two basic problems, especially in those areas which were not discussed or not sufficiently discussed during the previous stage; (b) the significance, objectives, and content of the movement; (c) problems related to methods--principally those concerned with how to stimulate the masses and whom we should rely upon for the completion of the movement; (d) assistance to members of the cadres in rectifying their errors and in bringing themselves to the examination and communication of their problems; and finally (e) the use of half a day for the organization of production and the channeling of the enthusiasm of the meeting into production.

Based on this content, the brigade meetings should not be too short. The second and fourth problems, particularly, will require a somewhat longer period. Thus, the full session of meetings will require three to four days.

(3) Discussion of the significance, objectives, and content (the last two may be discussed together until the point of the concrete boundary between them is reached). --Three points should be grasped by the leaders. (a) Problems should be raised, guidance initiated, and understanding increased in a direct manner and on the basis of the level of the production-team cadre. For example, the Shang-shan brigade raised questions as to why we should conduct a movement and whether we must continue with it, what we advocated, and what we opposed. In this way, the discussion of problems was made easy for the cadre to accept. (b) They must be allowed to disclose fully the widespread character and severity of the Three Evil Tendencies with reference to conditions in their own teams. After these have been disclosed, their harmfulness should be analyzed. In this way, the brigade can be made to understand that the previous phase of the movement was not deep and thorough, and that this phase of the movement has great significance. (c) Emphasis should be given to using living persons and events from a given region and to persuasion by personal example. It is also beneficial to use examples of one good and one bad, and one positive and one negative, for the purpose of education by contrast.

(4) The crux of the successful completion of the movement is the solution of the cadre's own problems. This should make up the major content of the expanded brigade cadre meetings. This is a point that the Chu-ch'i brigade handled very well. Their principal methods were repeated communication of policy, taking the lead and giving assistance at important points, and individual conversations. It would appear that it was very important for the leadership cadre members in the brigades to take the initiative in self-examination, for the examination to be sincere, and for problems to be thoroughly communicated without confusion. In this way the members of the brigade cadre can be stimulated to have the courage for examination. For example, when the Chu-ch'i brigade chief did not conduct a thorough self-examination, neither did the team cadre

members. After a supplementary session was given to the brigade chief, every-one communicated his problems.

Of course, there are some people (including team chiefs) who have many problems involving the masses. For them, in addition to examination at the cadre meetings, there should be a further stimulation of awareness and self-examination at mass meetings.

(5) The problem of integrating the movement with production. --At the beginning, both brigades made conscientious arrangements for production and detailed specialized personnel for the management of production. The Chu-ch'i brigade also issued a regulation to the effect that in the initial stage cadre members should use their free time in the morning, at noon, and in the evening to inspect and supervise production. The Shang-shan brigade, before the con-clusion of the meetings, displayed examples of good persons, good acts, and good production teams, and established model teams. Afterwards, everyone was allowed to talk about his experience in production and to resolve to compete in production and in developing a high tide of study, comparison, and emulation of those who are advanced.[2] These are all good methods for expanding pro-duction and should be used in every region.

(6) After the conclusion of the brigade cadre expanded meetings, Class Corps should be organized at once. The principal method is to rely on the positive elements who participated in the meetings to act as a nucleus for uniting the poor and lower-middle peasants. Later, with the brigade as the unit, the positive elements among the poor and lower-middle peasants of the teams should meet for the purpose of conducting class education and class analysis of evil tendencies currently in existence. This is for the purpose of raising their class awareness. Finally, we should tell them of the purposes and methods of the movement. In this way they can act as the backbone of the movement.

We hope that each commune, in the last stage of the expanded meetings of commune cadre members (or at a party branch secretaries' meeting after the conclusion of the expanded cadre meetings) will study the above opinions, and that any having differing opinions will report them to us. If there are unsatis-factory points, we request the Municipal Committees so to indicate!

LIEN-CHIANG COMMITTEE,
CHINESE COMMUNIST PARTY

February 23, 1963

REPORT ON THE EXPANDED CADRE MEETING OF THE SHANG-SHAN BRIGADE

This session of expanded cadre meetings began on February 19 and was con-ducted in the following way.

(1) Participants in the meetings. --Those participating in the meetings were the chiefs and assistant chiefs of the production teams, the Four Personnel of the production teams, the women's representatives, the militia company commanders, all party and Youth Corps members, all positive elements, demobilized military persons, cadre who have been sent down [hsia-fang], and elementary school-teachers. There were, in all, 425 persons, or 40 per cent of the adult population

---

[2] See Glossary, "Compare, Study, Emulate, and Assist movement."

and 63 per cent of the total number of households (618). We emphasized two problems. The first was to select, on the basis of conditions in the given team, poor and lower-middle peasants who were ideologically sound to take the lead in handling the collective and to select steadfast, positive elements for participation in the meetings. The second was to select from teams in distress, backward teams, and teams having deficiencies in their work, commune members of good abilities, ideology, and collective labor to act as a nucleus. From the entire brigade 89 positive elements were selected. This was 21 per cent of the total number of persons attending the meetings. These persons provided the nucleus for the establishment of a Class Corps having poor and lower-middle peasants as its core.

(2) The arrangement of meeting times. --Originally we had planned to hold a 24 hour day and night meeting. However, discussion time was a little too short. Everyone felt that problems had not been solved well and requested an extension. Many team chiefs said, "It would pay to spend another day on this kind of meeting." Therefore we extended it for one day and held a two-day meeting. It appeared that in this way problems were quite thoroughly solved and enthusiasm was high, with more people attending each meeting.

(3) Content of meeting report. --In making reports, attention was given to the following points. First, there were direct, simple, and short introductory talks on problems on a level that could be comprehended by those attending the meeting. Second, in accord with the spirit of higher-level directives, living persons, events, and ideology in the brigade were organized into living teaching materials. Third, the meetings were principally for the education and training of cadre members and not for the general arrangement of work. Three problems were discussed in the report. First, why must we continue to expand the Socialist Education movement? Second, must we oppose the Three Evil Tendencies? In this, in addition to using facts, clarification of the seriousness and harmfulness of the Three Evil Tendencies was emphasized. Third, on whom must the movement rely for its execution, and how will it be carried out? This is to resolve the problems of cadre members' attitudes toward the movement. We should indicate that this movement is a result of the demand of the cadre members and of the masses themselves and that its successful completion requires the true awakening of the masses in order that basic problems be solved.

(4) We organized discussion meetings in the following ways.

(a) Eighteen members of the leading brigade cadres and the branch committee work-groups participated in the work of the sixteen groups (thirty-three production teams), strengthened their leadership, and carried on discussions together.

(b) Based on the content of the report, three discussion topics were raised. (i) Should the movement be continued? (ii) What must we oppose and what must we advocate? (iii) Upon whom does the movement rely for its execution?

(c) We began with a discussion of general problems, after which these were related to the conditions of our brigades and predominant problems were solved.

(d) In discussion, by means of displaying facts, reasoning, recollection, contrast, and reckoning of accounts, causes were found and their roots were dug out so that problems could be thoroughly solved. During the discussion, education was conducted, using the method of contrast. A contrast was drawn between the Chih-sai production team, which maintained the collective and obtained increased production and income, and the Li-ssu production team, in which the spirit of individual enterprise severely decreased production and income. A contrast was drawn between Lin Tse-jui, a commune member who loved collective production, and the younger brother of Ch'en Ch'ing-kuan, who left the collective to hire himself out as a laborer. A contrast was drawn between the free marriage of Hsieh Chih-chien and the marriage-arranged-by-parents of his brother Hsieh Chih-hsiang, and between Commune Member Yang Ts'ung-t'ai, who practised superstition and extravagance, and Commune Member Cheng Shui-chu, who managed her household diligently and frugally. Party Member Liu Hsüan-chung said, "The more I think about silver and gold, the poorer I get." In self-examination he said: "After the autumn season last year, I did not participate in collective labor for two months. All I could think about was making money. I ran off to Nan-p'ing to work, and ended up by not making any money at all and having to sell a wool suit and a cotton overcoat. If we do not dig out the roots of capitalism, sooner or later we will run into trouble."

(5) At this meeting the following points concerning branch leadership of the party were emphasized.

(a) Thorough preparations were made for the meetings. After returning from the commune meetings, a Branch Party Committee meeting was first held for the discussion of the arrangement of the meetings and of production, and to determine who should attend the meetings. Living persons and events from the brigade were assembled, the content of the report discussed, and preparations were made for talks based on personal example. The brigade land was put under the supervision of the Branch Committee, and members were encouraged to come to the meetings on time.

(b) In order to unite the movement with current production, production arrangements were made before the meeting. At the end of the meetings, two hours were taken for a discussion of the current production tasks and the expansion of a new production competition. Nine team chiefs came to the platform to express their resolve, and they inspired everyone. The entire body of cadre members expressed a resolve to make 1963 another 1957 in the richness of its harvest.

The scale of these meetings was large, enthusiasm ran high, pressure was light, and results were great. By means of education, understanding was raised, doubts eliminated, faith strengthened, and backs stiffened. As people said: "Before the meeting, we were stumbling along as if we were blind. At the meeting we found our directions and got back on the highway." Everyone expressed the feeling that the movement should be completed and that production should not be relaxed. Those comrades attending the meetings also drew up a socialist agreement consisting of the "six requirements" for cadre members and the "six goods" for commune members.

The schedule of the meeting was tight, and preparatory work before the meeting was insufficient. There were thirteen persons who did not participate. In addition, we did not assemble enough living persons and events from the region to conduct sufficiently forceful education by contrast, reckoning of accounts, and persuasion.

SHANG-SHAN BRIGADE BRANCH,
CHINESE COMMUNIST PARTY

February 21, 1963

REPORT ON THE EXPANDED CADRE MEETING
OF THE CHU-CH'I BRIGADE

After the conclusion of the County Committee three-level cadre meeting, on the basis of the directives of the commune Party Committee, we began by holding an expanded meeting of cadre members on February 18. It lasted four-and-a-half days, and 120 persons, including the entire body of brigade and team cadre members, party members, and cadres of young people's, women's and military organizations participated in it. In addition, sixteen positive elements (including old peasants and poor peasants) were absorbed, making a total attendance of 136 persons. To bring about an even more successful meeting, on the afternoon of the 17th we held specialized half-day production-team meetings for the study of items related to the meetings and for making concrete arrangements for production during the period of the meetings.

The meetings were arranged in the following manner. Reports (reading of the communiqué of the Tenth Plenum of the Eighth Central Committee, the fourth, fifth, and sixth chapters of the Draft Regulations, and the six Provincial Committee decisions), a full half day; discussion of the two basic problems, a half day and one evening; discussion of the significance, objectives, and content of the movement, two days; discussion of methodological problems, half a day; and cadre examination, one day and one evening. Finally, there was a summary.

By means of this meeting, members of the cadre received a most profound and thorough Socialist Education. Their feelings ran high, and they expressed general enthusiasm. Attendance at the meetings was regular, and there were no absences or withdrawals during their course. Just as Team Chief Cheng Shih-shih said, "The banners and direction of this meeting were clear and its measures forceful, so that the more we listened, the more enthusiastic we became." As it was commonly said, "We can really solve problems when a movement is conducted in this way." It was especially after examinations that faith was raised even higher. There was a general expression of a desire to teach and influence the broad masses through one's own example. According to the meeting statistics, before the meeting there were eight persons who did not wish to serve as team chiefs. After the meetings, there were none who did not wish to serve and, moreover, they were very positive (as for example, Cheng Shih-shih). Before the meeting, nine cadre members were engaged in selling turnips. After the meeting, they resolved to go out of business.

The meeting also had a great stimulating effect on production. Although the cadre members were in meetings during the day, this did not affect production. The number of persons (excluding cadre members) participating in labor rose from 150 to 180 and more than 500 tan of fertilizer were collected each day.

We believe that the success of the meeting was due to the following points.

(1) We concentrated our forces in clarifying the reasons why such a big movement was necessary. The longest period of time was spent in discussing this problem and that of the content of the movement. The discussion was related to actual conditions; problems were pointed out and their harmfulness analyzed. Facts show that the more concretely the problems were set out, the deeper was the education. Everyone felt that although the previous phase had remedied the symptoms, ideological problems had still not been resolved and that after the movement new problems arose. Nine persons (among them, three cadre members) were engaged in the selling of turnips, and, as was disclosed at the meeting, there were in the entire brigade 12 persons following superstitious

practices, 16 gamblers, two sorcerers and priests, 11 persons engaged in odd jobs, 25 persons who had abandoned farming for peddling, three persons hiring labor, one person loaning money at high interest, and 30 persons felling trees. As for the cadre members, there were four who had committed graft and theft and 11 who had surreptitiously engaged in excess consumption. After the facts had been presented, everyone was permitted to analyze the harmfulness [of these acts], and it was generally recognized that if the three evil tendencies were not stopped, there would be even greater losses to production and commune members would suffer ideological disorientation. As Team Chief Cheng Ju-k'uo said: "We have a labor force of 23 on our team. Of these, there were two who engaged in speculation, three who wanted to go to Hong Kong, and one who did odd jobs. Only five or six persons went out to work in the collective. How could we complete production that way?" As a consequence, he expressed the wish to root out the three evil tendencies.

After these conditions had been presented in their entirety, an analysis was made in which the differences between improper and proper forms of the turnip business were contrasted (there are 120 persons in the brigade engaged in it). Everyone felt that a person should be permitted to sell in the market what he has produced and processed himself, but that if he buys turnips and takes them to Foochow and other places for sale, this should be considered as peddling and should be firmly stopped.

(2) Another important content of the meeting was the conscientious assistance given to cadre members, Youth Corps members, and party members in solving their own problems. Ideological struggle in these problems was quite intense. If we are not determined to solve the existing problems of lower-level attitudes toward higher levels, of party-member attitudes toward the branch committees, and of Youth Corps attitudes toward party members and the leadership cadre, then it will be very difficult to solve general problems among the cadre members, let alone educate the masses. As seen from the present situation, the overwhelming majority of comrades were very well examined. According to statistics, 84 persons (70 per cent) were thoroughly examined, and there were eight persons (principally, ordinary production-team cadre members), or 7 per cent, whose examination was deficient. In the course of solving this problem, we mastered the following three points. (a) We repeatedly clarified policy and direction for the benefit of the cadre, party, and Youth Corps members. (b) The leadership cadre members took the initiative in examining their own problems and instructed and influenced the entire body of comrades attending the meetings through their own actual conduct. This is an extremely important point. For example, when the branch secretary examined himself well, this was welcomed by everyone, but when the brigade chief began by not making a sufficient examination of his problem of house building, everyone was critical. Later, a "make-up session" was conducted, at which the team chiefs also conscientiously made self-examinations. For example, Production Team Chief Cheng Shih-yu at first decided that he would not make a self-examination, but after listening to the self-examinations of the commune party secretary and several of the brigade leadership cadre members he took the initiative in revealing his incorrect conduct of emigrating to engage in peddling and stated that he would sell the remaining 50 tan of turnips to the production team at a discount. He then guaranteed that in the future he would give up this activity. (c) For the benefit of some persons having serious problems and many ideological doubts, the Brigade Branch Committee and the work groups conducted individual assistance and education. This kind of treatment was accorded nine persons, and after receiving assistance, their examinations were well carried out.

(3) The meeting did not discuss the concrete methods of the movement to any extent, but looked only into the problem of how to mobilize the masses. Three major methods resulted from this study: (a) Work responsibilities were divided among the cadre members, party members, and Youth Corps members. Brigade cadre members were given charge of the strips of land and the teams. The production-team cadre members and party and Youth Corps members were assigned the households and individual persons. They then carried out the "three leads" (taking the lead in participation in the movement, taking the lead in the examination of one's own problems in the production team, and taking the lead in stimulating one's own family and relatives to participate in the meeting) and the "five guarantees" (guaranteeing to stimulate the commune members' participation in the meetings, to complete work in ideological education, to understand and reflect conditions beneath them, to assist in the solution of various concrete problems, and to lead and participate in production. (b) Through the activity of cadre members, party members, and Youth Corps members in succession, we cultivated Class Corps having poor and lower-middle peasants as their nuclei. (c) We selected thirty persons having high ideological awareness and strong propaganda capacities as a nucleus, and organized a small but active mobile propaganda group.

(4) In integrating the movement with production, we adopted the following principal methods. Before the meetings, we held a special meeting in which we made arrangements for production and in which we presented to the masses the production requirements at this stage. During the meetings, one assistant brigade chief was especially assigned to the production teams and irrigation-project districts to inspect and supervise the work. The production-team cadre members, for the most part, made use of their rest periods in the morning, at noon, and after their evening meals to return and assist the commune members in work arrangements and in the evaluation and the recording of work-points, as well as in the solution of their concrete problems. As a consequence, it was assured that neither the meetings nor production would be impeded.

Some problems still exist. For example, there was not a satisfactory study of the arrangements of the next stage of production work, and insufficient study was made on mounting an attack against serious opponents and on the selection of cadre members. These problems must be further studied and solved.

February 22, 1963

XXII

CADRE AND PARTY MEMBER CLASSIFICATION STANDARDS

    I. FIRST CLASS: Correct in orientation; firm in standpoint; able to act collectively; no three tendencies.

    II. SECOND CLASS: Not so correct in orientation; having a certain degree of the three tendencies; vacillating toward the collective.

    III. THIRD CLASS: Not clear in orientation; having the three tendencies, sometimes severely, while completely lacking a concept of them.

The brigade party personnel and cadre members, and the production-team chiefs and other production-team cadre members, should be classified on the basis of the above criteria. If a person to be classified is both a party member and a cadre member, he should be classified in both capacities. If a person holds several positions, he should be considered as belonging to the major one among his positions. When making reports, the following details should be given:

(1) Party members: total number and number in each class.

(2) Brigade: chief branch secretary and brigade chiefs; number of persons and number in each class.

(3) Assistant branch secretaries and assistant brigade chiefs: number of persons and number in each class.

(4) Brigade: Youth Corps party branch secretaries, Women's Corps chairmen, Militia Corps chiefs, secretaries, storage clerks, accountants, cashiers, and credit society chiefs: number of persons and number in each class.

(5) Production teams, production-team chiefs: number of persons and number in each class.

(6) Production teams, other production-team cadre members: number of persons and number in each class.

Please report the above data by telephone before the seventh of the month.

P'U-K'OU PARTY COMMITTEE

March 5, 1963

XXIII

NOTIFICATION ON THE PREPARATION
OF REPORT DATA

CLASSIFICATION NUMBER: Number 008 of the P'u-k'ou Party Committee

TO: All Brigade Party Branch and Work Groups

At present all the expanded meetings of brigade cadre members have been concluded, and the results of some have already been thoroughly circulated among the masses. In order that we may master the cadre situation, we hope that you will, within days, make a written report of the problems within the ranks of the cadre that have been revealed during this movement and send it to us. There are two methods that may be used in writing. The first is that of separate classification, that is, the classification into various types of errors and deficiencies which you have encountered among cadre members. For example, "graft" may be one classification (graft may be further classified into graft in cash, in cloth-ration coupons, and in food); "misappropriation" another, "speculation" another, "hiring and exploiting labor" another, and so on. After this, for each classification there can be an explanation of how many and what cadre members were involved in a given classification. In addition, two or three of the more common and serious examples may be cited. The second method is based on individuals. For example, you can describe what problems Chang San has and what problems Li Ssu has. In adopting this method, it is most important to write about those with serious problems or perverse conduct, and it is not necessary to write about each brigade and team cadre member individually. However, faults should be written up in detail. (For example, under "graft," the amount, the place, the time, and the method should be written up.) If there are some persons in the brigade who have many problems that cannot be reported together by using the above-mentioned method, the data on these individuals can be drawn up and reported individually.

We request that the above notifications be assigned to a specialized person by the Brigade Branch Committee (for those with work groups, it is best handled by them) and that data and methods of communication be furnished to them. We hope that we can receive this information from you by the sixteenth or seventeenth of the month. In addition, if persons with severe problems and with perverse conduct are discovered among the masses (including hostile elements), you may prepare and report the data on them at the same time.

P'U-K'OU COMMUNE PARTY COMMITTEE

March 13, 1963

XXIV

[REPORT OF THE SHANG-SHAN BRIGADE ON CADRE RECTIFICATION]

THE LIEN-CHIANG COUNTY COMMITTEE OF THE CHINESE COMMUNIST PARTY,

FUKIEN PROVINCE

(Approved for transmission)

NUMBER: 031

TO: Each Commune Party Committee, and the Tung-hu
               Farm, 3 copies; each Brigade Branch, 1 copy,
               Municipal Committees, 14 copies; and the Pro-
               vincial Committee Socialist Education Office,
               3 copies

COPIES TO: The County Committee Standing Committee, each
               County Committee member, each County Committee
               Section, Youth Corps, Women's Corps, People's
               Committee Offices, the Public Security Bureau,
               the Court, and the Procurator's Office, one copy
               each; file, 2 copies

THIS ITEM: 4 pages, issued by the Office of the Secretary,
               Lien-chiang County Committee, Chinese Communist
               Party, March 27, 1963

The Lien-chiang County Committee approves for transmission the report of the Shang-shan brigade, Ao-chiang commune, on cadre rectification.

We hereby transmit to you the report of the Shang-shan brigade, Ao-chiang commune, on cadre rectification. The cadre members of the Shang-shan brigade had a strong resolve to reform, and rapid progress was made. Their experiences, methods, and policy delimitations are all practicable and worthy of general consideration. It is hoped that each region will, like the Shang-shan Brigade, repeatedly discuss from above to below and from below to above the problem of the return or restoration of goods and money by the cadre members (this includes political rectification), and that each will, on the basis of actual conditions in a given team, work out concrete lines of policy.

In the matter of the return or restoration of goods and money by the cadre members, it is of the utmost importance to communicate this policy to the masses and to carry on repeated and mass democratic discussion. As for concrete treatment, a policy should first be set up by the brigade branch and examined and approved by the Commune Party Committee.

After the reception of this document, a conscientious study should be conducted in each region. Please report good experiences to us.

LIEN-CHIANG COUNTY COMMITTEE
CHINESE COMMUNIST PARTY

March 27, 1963

REPORT OF THE SHANG-SHAN BRIGADE ON CADRE RECTIFICATION

During this stage of the Socialist Education movement in the Shang-shan brigade it was discovered that 113 members of brigade and production-team cadre, or more than 48 per cent of the total number of cadre members at the production-team level and above, had problems. Among these were 33 party members, or 51 per cent of the brigade's party membership.

As can be seen from the rectification of these cadre members, the majority are now very good and have set examples by correcting their own errors in their actual conduct. However, there remains a minority of cadre members whose ideology is in conflict with that of rectification. According to our classification, there were, during the movement, 106 persons, or 93.8 per cent, who were able to examine their own errors thoroughly and who resolved to reform; four persons, or 3.5 per cent, who still had ideological doubts about rectification; and three persons, or 2.7 per cent, who did not examine themselves with sufficient depth and whose ideology was in conflict with that of rectification.

(1) During the movement we adopted the methods of immediate reform after the discovery of problems, in order that the movement might be gradually deepened. Up until March 24, there were 72 cadre members, or 63.5 per cent, with problems who had completely reformed; 19 cadre members, or 17 per cent, who had partially reformed; and 22 cadre members, or 19.5 per cent, who had not yet begun to reform. In the economic sphere (including graft and misappropriation), 28 persons have already returned funds amounting to 1,068 yüan, or 80 per cent of the total funds that should be returned. In regard to food (including misappropriation and excess consumption), 24 persons have already returned a total of 985.5 catties, or 85 per cent of the total amount of food that should be returned. In regard to land, 34 persons have returned 10.3 mou of excess private plots and illegally occupied collective land. This is 90 per cent of the land that should be returned. In regard to the private slaughter of pigs, four persons have paid the taxes on four pigs. This is 68 per cent of the taxes that should be paid up.

(2) The principles of rectification were concretely determined after repeated discussions by cadre members and masses.

(a) There were 42 persons who misappropriated 3,412 yüan of public funds. In principle, the entire amount must be repaid. However, on the basis of actual conditions, it was decided that 23 persons should make complete restitution of 493 yüan and, with the agreement of the commune members, 19 persons who were in financial distress could make restitution of the remaining 2,919 yüan on a time-repayment basis. (Now 825 yüan have been repaid. After the sweet potato sale, 782 yüan will be repaid, and 1,312 yüan will be returned from the summer harvest distribution.

(b) There were nine persons who together misappropriated 1,786 catties of collective food. The entire amount should be returned to the collective. At present, five persons have returned 890 catties and, through discussion and agreement by the commune membership, four persons in financial distress will be allowed to return the remaining 896 catties on a time basis. (Now 275 catties have been returned, and 621 catties will be returned from the summer harvest.)

(c) One person who misappropriated 12 yüan of collective funds has returned the entire amount to the collective.

(d) There were 41 persons who occupied an area of 10.8 mou of collective land. Land that has not yet been planted must be returned immediately to the collective. Land that has been planted may be harvested by those who did the planting. We request that the land be returned to the collective as early as possible and before the rice seedlings are transplanted. The 1.2 mou of collective land that was occupied and on which houses were built was obtained previously without going through official approval procedures. Correction should be made through the confiscation of the private plots belonging to the respective households.

(e) There were four persons with excess shares of private plots, amounting to an area of 4 fen, 2 li. [1] These should be returned to the collective before the transplanting of rice seedlings.

(f) There were 47 persons who engaged in excess consumption. Of these, 32 persons consumed 221 catties of food in excess; 8 persons bought 6 catties of duck eggs in excess; 11 persons bought 95 catties of chemical fertilizer in excess; 2 persons bought 60 catties of rice bran in excess. After a thorough self-examination by these persons and after discussion and agreement with the commune members [it was decided that,] with the exception of those who had consumed excess food and who were required to make restitution for part of it (110 catties), no action would be taken against them.

(g) There were six persons who privately slaughtered six hogs and were required to pay the taxes on them.

(h) There were eleven persons who abandoned farming for trade and who made a profit of 870 yüan. With the exception of one person who made high profits and who was required to pay a tax, the rest underwent thorough self-examination and recognized their error. They were not punished.

(i) There were twelve persons who engaged in gambling, but only occasionally. After a thorough self-examination, they recognized their error and resolved to give up the practice. They were not punished.

(j) There was one person who made use of the authority of his position to employ the collective's facilities to manufacture privately brick and lime of an estimated value of 150 yüan. After a thorough investigation, the commune members agreed not to mete out punishment. However, he was required to make indemnification of 30 yüan for the damages resulting from his borrowing of collective vehicles and boats to transport the brick and lime.

(3) In this stage we grasped the following four points among the concrete methods for cadre rectification:

(a) We resolved the ideological problems of the cadre members and raised their understanding of the importance of rectification. At first, the cadre members had

---

[1] The fen is equivalent to 0.1 mou, the li to 0.01 mou.

three differing ways of thinking about rectification: fear that returning funds would cause difficulties; the attitude of wait and see; fear that after communicating their problems they would lose their prestige. We treated these views separately in party-member meetings, expanded cadre member meetings, and individual conversations. We repeatedly explained that the completion of rectification would not only stimulate the current movement, but would also evoke a positive spirit of production among the masses, thereby strengthening the collective economy. We also indicated to the cadre members what the correction of errors would mean for the future, that comrades who were willing to correct their errors would be considered good cadre members, and that frank communicating of problems and resolving to repay funds would not cause them to lose their authority among the masses, but rather would lead to their being accepted by the masses. On the foundation of an improved ideological level of the cadre members, we called upon them to make plans for the repayment of funds and to resolve to correct their errors. When making plans for the repayment of funds, we treated individually the cadre members who were in actual difficulty and assisted them in solving their difficulties.

(b) With the leadership cadre members taking the lead, all levels of cadre members resolved to reform. The Branch Secretary Hsieh T'ien-tseng, who had misappropriated 60 yüan of public funds, during the course of rectification gave back 28 yüan of his month's wages and borrowed another two yüan, making a total of 30 yüan [returned]. When the other cadre members saw that the branch secretary had taken the lead in returning funds, they also increased their self-awareness and repaid the collective. For example, the brigade chief had misappropriated 700 yüan, which he originally planned to return in installments at the summer harvest, in August, and after the autumn harvest. Upon seeing the branch secretary return funds, he borrowed 200 yüan from friends and relatives to return to the brigade and resolved to return 300 yüan at the summer harvest and another 200 yüan in August after selling his pigs. This raised the trust of the other cadre members with regard to returning funds and goods, and a high tide of rectification was formed.

(c) Discussion proceeded from above to below, and decisions from below to above. Thorough mass discussion was developed, and the opinion of the persons concerned was solicited. After the problems were first enumerated, the principles of rectification were determined through study by the Branch Committee. Preliminary suggestions on rectification were proposed and the agreement of the persons concerned was sought. After this, separate meetings of the production-team chiefs and production-team membership were held. Finally, the persons concerned gave pledges to the team members that the rectification would be carried out.

(d) During the course of rectification we emphasized that all who had harmed the welfare of the state and the collective should adopt a spirit of willingness to make restitution. We adopted the principle of treating infractions of laws and regulations severely, of treating ordinary problems leniently, and of treating errors incurring important mass criticisms severely and treating those which the masses forgave leniently. By this means, we carefully studied, treated, and gradually solved problems individually.

After these corrections had been made, the satisfaction of the cadre members and the masses was achieved. The commune members said in response: "If all the cadre members could correct their errors, we commune members should correct our faults as well. In this way, we can together complete collective production and strengthen the collective economy."

SHANG-SHAN BRIGADE BRANCH WORK GROUP,
CHINESE COMMUNIST PARTY

XXV

CH'ANG-SHA BRIGADE CADRE SELF-EXAMINATION RECORDS DURING THE SOCIALIST EDUCATION MOVEMENT

(THE SECOND GROUP: THE SECOND AND SIXTH PRODUCTION TEAMS)

Self-examination:

CHEN-T'AI

(1) During June of 1962, I was struggling against the ideology of the spirit of individual enterprise. Although I did not take part in it, I was influenced by it, and, at the beginning of the rectification movement, I had taken over a few mou of land.

(2) I was guilty of subjectivism in my work and did not dare to handle affairs courageously. I did not rely on the Seven Personnel and the strength of the commune members. Therefore I was not able to unite with the masses.

(3) I took over about 210 mou of land near the dam and privately planted it with sweet potatoes.

(4) I disbursed an excess of 200 yüan from the accounts (this includes other materials and extra meals during the night) and bought more fish than I should. I took special privileges and disbursed in excess of 40 yüan from the team's accounts. I thereby affected the production spirit of the commune members. I was not able to get back the funds owed by the commune members. I approved funds indiscriminately to commune members on the grounds of illness and other reasons.

(5) I did not investigate production-team property at the proper times. More than 10 catties of extra provisions were consumed by the cadre.

(6) I was not friendly enough in dealing with commune members.

(7) I bought some oysters and engaged in peddling once, but did not make any money and did not do it again.

(8) I had the capitalist ideology of not wanting to be a cadre member and of wanting to become a laborer.

Mass assistance:

FA-CHIH. His standpoint as a production-team chief was not firm. He did not dare to supervise the Seven Personnel, and usually did not control finances. He approved the lending of materials to other teams or individuals as he pleased.

I-SHU. He did not give public notice of commune-member work-points at the proper time, and the figures were not clear. He did not have a high sense of responsibility as a cadre member and did not inspect accounts at the proper time.

Self-examination:

CHUNG-JUI

(1) I did not want to serve as a cadre member. I had a quick temper, and when I got angry, I gave everything up. This affected the spirit of commune-member production. I was not able to lead the masses to go out to work, and delays and postponements resulted.

(2) I harbored the spirit of individual enterprise, believing that it would be best to divide up land among the commune members.

(3) I engaged in excess consumption. Finally, I obtained some oysters, summoned the Seven Personnel to eat them and then charged the expense to the team's account.

(4) I did not establish a sense of responsibility among the cadre members. I was not exact in my division of labor, and did not direct the commune members in their undertakings.

(5) My management of finances was not good. I did not evaluate the work-points at the proper time and, in general, only evaluated them about once a month. I did not make public announcement of finances, and was not familiar with the receipts and disbursements.

(6) I engaged in peddling two or three times and did not give serious attention to production-team work. Moreover, I took production-team funds for capital. The second time the money was advanced by Tsu Hsiang.

Mass assistance:

CHEN-T'AI. There were errors in his financial management, and more than 100 yüan was misappropriated by his assistants. The brigade decided that the team chief should also participate in sentry duties, and he ignored it.

CHO-CHIN. We think that the fund taken by the assistant was used by the team chief.

SUNG-T'AI. His standpoint was not firm. He feared the reaction of the masses, feared trouble, and did not want to serve as a cadre member.

Self-examination:

TUNG-CHIN

(1) I did not do my work sufficiently in 1962, and particularly where women were concerned, I ignored others' accomplishments. I did not want to serve as a cadre member, because of the trouble.

(2) I took special privileges. I bought an excess of fish and spent an excess of brigade funds.

(3) I did not regularly hold women's representatives meetings, did not regularly take part in production-team meetings, and did not have close contact with the masses.

(4) I was especially deficient in handling women's work, and did not solve the problems among the women.

Mass assistance:

CHEN-T'AI. He did not take part enthusiastically in production-team meetings, and was deficient in stimulating the masses and taking part in meetings. He did not accept the criticisms of the masses and did not fully observe the labor system.

Self-examination:

I-SHU

(1) I did not have a positive attitude about being a group chief, and did not take part in meetings. I did not handle commune production well, and did not dare to correct members who worked poorly.

(2) I thought that a group chief need not do anything unless a higher level told him to. If I did not get any orders, I did not do anything.

Mass assistance:

FA-CHIH. I-shu was a team chief in name only. He did not do anything.

CHEN-T'AI. He was afraid of trouble and afraid of being a cadre member. He did not accept his mission enthusiastically.

TUNG-CHIN. Conservative.

Self-examination:

FA-CHIH

(1) I did not handle my work well and did not take over the storage of farm tools at the proper time.

(2) I did not manage accounts accurately, and I managed food badly. My accounts were not clear. I even cooked food, especially a lot of fish, without getting the brigade chief's approval.

(3) I engaged in excess consumption of such things as sweet potatoes and broad beans.

Mass assistance:

YU-CH'IN. He took special privileges and used public farm tools for private purposes.

I-SHU. He took rice home, but when it was discovered, he returned it to the production team. He used up six slabs of bamboo, and his food figures were not clear.

CHEN-T'AI. He cooked food and beans whenever it pleased him. He was not thorough in his management of production-team farm tools and would not do anything unless he was prodded.

Self-examination:

YUNG-LIANG:

(1) I did not record the work-points of the commune members at the proper time. I regularly failed to record work-points, and sometimes failed to record those of an entire household.

(2) I had a stubborn attitude, and when the masses had doubts I did not explain to them in the proper manner.

Mass assistance:

FA-CHIH

(1) He did not have a high sense of responsibility about being a work-point recorder, and regularly altered the records.

(2) He did not acknowledge his borrowings of public farm tools, as, for example, a hoe and one tan of hemp rope.

CHEN-T'AI

(1) He regularly failed to record labor done by commune members and sometimes intentionally failed to record work-points for labor.

(2) He did not take the lead, and so fell behind the masses.

(3) His attitude and work attitude were bad.

CHEN-HSIUNG. He was self-satisfied and looked down on women. He had a stubborn attitude and would not accept the criticisms of the masses.

Self-examination:

CHO-CHIN

(1) I did not go regularly to the teams to investigate their work, and I did not have a high sense of production responsibility.

(2) I opened up much uncultivated collective land and was unconcerned with collective production.

Assistance from others:

CHUNG-JUI

(1) He did not have a high sense of responsibility about being a group chief, being one in name only. Other people had to remind him before he attended to his work.

(2) He did not have firm convictions.

Self-examination:

CHAO

(1) I did not manage farm tools well, and many were lost.

(2) I gave food to the commune members without following procedures, to the extent that I lost count of the amount that was given out.

Assistance:

CHUNG-JUI

(1) He gave out supplementary rations to the commune members without using his seal, to the extent that the figures were not clear.

(2) He did not manage farm tools properly, giving them to others as he pleased.

(3) He lost several scores of catties of chemical fertilizer.

Self-examination:

CHING-CHUN

(1) I did not shoulder my responsibilities as a work-point recorder and did not record work-points at the proper time. I regularly failed to record work-points.

(2) I did not manage production well, and I did not have a high spirit of labor.

Assistance:

CHUNG-JUI

(1) He did not bother about recording work-points, except his own, to the extent that he only recorded them once a month. He did not accept the criticisms of others. When the masses wanted him to correct the work-points, he did not pay any attention to them.

(2) He opened up uncultivated land on a large scale and abandoned collective production. He would not go to the team office in the evening, and did not concern himself with the collective.

CHEN-T'AI

(1) He damaged public interests for private advantage. He opened up uncultivated land on a large scale and turned the sidewalks into vegetable gardens.

(2) He let his geese loose on crop land and damaged a good deal of the crops.

Self-examination:

SUNG-T'AI

(1) Because I put too much emphasis on Small Freedoms and neglected the production team, I did not regularly go out to work and take part in production.

(2) I did not take the initiative in helping the production team to study production.

Assistance from others:

CHUNG-JUI

(1) His speech was not orthodox, and he fell behind the masses. He said a lot of nonsensical things.

(2) During the War Preparation period, when civil laborers were being selected, besides not obeying the assignments he influenced the masses so that the entire team did not respond.

(3) He opened up an excessive amount of uncultivated land. Except for fishing, he did not pay any attention to the production team.

Self-examination:

AI-CHU

(1) I did not accept the responsibility of being selected assistant team chief by the masses.

(2) I was concerned for myself but not for others.

Assistance from others:

CHUNG-JUI

(1) She was not courageous in work, and was indecisive in production.

(2) She has a stubborn character. Her family was not very well united and regularly argued without any reason.

[March 1963]

GLOSSARY

BRIGADE CONTRACT PRODUCTION. A system of production on land farmed by the brigade, which contracts to produce a fixed output at a fixed cost and a fixed number of work-points.

CADRE. The administrative personnel of a commune, brigade, or team; also an individual member of a cadre.

CATTY. Unit of weight, equal to 0.5 kg. or 1.1 lb.

CLASS CORPS. A group composed usually of poor and lower-middle peasants who serve as the activists in a movement and supervise work in the units of a commune.

COMPARE, STUDY, EMULATE, AND ASSIST MOVEMENT. A slogan exhorting a commune unit to compare itself with the advanced units, learn from the advanced units, and emulate the advanced units, and to assist the backward ones.

EIGHT CHARACTER CHARTER. (1) Water conservation, (2) application of fertilizer, (3) soil amelioration, (4) use of better seed strains, (5) rational close planting, (6) plant protection, (7) field management, and (8) tool reform.

EIGHT CHARACTER POLICY. The policy of "readjustment," "consolidation," "filling out," and "raising standards," so called from the four sets of two characters comprising these terms.

EIGHT POINTS TO BE OBSERVED BY CADRES. (1) Pay attention to the livelihood of the masses, (2) take part in collective labor, (3) treat people with an attitude of equality, (4) consult with the masses on one's work and handle affairs with impartiality, (5) identify oneself with the masses and prevent the formation of privileged classes, (6) do not claim the right to speak without investigation, (7) handle affairs according to the true situation, and (8) raise the class consciousness of the proletariat as well as one's own political level.

EQUALITARIANISM. Equal sharing of food and other supplies by all members of a commune, brigade, or team.

FIVE GUARANTEED HOUSEHOLDS. The households of the aged, the weak, the orphaned, the widowed, and the infirm or disabled. Persons of these categories were guaranteed their food, housing, clothing, and funeral.

FOUR CLASS ELEMENTS. Landlords, rich peasants, counterrevolutionaries, and "bad elements" such as thieves, vandals, and criminals.

FOUR FIXED SYSTEM. The assignment of land, labor, agricultural tools, and plow oxen to production teams on a permanent (i.e., fixed) basis.

FOUR PERSONNEL. The persons holding the four leading administrative offices in a production team. These would usually include the team chief, deputy team chiefs, and accountant.

GENERAL LINE OF SOCIALIST CONSTRUCTION. This refers to the over-all policy of the Communist Party on building socialism.

HSIA-FANG. Meaning "sent down," the term refers to the shifting of cadres, persons, land, agricultural tools, and plow oxen from a higher level of a commune to a lower level, or from the urban to the rural districts.

HOUSEHOLD CONTRACT PRODUCTION. Production on land farmed out to households which undertake to produce a fixed output for a fixed cost and a fixed number of work-points.

INDIVIDUAL-ENTERPRISE CONTRACTING. Entering into a contract for Household Contract Production.

MOU. Unit of area, equal to 733 1/2 sq. yds. or approximately one-sixth of an acre.

PAO-CHIA. Units of self-government below the township and village levels. Ten households were organized into a chia, and ten chia's into a pao. The system was in force on the Chinese mainland before the Communist takeover.

PEDDLERS. Persons who resell commodities bought from others, in contrast to those who sell what they themselves produce.

RAT WORK. Odd jobs done surreptitiously for pay.

SEVEN PERSONNEL. The seven leading cadre members in a production team, including the team chief, deputy chief or chiefs, accountant, stock controller, production manager, and work-point recorder. Sometimes the number of key personnel would be fewer--hence such a term as Four Personnel.

SIXTY DRAFT REGULATIONS. The "Draft Regulations Governing Rural People's Communes," promulgated May 12, 1961, which consisted of sixty articles. The Draft Regulations were revised in September 1962.

SMALL FREEDOMS. The meaning of the term is not known precisely, but probably the Small Freedoms would include not only freedom to cultivate one's private plot and one's reclaimed land, but also freedom to engage in Household Contract Production and private business and to sell one's produce in the free market.

SPIRIT OF INDIVIDUAL ENTERPRISE. The attitude reflected in Household Contract Production and such private behavior as abstention from collective work, drifting out of one's own commune unit to do odd jobs (rat work), engaging in peddling, and reclaiming waste land for private use.

STATE LEVY AND PURCHASE. Includes the state levy or agricultural tax and the compulsory sale to the state of food, cotton, and other specified products at prices and in quantities determined by the state.

TAN. Unit of weight, equal to 100 catties or 50 kg.

THREE EVIL TENDENCIES. Capitalism, feudalism, and extravagance.

THREE FIXED PRODUCTION. The undertaking by the team or household, as the
case may be, to produce a fixed quantity of output for a fixed amount of cost
and a fixed number of work-points.

THREE FUNDS. The reserve, welfare, and administrative funds.

THREE GREAT DISCIPLINES (for cadre members). Carrying out the policies
of the party Central Committee and the laws of the state strictly, and
participating positively in building socialism; practicing democratic centralism;
and reflecting the real situation truthfully.

THREE RED BANNERS. The General Line of Socialist Construction, the Great
Leap Forward, and the People's Communes.

THREE RETAINED FOODS. Seed, feed, and the human ration.

TWELVE ARTICLES. The twelve articles contained in the urgent directives
concerning work in rural regions issued by the Central Committee of the
Chinese Communist Party in January 1961. Among the more important
of the articles were:

   (1) In the present phase, a people's commune should consist
       basically of three levels, with the production brigade as
       its foundation.

   (5) Commune members should be permitted to cultivate small private
       plots and engage in small-scale domestic subsidiary enterprises.

   (7) The principle of "from everyone according to his ability and to
       everyone according to his labor" should be enforced.

   (10) Rural markets should be restored under proper leadership and
        planning, in order to activate the rural economy.

   (12) Rectification movements and the betterment of the communes
        should be encouraged.

               (Source: Fei-ch'ing Yüeh-pao [Mainland Conditions Monthly],
               Taiwan, March 1961, pp. 8-9.)

TWO ROADS STRUGGLE. Refers to the struggle between the "two roads" of
socialism and capitalism.

WAR PREPARATION PERIOD. Refers to the latter part of 1962, a period when
an invasion of the mainland by the Nationalist Chinese was feared and preparations were made for this contingency.

YÜAN. Monetary unit of Communist China. No official rates of exchange between
the yüan and the U.S. dollar are published. The official rates between the
yüan and the pound sterling are 685.90 yüan (buying) and 692.70 yüan (selling)
for each 100 pounds sterling, indicating an average of 2.46 yüan to one U.S.
dollar.